privilege

privilege

A Reader

THIRD EDITION

Michael S. Kimmel and Abby L. Ferber
EDITORS

WESTVIEW
PRESS
A Member of the Perseus Books Group

Westview Press was founded in 1975 in Boulder, Colorado, by notable publisher and intellectual Fred Praeger. Westview Press continues to publish scholarly titles and high-quality undergraduate- and graduate-level textbooks in core social science disciplines. With books developed, written, and edited with the needs of serious nonfiction readers, professors, and students in mind, Westview Press honors its long history of publishing books that matter.

Find us on the World Wide Web at www.westviewpress.com.
Every effort has been made to secure required permissions for all text, images, maps, and other art reprinted in this volume.
Westview Press books are available at special discounts for bulk purchases in the United States by corporations, institutions, and other organizations. For more information, please contact the Special Markets Department at the Perseus Books Group, 2300 Chestnut Street, Suite 200, Philadelphia, PA 19103, or call (800) 810-4145, ext. 5000, or e-mail special.markets@perseusbooks.com.

A CIP catalog record for the print version of this book is available from the Library of Congress.

PB ISBN: 978-0-8133-4871-1
10 9 8 7 6 5 4 3 2 1

For our children, Sydney and Zachary

contents

preface

Confronting privilege can be extremely uncomfortable—a productive and healthy discomfort, to be sure, but discomfort just the same. And once the process of confrontation has begun, it's difficult to resist what a colleague once called "premature self-congratulation," the often earnest, if insufferable, proclamations of the newly converted. "Thanks so much for bringing this privilege thing to our attention," we might be tempted to say. "We'll take it from here."

The ability to live with that discomfort and without that preachy self-congratulatory tone is the hallmark of the works we have collected here. It is a struggle, both politically and stylistically, and we hope that these essays will prove to be as unsettling and as discomfiting as they have been for the editors.

After all, we found our way to these essays, and to editing this book together, because we were so unsettled and challenged by the process of confronting our own unearned privilege. The essays in this volume proved both provocative and helpful, not only as we first began to think our way through these issues, but also as we continue the process of confronting privilege today.

A Note to Students

If you are reading this book, odds are your instructors are already themselves engaged in this process. Don't be afraid to talk about it, and to disagree. The way we've organized the book is sort of like peeling back the layers of an onion—the first articles describe the initial shock of realizing that in some way you, too, have experienced both privilege and the absence of privilege. Perhaps you are a working-class student on a scholarship at a private college or university where the students are so wealthy that they often drive nicer cars than the professors. But perhaps you are also white, or straight, or male. But then again, you might be Muslim or Jewish and experience feelings of exclusion around Christmastime. Or an older student, or disabled.

Subsequent sections complicate matters by looking at the ways these different statuses—sexuality, ability, race, class, gender, religion, and the like—each modify and shape the others. Such complication changes the "or" in the preceding paragraph to an "and," or a "but also": What if you are black *and* female? What if you are white *but also* Jewish? As you'll see, these statuses sometimes reinforce one another—as in straight white Protestant male—and sometimes collide with and undercut one another.

Some years ago, the great sociologist Erving Goffman described the ways these statuses all might coalesce into the "perfect" American male—the one who really has all the privilege:

> In an important sense there is only one complete unblushing male in America: a young, married, white, urban, northern, heterosexual, Protestant, father, of college education, fully employed, of good complexion, weight, and height, and a recent record in sports. . . . Any male who fails to qualify in any one of these ways is likely to view himself—during moments at least—as unworthy, incomplete, and inferior.*

This dynamic is critical. Goffman is saying that every single man, at some point in life, will "fail to qualify" and will feel, at least at moments, "unworthy, incomplete, and inferior." It is those feelings of inadequacy and inferiority that, we think, often motivate us to resist facing the kinds of privilege we *do* have, because we are so painfully aware of the places and arenas in which we don't measure up. Privilege is far less visible to us than its absence; when we are discriminated against, it is much more painfully obvious than when we belong to the groups that benefit from that discrimination.

One of the editors of this book has a friend—"Jane"—who is a black lesbian. Jane says that when she hangs out with a bunch of her black friends, all she can think about is being a lesbian who doesn't fit in. (That is, because virtually all the black people at her school seem to be straight.) But when

---

*Erving Goffman, *Stigma* (Englewood Cliffs, NJ: Prentice-Hall, 1963), p. 128.

Jane hangs out with her lesbian friends, all she can think about is how she's black and doesn't fit in (because all the lesbians at her school are white). We see where we *don't* fit in far better than where we *do*.

One more thing. Sometimes confronting privilege can be painful, but it can also be really funny. When you have a spare 2:40, check out this video of the comedian Louis CK describing his moment of realization of the privilege he gets for being a white man in America (warning: NSFW—*or school!*): www.youtube.com/watch?v=xqbw4nHrHc0.

Feeling Conscious, Not Guilty

Realizing that you do have privileges—no matter who you are—does not mean feeling miserable and guilty for the rest of your life. Just conscious, of both the advantages and the disadvantages that every one of us has because of the statuses we occupy, some by birth and some by choice. Conscious that there simply *are* no level playing fields anywhere—and that every single arena, whether class or race or gender or sexuality or religion or anything else, is not just a source of identity but also a site of social inequality that is arbitrary and unfair. Knowing how it feels to experience that inequality in one arena should inspire you to help level the playing field in all arenas.

But feeling conscious is an ongoing process, not a state of being. Consider this: following all the recent controversies about rape—from politicians making pronouncements about "real rape" or the role of God's will in pregnancies resulting from rape to gang rapes as far away as India and as close to home as Ohio—a guy who truly considers himself an ally to feminist women felt . . . weary. "I will not think about rape for the entire weekend," vowed "Jack" in a Facebook update.

Almost instantly some of Jack's female friends pointed out, gently but firmly, that they do not have that luxury, that they can't "opt out" of thinking about rape. His response was eloquent; he was so grateful to his friends both for pointing out what he hadn't seen (privilege makes you blind to some things and enables you to see others) and for doing so in such a way that he could react openly, without being defensive.

Here was a moment, in miniature, of the sort of experiences you will have reading this book. Your task is to be as gentle and as firm when explaining your experiences as Jack's friends were, and to be as open as Jack was to accepting the possibility of a different point of view. To facilitate this process, at the end of each section we have provided issues for discussion and activities for you to engage in. Instead of "busy work" questions to make sure you're really reading, these are designed specifically to help you engage in the very difficult work of self-examination. Our goal with this volume is not to simply provide you with the latest and most important scholarship on the subject of privilege. Learning about privilege entails examining your own life and experience as well. After all, each one of us has been deeply shaped by the systems and processes examined in these chapters. Understanding privilege is one step in the process of working to dismantle systems of inequality.

There's an old saying, attributed to Native Americans, that you can't really understand another's experience until you've walked a mile in their moccasins. (Some college campuses help men do just that by "Walking a Mile in Her Shoes"—an organized activity in which men don high heels and attempt to walk across their own campuses.) Truth is, you can't walk a mile in *everyone's* moccasins; you have to trust people when they tell you about their experiences. But only if you really do trust them will they be able, in turn, to really listen to your explanation of what it's like to live inside *your* skin.

Acknowledgments

We are so grateful to the authors of the essays in this book for their courage and wisdom. We're grateful to the instructors who feel they can use this book to challenge themselves and their students to think about these issues, all while maintaining a safe space for doing so. And we're grateful to all of the students—past, present, and future—who take the risk of confronting privilege with us.

The process of producing a book like this is as much form as it is content, as much practical concerns as it is political engagement, as much technical as theoretical. And we have been ably assisted by Rosemary Kelbel, Abby's departmental program assistant, who helped tremendously with the logistics of the book's assembly.

We've also had a dedicated staff at Westview Press. Over the years and editions, our editors at Westview have been supportive and enthusiastic, none more so than Leanne Silverman, who embraced the project with open arms! Priscilla McGeehon has overseen it all with a sharp grace. Brooke Smith oversaw production with one eye on the keenest of detail and the other on the big picture. A thank-you is also due to Westview's reviewers, who provided valuable advice as we shaped this third edition: Marni Brown

(Georgia State University), Ingrid Castro (Massachusetts College of Liberal Arts), Henry Codjoe (Dalton State College), Judith Ezekiel (Wright State University), Katherine Flower-Kim (Austin Peay State University), Rachel Griffen (Southern Illinois University), Cecily Hazelrigg-Hernandez (Western Washington University), Tony Juge (Pasadena City College), Lisa Munoz (Hawkeye Community College), Deborah Thien (California State University), Larry Van Sickle (Rollins College), William Weston (Centre College), and Kyong Yoon (University of British Columbia–Okanagan). We're grateful to them all.

In addition, Abby thanks: my wonderful graduate students in my Privilege and Power class who engaged this text thoroughly and offered suggestions about which readings to keep or cut, and reviewed a number of new readings that we considered including in this edition. Their insights were invaluable and their open willingness to challenge themselves and grow served to remind me why I do this work: Khaled Alsubaiee, Audrey Brehm, Latoya Council, Jasmine Fuller, Janene Krieger, Allison Monterrosa, Kimberlee McWhirter, and Kevin Walsh.

I thank my dear friends Eddie Moore Jr., Marqita Jones, and Brenda J. Allen, who have taught me more about privilege and the value and necessity of working in multiracial teams than I could ever learn from any book. My involvement with them in the White Privilege Conference keeps me accountable and provides me a supportive and compassionate space for examining my privilege all year long. I am grateful to the many, many committed volunteers and participants who have nurtured this conference for the past fourteen years, providing a truly challenging space and community for people committed to dismantling systems of privilege to do this hard work together. And I am quite fortunate to have found a home in the Department of Sociology, and Women's and Ethnic Studies, at the University of Colorado, Colorado Springs, where this urgent work is truly valued. I am sustained in everything I do by the love and support of Joel, my life partner, and Andrea Herrera, my dear friend and colleague. And finally, I want to thank my mentor, Michael Kimmel, whose work has been truly inspirational for me, and whose friendship, support, and collaboration I value more than he can possibly know.

And then there is Sydney, who is finally old enough to read this book and, much more important, passionate about this subject matter. I am so proud of her accomplishments, leadership, and commitment to everything she takes on.

Michael thanks: a group of friends (Lillian Rubin, Troy Duster, Martin Sanchez-Jankowski, Angela Harris, Jerry Karabel, and the late and dearly missed Michael Rogin) who began discussing whiteness twenty years ago in a little study group; my longtime friends Harry Brod, Marty Duberman, Michael Kaufman, Mike Messner, and Don Sabo, who have sustained the endless conversation; my European colleagues and friends, notably Chris Beasley, Harry Ferguson, Debra Gimlin, Jeff Hearn, Oystein Holter, Lars Jalmert, and Jorgen Lorentzen; and my friend and coeditor Abby Ferber, for her insightful work and deeply ethical vision; she inspires me constantly. I'm also grateful to my colleagues and students at State University of New York, Stony Brook, my intellectual home for more than two decades, and to Amy and Zachary, my home forever.

We live in a nation where—despite all ideological assertions about meritocracy and about how individuals are free to rise as high as they can based solely on their individual achievements—race, class, and gender are the best predictors of what we social scientists call "life chances": your level of wealth, occupation, health, even marital happiness. Ours is a nation where characteristics of your birth are the best predictors of where you will end up at your death. On the other hand, we actually do want to live in a nation in which those ideals of individual achievement are actually realized, where talent, motivation, ambition, and hard work actually do pay off, where race, class, sexuality, and gender predict very little about your economic and social life.

Every single day, we are inspired by all the people who have done so much work already to reveal the workings of oppression; all the scholars, writers, and activists who have struggled to make the unseen visible, teaching the privileged about privilege; those who had virtually no choice but to examine race, class, gender, and sexuality as they confront daily the effects of inequality based on those experiences.

introduction

toward a sociology of the superordinate

Michael S. Kimmel

This Breeze at My Back

To run or walk into a strong headwind is to understand the power of nature. You set your jaw in a squared grimace, your eyes are slits against the wind, and you breathe with a fierce determination. And still you make so little progress.

To walk or run with that same wind at your back is to float, to sail effortlessly, expending virtually no energy. You do not feel the wind; it feels you. You do not feel how it pushes you along; you feel only the effortlessness of your movements. You feel like you could go on forever. Only when you turn around and face that wind do you realize its strength.

Being white, or male, or heterosexual in this culture is like running with the wind at your back. It feels like just plain running, and we rarely if ever get a chance to see how we are sustained, supported, and even propelled by that wind.

This book tries to make the wind visible.

In recent years, the study of discrimination based on gender, race, class, and sexuality has mushroomed, creating a large literature and increasing courses addressing these issues. Of course, the overwhelming majority of

1

the research has explored the experiences of the victims of racism, sexism, homophobia, and class inequality. These are the "victims," the "others" who have begun to make these issues visible to contemporary scholars and laypeople alike. This is, of course, politically as it should be: the marginalized always understand first the mechanisms of their marginalization; it remains for them to convince the center that the processes of marginalization are in fact both real and remediable.

When presented with evidence of systematic discrimination, majority students are often indifferent, and sometimes even defensive and resistant. "What does this have to do with me?" they ask. The more defensive of them immediately mention several facts that, they believe, will absolve them of inclusion into the *superordinate* category. "My family never owned slaves," "I have a gay friend," and "I never raped anyone" are fairly typical responses. Virtually none seems able to discuss white people as a group. Some will assert that white people differ dramatically from one another, that ethnicity and religion are more important than race. Others maintain that white people, as a group, are not at all privileged. And virtually all agree that racism is a problem of individual attitudes, prejudiced people, and not a social problem.

What's more, we seem to be even *more* eager to let ourselves off the collective hook, to refuse to examine these issues from the point of view of the superordinate, than we were even a decade ago. We triumphantly declare America a "postracial" society because we now have an African-American president, and it's not uncommon to hear people "opt out" of understanding racism because they voted for Barack Obama (as if racism were a personal lifestyle option). Indeed, it seems that this self-congratulatory moment has also permitted the return of a more virulent public expression of racism than we've witnessed in decades.

Equally true, try finding a female student who calls herself a feminist. My female students often tell me that feminism was really important back in the day, when, for example, their baby-boomer professor was in college, because things were so unequal then. "But now I can do anything I want; I have completely free choice," the women declare. Gender inequality is a thing of the past; feminism is no longer necessary. "Thank you very much," they seem to be saying to the generations of women who came before them. "We won." (These same students often return to campus a few years later and confess how naive they were, not having entered the labor market or experienced wage discrimination, glass ceilings for promotion, or well-intentioned husbands who can't seem to remember how to wash a dish.)

Such statements are as revealing as they are irrelevant. They tell us far more about the way we tend to individualize and personalize processes that are social and structural. They also tell us that majority students resist discussing inequality because it will require that they feel guilty for crimes someone else committed, as well as to recognize the ways they have benefited from those actions.

Even those students who are willing to engage with these questions tend to personalize and individualize them. They may grudgingly grant the systematic nature of inequality, but to them, racism, sexism, and heterosexism are bad attitudes held by bad people. They are eager to help those bad people see the error of their ways and change their attitudes to good attitudes. This usually will come about through better education.

Those of us who are white, heterosexual, middle class, and/or male need to go further; we need to see how we are stakeholders in understanding structural inequality, how the dynamics that create inequality for some also benefit others. Privilege needs to be made visible.

For the past couple of decades, a spate of exciting new research in a variety of disciplines, including sociology, literature, and cultural studies, has been examining what previously passed as invisible, neutral, and universal. We now can begin to see how the experience of "privilege" also shapes the lives of men, white people, and heterosexuals. Such inquiries, long overdue, are enabling us to more fully understand the social dynamics of race, class, gender, and sexuality, and how they operate in all our lives.

Making Privilege Visible

To be white, or straight, or male, or middle class is to be simultaneously ubiquitous and invisible. You're everywhere you look, you're the standard against which everyone else is measured. You're like water, like air. People will tell you they went to see a "woman doctor," or they will say they went to see "the doctor." People will tell you they have a "gay colleague" or they'll tell you about a "colleague." A white person will be happy to tell you about a "black friend," but when that same person simply mentions a "friend," everyone will assume the person is white. Any college course that doesn't have the word "woman" or "gay" or "minority" in the title is, de facto, a course about men, heterosexuals, and white people. But we call those courses "literature," "history," or "political science."

This invisibility is political. I first confronted this invisibility in the early 1980s, when I participated in a small discussion group on feminism. In one meeting, a white woman and a black woman were discussing whether all women were, by definition, "sisters," because they all had essentially the same experiences and because all women faced a common oppression by men. The white woman asserted that the fact that they were both women bonded them, in spite of racial differences. The black woman disagreed.

"When you wake up in the morning and look in the mirror, what do you see?" she asked.

"I see a woman," replied the white woman.

"That's precisely the problem," responded the black woman. "I see a *black* woman. To me, race is visible every day, because race is how I am *not* privileged in our culture. Race is invisible to you, because it's how you are privileged. It's why there will always be differences in our experience."

As I witnessed this exchange, I was startled, and groaned—more audibly, perhaps, than I had intended. Someone asked me, the only man in the room, what my response had meant.

"Well," I said, "when I look in the mirror, I see a human being. I'm universally generalizable. As a middle-class white man, I have no class, no race, and no gender. I'm the generic person!"

Sometimes I like to think that it was on that day that I *became* a middle-class white man. Sure, I had been all those before, but they had not meant much to me. Since then I've begun to understand that race, class, and gender don't refer only to other people, who were marginalized by race, class, or gender privilege. Those terms also described me. I enjoyed the privilege of invisibility. The very processes that confer privilege to one group and not another group are often invisible to those upon whom that privilege is conferred. What makes us marginal or powerless are the processes we see, partly because others keep reminding us of them. Invisibility is a privilege in a double sense—describing both the power relations that are kept in place by the very dynamics of invisibility, and in the sense of privilege as luxury. It is a luxury that only white people have in our society not to think about race every minute of their lives. It is a luxury that only men have in our society to pretend that gender does not matter.

That discussion took place several decades ago, but I was reminded of it recently when I went to give a guest lecture for a female colleague at my university. We teach the same course on alternate semesters, so she always gives a guest lecture for me, and I do one for her. As I walked into the auditorium, one student looked up at me and said, "Oh, finally, an objective opinion!"

All that semester, whenever my female colleague opened her mouth, what this student saw was "a woman." Biased. But when I walked in, I was, in this student's eyes, *unbiased*, an objective opinion. Disembodied western rationality—standing right in front of the class! This notion that middle-class white men are "objective" and everyone else is "biased" is the way that inequalities are reproduced.

Let me give you another example of how power is so often invisible to those who have it. You all have e-mail addresses, and you write e-mail messages to people all over the world. You've probably noticed that there is one big difference between e-mail addresses in the United States and e-mail addresses of people in other countries: their addresses have "country codes" at the end of the address. So, for example, if you were writing to someone in South Africa, you'd put "za" at the end, or "jp" for Japan, or "uk" for England (United Kingdom), or "de" for Germany (Deutschland). Even if you write to someone at a university in another country, you have to use the country code, so, for example, it would be "ac.uk" for an academic institution in Britain, or "edu.au" for an educational institution in Australia. But when you write to people in the United States, the e-mail address ends with "edu" for an educational institution, "org" for an organization, "gov" for a federal government office, or "com" or "net" for commercial Internet providers. Why is it that the United States doesn't have a country code?

It is because when you are the dominant power in the world, everyone else needs to be named. When you are "in power," you needn't draw attention to yourself as a specific entity, but rather you can pretend to be the generic, the universal, the generalizable. From the point of view of the United States, all other countries are "other" and thus need to be named, marked, noted. Once again, privilege is invisible.

There are consequences to this invisibility: privilege, as well as gender, remains invisible. And it is hard to generate a politics of inclusion from invisibility. The invisibility of privilege means that many men, like many white people, become defensive and angry when confronted with the statistical realities or the human consequences of racism or sexism. Since our privilege is invisible, we may become defensive. Hey, we may even feel like victims ourselves.

In *The Envy of the World, Newsweek* writer Ellis Cose underscores this issue when he counsels other black people in this way:

> Given such psychologically complex phenomena as racial guilt and racial pain, you are not likely to find much empathy or understanding when you bring racial complaints to whites. The best you can generally hope for is an awkward silence accompanied by the suspicion that you are crying wolf. (excerpted in *Newsweek*, January 28, 2002, p. 52)

I was reminded of this sort of reaction from the privileged when I appeared on a television talk show opposite three "angry white males"—three men who felt that they had been the victims of workplace discrimination. The show's title, no doubt to entice a large potential audience, was "A Black Woman Took My Job." In my comments to these angry men, I invited them to consider what the word "my" meant in that title, that they felt that the jobs were originally "theirs," that they were entitled to them, and that when some "other" person—black, female—got the job, that person was really taking "their" job. But by what right is that his job? By convention, by a historical legacy of such profound levels of discrimination that we have needed decades of affirmative action to even begin to make slightly more level a playing field that has tilted so decidedly in one direction.

Our task is to begin to make visible the privilege that accompanies and conceals that invisibility.

The Invisible Knapsack

One way to understand how privilege works—and how it is kept invisible—is to look at the way we think about inequality. We always think about inequality from the perspective of the one who is hurt by the inequality, not the one who is helped. Take, for example, wage inequality based on gender. We're used to hearing that women make about 78 cents for every dollar made by a man. In that statistic women's wages are calculated as a function of men's wages; men's wages are the standard (the $1) against which women's wages are calculated. In this way, the discrimination against women is visible—doing the same job, they earn less, just because they are women.

But what if we changed the statistics? What if we expressed men's wages as a function of women's wages? What if we said that for every dollar earned by a woman, men make $1.28? Then it wouldn't be the discrimination that was visible—it would be the privilege. Just for being a male, a male worker received an additional 28 cents. This is what sociologist R. W. Connell calls the "masculinity dividend"—the unearned benefits that accrue to men, just for being men.

One could easily apply this model to race, class, and sexuality. And several of the authors in this volume probe their own experiences as a way to enable others to see what had earlier been invisible. Perhaps no one has done that more successfully than Peggy McIntosh, in her celebrated essay on what she calls the "invisible knapsack." The invisible knapsack contains all the little benefits that come to us simply because we are white, or straight, or middle class, or male. We have to open up that knapsack, dump its contents out, and take a look at all the very different ways that these ascribed characteristics (those we were born with) have become so obscured that we have come to believe that the events of our lives are the results of achieved characteristics.

Making gender, race, class, and sexuality visible—both as the foundations of individual identity and as the social dynamics of inequality—means that we pay some attention to the differences among them as well. Often students argue that gender is different from race, because, as one of my students put it, "you have to live every day with a person of the opposite sex, but you don't have to live so intimately with people of another race." Leaving aside the potential racism or heterosexism of such a statement—one might, after all, live intimately with someone of a different race, or one might not live with someone of the opposite sex—this student does point to an important issue: *just as all forms of inequality are not the same, all forms of privilege are not the same.*

For example, two of the dimensions we discuss in this book—race and gender—appear, at least on the surface, to be based on characteristics present at birth: one's sex or race. That means that they are always visible to an observer. (Well, at least nearly always. There are, of course, people who change their biological sex, or who dress differently from established norms, and those who try to pass as members of another race, and even those, like the late Michael Jackson, who seem to be using draconian surgical techniques to be taken for the other.) Thus the privileges based on gender or race may feel even more invisible because those privileged by race and gender did nothing to earn their privilege.

Privilege based on physical ability is difficult to navigate because the world was made largely by physically able people *for* physically able people.

The idea that sidewalks and curbs were not "neutral" would have been a foreign concept indeed to people as recently as the 1970s, when a group in California, at the Center for Independent Living, began the first campaign for ramps. Equal access to public buildings has to, in fact, provide *equal* access to everyone. Equality doesn't mean we all can use the same stairs (e.g., that there is no longer a separate entrance for "white" and for "colored" or for "boys" and "girls"). Equality means we all may have to use *different* means to arrive at the *same* place.

The other dimensions—sexuality, religion, class—however, are not immediately visible to the public. One can more easily pass as a member of a privileged group. But sexual minorities also may feel that their identity is not a social construction but the fulfillment of an inner essence—that is, it is more like race and gender than it is like class. While race and biological sex may seem to be evidently inborn, biologically based, and/or "God-given," sexuality also feels like that to both heterosexuals and homosexuals.

Class, however, does not. In fact, class seems to feel exactly the opposite—as a status that one was not born with but that one has earned. Class is less visible than the other dimensions because while our objective position in an economic order depends on empirically measurable criteria (income, occupation, education), class as an everyday experience rests on other people's evaluation of our presentation of self. It is far easier to pass as something we are not—both for people of modest means to affect the lifestyle of the rich and famous and for very wealthy people to affect the styles of the poor. While most of us would like to have everyone think we are wealthier than we actually are, it is often the case that the truly wealthy want everyone to think they are *less* wealthy than they are. We may dress "up" while they dress "down."

Often we will associate ourselves with the trappings of the class to which we aspire as opposed to the class from which we actually come. Take, for example, fashion. I am reasonably certain that most of the readers of this essay have, at some point in their lives, gone bowling. And I am equally certain that very few readers, if any, have ever played polo. And yet I would bet that many of you would be very happy to shell out a lot of money for a garment that identified you as a polo player (for example, a Ralph Lauren "Polo" shirt with a little polo player on it) than for an equally well-made garment with a little bowler on it. In fact, you would be eager to pay a premium on that Polo shirt precisely because the brand has become associated with a class position to which you can only aspire.

Class can be concealed and class feels like something we have earned all by ourselves. Therefore, class privilege may be the one set of privileges we are least interested in examining because they feel like they are ours by right, not by birth. All the more reason to take a look at class.

Religious privilege can be equally invisible. Imagine that you are Buddhist or Muslim or Taoist, or Jewish or Hindu or any one of the thousands of religions in the world, and you live in a country in which people routinely proclaim, "America is a Christian nation!" Just how welcome would you feel? Just how much a part of the nation would you feel? Or imagine you are an atheist, as fully 20 percent of all Americans are, and you have to clench your teeth every single time you say the Pledge of Allegiance and mouth the words "under God" without actually saying them? Religious privilege is when you assume that everyone has a faith, and that everyone's faith is the same generic Christianity as yours. It's called "christonormativity"—the assumption that everyone else is also Christian. And when you wish someone a "Merry Christmas," you might think you are being *inclusive* and genuinely warm and friendly toward them. But the other person may experience this as *exclusionary*, making him or her feel you are cold and unfeeling. If you don't assume someone's religion, or even that they *have* one, you can't offend them.

The Souls of White (and Straight and Middle-Class and Male) Folk

Taking a look at class is a difficult thing to do, and there is no question that it will make us feel uncomfortable. It's unpleasant to acknowledge that all the good things that have happened to you are not simply the result of your hard work and talent and motivation but the result of something you had no power over. Sometimes it will make us feel guilty, other times defensive. Sometimes we just feel powerless. "What can I possibly do to change this massive system of inequality?"

In a culture such as ours, all problems are thought to be individual problems, based on bad attitudes, wrong choices, or our own frailties and addictions. When confronted with structural or social problems, we think the solutions are either aggregated individual solutions—*everyone* needs to change their attitudes—or that the solutions don't exist. A single, lone individual has no chance, we think, to change the system. You can't fight City Hall.

We feel powerless, impotent. We can become mired in guilt. Some people argue that guilt is a negative emotion and that we shouldn't have to feel guilty for the things that happened generations—even centuries—ago. Occasionally someone is moved by that guilt to attempt to renounce his or her privilege. Books counsel us to become "race traitors," or to "refuse" to be a man.

And sometimes a posture of self-negation feels moral and self-righteous. Guilt isn't always a "bad" emotion after all. How would you feel about a German student who says that he really didn't want to feel guilty about genocide in World War II? "After all, I never personally sent a Jew to the gas chamber." Or a white South African who proclaimed that she never actually benefited from apartheid, since she got her job and her wealth by virtue of her hard work and determination.

Guilt may be appropriate, even a necessary feeling—for a while. It does not freeze us in abjection, but can motivate us to transform the circumstances that made us feel guilty in the first place, to make connections between our experiences and others' and to become and remain accountable to the struggles for equality and justice around the world. Guilt can politicize us. (Perhaps that's one reason we often resist it?)

While noble in its intention, however, this posture of guilty self-negation cannot be our final destination as we come to understand how we are privileged by race, class, gender, and sexuality. Refusing to be men, white, or straight does neither the privileged nor the unprivileged much good. One can no more renounce privilege than one can stop breathing. It's in the air we breathe.

And it is embedded in the architecture that surrounds us. Renouncing privilege ultimately substitutes an individual solution for a structural and social problem. Inequality is structural and systematic, as well as individual and attitudinal. Eliminating inequalities involves more than changing everyone's attitudes.

Trying to rid oneself of bad attitudes, renouncing one's unearned privilege also, finally, brings us no further than the feelings of impotent despair that we often feel in the face of such overwhelming systemic problems. We feel lonely. We feel isolated from our friends, our families, or our classmates. It's the loneliness of the long-distance runner against the wind.

The struggles against inequality are, however, collective struggles, enormous social movements that unite people across geography, race, religion, class, sexuality, and gender. Participating in these struggles to end inequality brings one into a long history of those who have stood alongside the victims of oppression, those who have added their voices to the voices of those who had been earlier silenced. Examining our privilege may be uncomfortable at first, but it can also be energizing, motivating, and engaging.

A Method of Analysis

In this book, we try to use an "intersectional approach" to explore the ways in which race, class, gender, sexuality, (dis)ability, and religion intersect and interact. This theory was first developed by women of color who argued that the variables of race, class, gender, and sexuality could not be separated in understanding their experiences. This was a response to the traditional studies of race, which focused on race alone and usually ended up focused narrowly on men of color, and women's studies, which often focused only on the experiences of white women. But some of these theorists asked different questions: Where does the black person stop and the woman begin? How can one analyze the totality of one's experience without examining the ways in which all these categories coincide, collide, contradict?

Intersectionality has now become a buzzword in academia, though it still has virtually no currency outside of colleges and universities. It's clear that the different statuses we occupy—by race, class, gender, sexuality, age, etc.— all shape and modify one another. Sometimes one of these becomes a master status through which all others are filtered and in which all others become sort of adjectives to its noun. At other times, they shift and sort and collide in ways that can give you a headache. It's complex, and one always runs the risk of a slippery slope into an infinite regress, and by the time you're done enumerating all the different statuses you occupy, you are the only one of that specific combination, and therefore immune to any and all generalizations. Individualism is not the corrective to a social analysis; it's part of it.

What does seem clear, from surveys of young people, is that the places in which we are not privileged are the ones of which we are most aware. In a well-known study, students were asked to list five characteristics about themselves. Not "cool" or "pretty" or "awesome," but five social characteristics. Virtually all the African-American students listed their race; virtually no white students did. (Asian students and Latinos were split about 50/50.) About 25 percent of the students listed "Christian" (they were largely evangelicals), but nearly 100 percent of the Jews and Muslims listed their faith. (Virtually no atheists listed that; it's just not that important to them, I guess.)

None of the heterosexual students wrote "straight" but virtually all the LGBT students listed something to do with their sexuality. Many students listed their ethnicity—Irish, Italian, Dominican, Russian. Not one student who did not have a disability wrote anything about that; every single physically disabled student noted it. And no one wrote anything to do with class. No one at all.

It's still the case that those parts of our lives in which we feel we stick out, by which we feel marginal, are the most visible to us. We are more aware of where we don't fit in to the dominant groups than where we do. Yet both— our membership in dominant if invisible groups and our membership in visible yet marginalized groups—define us, providing the raw materials from which we fashion an identity. Subordinate and superordinate—these are the statuses that enable us to define who we are.

We need to understand both if we are to understand ourselves, as well as others. We need to see how these different statuses combine and collide, reinforce and contradict one another. This volume uses an intersectional analysis to explore the ways in which race, gender, class, religion, physical ability, and sexuality interact in the lives of those who are privileged by one or more of these identities. We bring together leading thinkers and writers on all of these dimensions, to examine both the parallels and the ruptures among these different but connected relationships. Written both personally and analytically, these essays can bring the reader inside the experiences, and enable us all to begin to theorize our own lives, as well as to explore the ways in which these systems intersect in people's lives.

Ultimately we believe that examining those arenas in which we are privileged as well as those arenas in which we are not privileged will enable us to understand our society more fully, and engage us in the long historical process of change.

part one

making privilege visible

1

white privilege and male privilege

Peggy McIntosh*

Through work to bring materials and perspectives from Women's Studies into the rest of the curriculum, I have often noticed men's unwillingness to grant that they are over-privileged in the curriculum, even though they may grant that women are disadvantaged. Denials which amount to taboos surround the subject of advantages which men gain from women's disadvantages. These denials protect male privilege from being fully recognized, acknowledged, lessened, or ended.

Thinking through unacknowledged male privilege as a phenomenon with a life of its own, I realized that since hierarchies in our society are interlocking, there was most likely a phenomenon of white privilege which was similarly denied and protected, but alive and real in its effects. As a white person, I realized I had been taught about racism as something which puts others at a disadvantage, but had been taught not to see one of its corollary aspects, white privilege, which puts me at an advantage.

---

*"White Privilege and Male Privilege: A Personal Account of Coming to See Correspondences Through Work in Women's Studies," by Peggy McIntosh. Copyright © 1988 by Peggy McIntosh, Working Paper 189, Wellesley College. Center for Research on Women, Wellesley, MA 02481.

I think whites are carefully taught not to recognize white privilege, as males are taught not to recognize male privilege. So I have begun in an untutored way to ask what it is like to have white privilege. This paper is a partial record of my personal observations, and not a scholarly analysis. It is based on my daily experiences within my particular circumstances.

I have come to see white privilege as an invisible package of unearned assets which I can count on cashing in each day, but about which I was "meant" to remain oblivious. White privilege is like an invisible weightless knapsack of special provisions, assurances, tools, maps, guides, codebooks, passports, visas, clothes, compass, emergency gear, and blank checks.

Since I have had trouble facing white privilege, and describing its results in my life, I saw parallels here with men's reluctance to acknowledge male privilege. Only rarely will a man go beyond acknowledging that women are [dis]advantaged to acknowledging that men have unearned advantage, or that unearned privilege has not been good for men's development as human beings, or for society's development, or that privilege systems might ever be challenged and *changed.*

I will review here several types or layers of denial which I see at work protecting, and preventing awareness about, entrenched male privilege. Then I will draw parallels, from my own experience, with the denials which veil the facts of white privilege. Finally, I will list 46 ordinary and daily ways in which I experience having white privilege, within my life situation and its particular social and political frameworks.

Writing this paper has been difficult, despite warm receptions for the talks on which it is based.[1] For describing white privilege makes one newly accountable. As we in Women's Studies work to reveal male privilege and ask men to give up some of their power, so one who writes about having white privilege must ask, "Having described it, what will I do to lessen or end it?"

The denial of men's overprivileged state takes many forms in discussions of curriculum change work. Some claim that men must be central in the curriculum because they have done most of what is important or distinctive in life or in civilization. Some recognize sexism in the curriculum but deny that it makes male students seem unduly important in life. Others agree that certain *individual* thinkers are blindly male-oriented but deny that there is any systemic tendency in disciplinary frameworks or epistemology to over-empower men as a group. Those men who do grant that male privilege takes institutionalized and embedded forms are still likely to deny that male hegemony has opened doors for them personally. Virtually all men deny that male overreward alone can explain men's centrality in all the inner sanctums of our most powerful institutions. Moreover, those few who will acknowledge that male privilege systems have over-empowered them usually end up doubting that we could dismantle these privilege systems. They may say they will work to improve women's status, in the society or in the university, but they can't or won't support the idea of lessening men's. In curricular terms, this is the point at which they say that they regret they cannot use any of the interesting new scholarship on women because the syllabus is full. When the talk turns to giving men less cultural room, even the most thoughtful and fair-minded of the men I know well tend to reflect, or fall back on, conservative assumptions about the inevitability of present gender relations and distributions of power, calling on precedent or sociobiology and psychobiology to demonstrate that male domination is natural and follows inevitably from evolutionary pressures. Others resort to arguments from "experience" or religion or social responsibility or wishing and dreaming.

After I realized, through faculty development work in Women's Studies, the extent to which men work from a base of unacknowledged privilege, I understood that much of their oppressiveness was unconscious. Then I remembered the frequent charges from women of color that white women whom they encounter are oppressive. I began to understand why we are justly seen as oppressive, even when we don't see ourselves that way. At the very least, obliviousness of one's privileged state can make a person or group irritating to be with. I began to count the ways in which I enjoy unearned skin privilege and have been conditioned into oblivion about its existence, unable to see that it put me "ahead" in any way, or put my people ahead, overrewarding us and yet also paradoxically damaging us, or that it could or should be changed.

My schooling gave me no training in seeing myself as an oppressor, as an unfairly advantaged person, or as a participant in a damaged culture. I was taught to see myself as an individual whose moral state depended on her individual moral will. At school, we were not taught about slavery in any depth; we were not taught to see slaveholders as damaged people. Slaves were seen as the only group at risk of being dehumanized. My schooling followed the pattern which Elizabeth Minnich has pointed out: whites are taught to think of their lives as morally neutral, normative, and average, and also ideal, so that when we work to benefit others, this is seen as work which will allow "them" to be more like "us." I think many of us know how obnoxious this attitude can be in men.

After frustration with men who would not recognize male privilege, I decided to try to work on myself at least by identifying some of the daily effects of white privilege in my life. It is crude work, at this stage, but I will give here a list of special circumstances and conditions I experience which I did not earn but which I have been made to feel are mine by birth, by citizenship, and by virtue of being a conscientious law-abiding "normal" person of goodwill. I have chosen those conditions which I think in my case *attach somewhat more to skin-color privilege* than to class, religion, ethnic status, or geographical location, though of course all these other factors are intricately intertwined. As far as I can see, my Afro-American co-workers, friends, and acquaintances with whom I come into daily or frequent contact in this particular time, place, and line of work cannot count on most of these conditions.

1. I can, if I wish, arrange to be in the company of people of my race most of the time.
2. I can avoid spending time with people whom I was trained to mistrust and who have learned to mistrust my kind or me.
3. If I should need to move, I can be pretty sure of renting or purchasing housing in an area which I can afford and in which I would want to live.
4. I can be pretty sure that my neighbors in such a location will be neutral or pleasant to me.
5. I can go shopping alone most of the time, pretty well assured that I will not be followed or harassed.
6. I can turn on the television or open to the front page of the paper and see people of my race widely represented.
7. When I am told about our national heritage or about "civilization," I am shown that people of my color made it what it is.
8. I can be sure that my children will be given curricular materials that testify to the existence of their race.
9. If I want to, I can be pretty sure of finding a publisher for this piece on white privilege.
10. I can be pretty sure of having my voice heard in a group in which I am the only member of my race.
11. I can be casual about whether or not to listen to another woman's voice in a group in which she is the only member of her race.

12. I can go into a music shop and count on finding the music of my race represented, into a supermarket and find the staple foods which fit with my cultural traditions, into a hairdresser's shop and find someone who can cut my hair.
13. Whether I use checks, credit cards, or cash, I can count on my skin color not to work against the appearance of financial reliability.
14. I can arrange to protect my children most of the time from people who might not like them.
15. I do not have to educate my children to be aware of systemic racism for their own daily physical protection.
16. I can be pretty sure that my children's teachers and employers will tolerate them if they fit school and workplace norms; my chief worries about them do not concern others' attitudes toward their race.
17. I can talk with my mouth full and not have people put this down to my color.
18. I can swear, or dress in secondhand clothes, or not answer letters, without having people attribute these choices to the bad morals, the poverty, or the illiteracy of my race.
19. I can speak in public to a powerful male group without putting my race on trial.
20. I can do well in a challenging situation without being called a credit to my race.
21. I am never asked to speak for all the people of my racial group.
22. I can remain oblivious of the language and customs of persons of color who constitute the world's majority without feeling in my culture any penalty for such oblivion.
23. I can criticize our government and talk about how much I fear its policies and behavior without being seen as a cultural outsider.
24. I can be pretty sure that if I ask to talk to "the person in charge," I will be facing a person of my race.
25. If a traffic cop pulls me over or if the IRS audits my tax return, I can be sure I haven't been singled out because of my race.
26. I can easily buy posters, post-cards, picture books, greeting cards, dolls, toys, and children's magazines featuring people of my race.
27. I can go home from most meetings of organizations I belong to, feeling somewhat tied in rather than isolated, out-of-place, outnumbered, unheard, held at a distance, or feared.

28. I can be pretty sure that an argument with a colleague of another race is more likely to jeopardize her chances for advancement than to jeopardize mine.

29. I can be pretty sure that if I argue for the promotion of a person of another race, or a program centering on race, this is not likely to cost me heavily within my present setting, even if my colleagues disagree with me.

30. If I declare there is a racial issue at hand, or there isn't a racial issue at hand, my race will lend me more credibility for either position than a person of color will have.

31. I can choose to ignore developments in minority writing and minority activist programs, or disparage them, or learn from them, but in any case, I can find ways to be more or less protected from negative consequences of any of these choices.

32. My culture gives me little fear about ignoring the perspectives and powers of people of other races.

33. I am not made acutely aware that my shape, bearing, or body odor will be taken as a reflection on my race.

34. I can worry about racism without being seen as self-interested or self-seeking.

35. I can take a job with an affirmative action employer without having my co-workers on the job suspect that I got it because of my race.

36. If my day, week, or year is going badly, I need not ask of each negative episode or situation whether it has racial overtones.

37. I can be pretty sure of finding people who would be willing to talk to me and advise me about my next steps, professionally.

38. I can think over many options, social, political, imaginative, or professional, without asking whether a person of my race would be accepted or allowed to do what I want to do.

39. I can be late to a meeting without having the lateness reflect on my race.

40. I can choose public accommodation without fearing that people of my race cannot get in or will be mistreated in the places I have chosen.

41. I can be sure that if I need legal or medical help, my race will not work against me.

42. I can arrange my activities so that I will never have to experience feelings of rejection owing to my race.

43. If I have low credibility as a leader I can be sure that my race is not the problem.
44. I can easily find academic courses and institutions which give attention only to people of my race.
45. I can expect figurative language and imagery in all of the arts to testify to experiences of my race.
46. I can choose blemish cover or bandages in "flesh" color and have them more or less match my skin.

I repeatedly forgot each of the realizations on this list until I wrote it down. For me, white privilege has turned out to be an elusive and fugitive subject. The pressure to avoid it is great, for in facing it I must give up the myth of meritocracy. If these things are true, this is not such a free country; one's life is not what one makes it; many doors open for certain people through no virtues of their own. These perceptions mean also that my moral condition is not what I had been led to believe. The appearance of being a good citizen rather than a troublemaker comes in large part from having all sorts of doors open automatically because of my color.

A further paralysis of nerve comes from literary silence protecting privilege. My clearest memories of finding such analysis are in Lillian Smith's unparalleled *Killers of the Dream* and Margaret Andersen's review of Karen and Mamie Fields' *Lemon Swamp*. Smith, for example, wrote about walking toward black children on the street and knowing they would step into the gutter; Andersen contrasted the pleasure which she, as a white child, took on summer driving trips to the South with Karen Fields' memories of driving in a closed car stocked with all necessities lest, in stopping, her black family should suffer "insult, or worse." Adrienne Rich also recognizes and writes about daily experiences of privilege, but in my observation, white women's writing in this area is far more often on systemic racism than on our daily lives as light-skinned women.[2]

In unpacking this invisible knapsack of white privilege, I have listed conditions of daily experience which I once took for granted, as neutral, normal, and universally available to everybody, just as I once thought of a male-focused curriculum as the neutral or accurate account which can speak for all. Nor did I think of any of these perquisites as bad for the holder. I now think that we need a more finely differentiated taxonomy of privilege, for some of these varieties are only what one would want for everyone in a just society, and others give license to be ignorant, oblivious, arrogant, and destructive.

Before proposing some more finely tuned categorization, I will make some observations about the general effects of these conditions on my life and expectations.

In this potpourri of examples, some privileges make me feel at home in the world. Others allow me to escape penalties or dangers which others suffer. Through some, I escape fear, anxiety, or a sense of not being welcome or not being real. Some keep me from having to hide, to be in disguise, to feel sick or crazy, to negotiate each transaction from the position of being an outsider or, within my group, a person who is suspected of having too close links with a dominant culture. Most keep me from having to be angry.

I see a pattern running through the matrix of white privilege, a pattern of assumptions which were passed on to me as a white person. There was one main piece of cultural turf; it was my own turf, and I was among those who could control the turf. I could measure up to the cultural standards and take advantage of the many options I saw around me to make what the culture would call a success of my life. *My skin color was an asset for any move I was educated to want to make,* I could think of myself as "belonging" in major ways, and of making social systems work for me. I could freely disparage, fear, neglect, or be oblivious to anything outside of the dominant cultural forms. Being of the main culture, I could also criticize it fairly freely. My life was reflected back to me frequently enough so that I felt, with regard to my race, if not to my sex, like one of the real people.

Whether through the curriculum or in the newspaper, the television, the economic system, or the general look of people in the streets, we received daily signals and indications that my people counted, and that others *either didn't exist or must be trying, not very successfully, to be like people of my race.* We were given cultural permission not to hear voices of people of other races, or a tepid cultural tolerance for hearing or acting on such voices. I was also raised not to suffer seriously from anything which darker-skinned people might say about my group, "protected," though perhaps I should more accurately say *prohibited,* through the habits of my economic class and social group, from living in racially mixed groups or being reflective about interactions between people of differing races.

In proportion as my racial group was being made confident, comfortable, and oblivious, other groups were likely being made inconfident, uncomfortable, and alienated. Whiteness protected me from many kinds of hostility, distress, and violence, which I was being subtly trained to visit in turn upon people of color.

For this reason, the word "privilege" now seems to me misleading. Its connotations are too positive to fit the conditions and behaviors which "privilege systems" produce. We usually think of privilege as being a favored state, whether earned or conferred by birth or luck. School graduates are reminded they are privileged and urged to use their (enviable) assets well. The word "privilege" carries the connotation of being something everyone must want. Yet some of the conditions I have described here work to systematically overempower certain groups. Such privilege simply *confers dominance,* gives permission to control, because of one's race or sex. The kind of privilege which gives license to some people to be, at best, thoughtless, and at worst, murderous should not continue to be referred to as a desirable attribute. Such "privilege" may be widely desired without being in any way beneficial to the whole society.

Moreover, though "privilege" may confer power, it does not confer moral strength. Those who do not depend on conferred dominance have traits and qualities which may never develop in those who do. Just as Women's Studies courses indicate that women survive their political circumstances to lead lives which hold the human race together, so "under-privileged" people of color who are the world's majority have survived their oppression and lived survivors' lives from which the white global minority can and must learn. In some groups, those dominated have actually become strong through *not* having all of these unearned advantages, and this gives them a great deal to teach the others. Members of so-called privileged groups can seem foolish, ridiculous, infantile, or dangerous by contrast.

I want, then, to distinguish between earned strength and unearned power conferred systemically. Power from unearned privilege can look like strength when it is in fact permission to escape or to dominate. But not all of the privileges on my list are inevitably damaging. Some, like the expectation that neighbors will be decent to you, or that your race will not count against you in court, should be the norm in a just society and should be considered as the entitlement of everyone. Others, like the privilege not to listen to less powerful people, distort the humanity of the holders as well as the ignored groups. Still others, like finding one's staple foods everywhere, may be a function of being a member of a numerical majority in the population. Others have to do with not having to labor under pervasive negative stereotyping and mythology.

We might at least start by distinguishing between positive advantages which we can work to spread, to the point where they are not advantages at all but simply part of the normal civic and social fabric, and negative types of advantage which unless rejected will always reinforce our present hierarchies. For example, the positive "privilege" of belonging, the feeling that one belongs within the human circle, as Native Americans say, fosters development and should not be seen as privilege for a few. It is, let us say, an entitlement which none of us should have to earn; ideally it is an *unearned entitlement.* At present, since only a few have it, it is an *unearned advantage* for them. The negative "privilege" which gave me cultural permission not to take darker-skinned Others seriously can be seen as arbitrarily conferred dominance and should not be desirable for anyone. This paper results from a process of coming to see that some of the power which I originally saw as attendant on being a human being in the United States consisted in *unearned advantage* and *conferred dominance,* as well as other special circumstances not universally taken for granted.

In writing this paper I have also realized that white identity and status (as well as class identity and status) give me considerable power to choose whether to broach this subject and its trouble. I can pretty well decide whether to disappear and avoid and not listen and escape the dislike I may engender in other people through this essay, or interrupt, take over, dominate, preach, direct, criticize, or control to some extent what goes on in reaction to it. Being white, I am given considerable power to escape many kinds of danger or penalty as well as to choose which risks I want to take.

There is an analogy here, once again, with Women's Studies. Our male colleagues do not have a great deal to lose in supporting Women's Studies, but they do not have a great deal to lose if they oppose it either. They simply have the power to decide whether to commit themselves to more equitable distributions of power. They will probably feel few penalties, whatever choice they make; they do not seem, in any obvious short-term sense, the ones at risk, though they and we are all at risk because of the behaviors which have been rewarded in them.

Through Women's Studies work I have met very few men who are truly distressed about systemic, unearned male advantage and conferred dominance. And so one question for me and others like me is whether we will be like them, or whether we will get truly distressed, even outraged, about unearned race advantage and conferred dominance, and if so, what we will do to lessen them. In any case, we need to do more work in identifying how they actually affect our daily lives. We need more down-to-earth writing by people about these taboo subjects. We need more understanding of the ways in which white "privilege" damages white people, for these are not the same ways in which it damages the victimized. Skewed white psyches are an inseparable part of the picture, though I do not want to confuse the kinds of damage done to the holders of special assets and to those who suffer the deficits. Many, perhaps most, of our white students in the United States think that racism doesn't affect them because they are not people of color; they do not see "whiteness" as a racial identity. Many men likewise think that Women's Studies does not bear on their own existences because they are not female; they do not see themselves as having gendered identities. Insisting on the universal *effects* of "privilege" systems, then, becomes one of our chief tasks, and being more explicit about the *particular* effects in particular contexts is another. Men need to join us in this work.

In addition, since race and sex are not the only advantaging systems at work, we need to similarly examine the daily experience of having age advantage, or ethnic advantage, or physical ability or advantage related to nationality, religion, or sexual orientation. Professor Marnie Evans suggested to me that in many ways the list I made also applies directly to heterosexual privilege. This is a still more taboo subject than race privilege: the daily ways in which heterosexual privilege makes married persons comfortable or powerful, providing supports, assets, approvals, and rewards to those who live or expect to live in heterosexual pairs. Unpacking that content is still more difficult, owing to the deeper imbeddedness of heterosexual advantage and dominance, and stricter taboos surrounding these.

But to start such an analysis I would put this observation from my own experience: The fact that I live under the same roof with a man triggers all kinds of societal assumptions about my worth, politics, life, and values, and triggers a host of unearned advantages and powers. After recasting many elements from the original list, I would add further observations like these:

1. My children do not have to answer questions about why I live with my partner (my husband).
2. I have no difficulty finding neighborhoods where people approve of our household.
3. My children are given texts and classes which implicitly support our kind of family unit, and do not turn them against my choice of domestic partnership.
4. I can travel alone or with my husband without expecting embarrassment or hostility in those who deal with us.

5. Most people I meet will see my marital arrangements as an asset to my life or as a favorable comment on my likability, my competence, or my mental health.
6. I can talk about the social events of a weekend without fearing most listeners' reactions.
7. I will feel welcomed and "normal" in the usual walks of public life, institutional and social.
8. In many contexts, I am seen as "all right" in daily work on women because I do not live chiefly with women.

Difficulties and dangers surrounding the task of finding parallels are many. Since racism, sexism, and heterosexism are not the same, the advantaging associated with them should not be seen as the same. In addition, it is hard to disentangle aspects of unearned advantage which rest more on social class, economic class, race, religion, sex, and ethnic identity than on other factors. Still, all of the oppressions are interlocking, as the Combahee River Collective statement of 1977 continues to remind us eloquently.[3]

One fact seems clear about all of the interlocking oppressions. They take both active forms which we can see and embedded forms which, as a member of the dominant group, one is taught not to see. In my class and place, I did not see myself as racist because I was taught to recognize racism only in individual acts of meanness by members of my group, never in invisible systems conferring unsought racial dominance on my group from birth. Likewise, we are taught to think that sexism or heterosexism is carried on only through individual acts of discrimination, meanness, or cruelty toward women, gays, and lesbians, rather than in invisible systems conferring unsought dominance on certain groups. Disapproving of the systems won't be enough to change them. I was taught to think that racism could end if white individuals changed their attitudes; many men think sexism can be ended by individual changes in daily behavior toward women. But a man's sex provides advantage for him whether or not he approves of the way in which dominance has been conferred on his group. A "white" skin in the United States opens many doors for whites whether or not we approve of the way dominance has been conferred on us. Individual acts can palliate, but cannot end, these problems. To redesign social systems, we need first to acknowledge their colossal unseen dimensions. The silences and denials surrounding privilege are the key political tool here. They keep the thinking about equality or equity incomplete, protecting unearned advantage and conferred dominance by making these subjects taboo. Most talk by whites about equal opportunity seems to me now to be about equal opportunity to try to get into a position of dominance while denying that *systems* of dominance exist.

It seems to me that obliviousness about white advantage, like oblivious- ness about male advantage, is kept strongly inculturated in the United States so as to maintain the myth of meritocracy, the myth that democratic choice is equally available to all. Keeping most people unaware that freedom of con- fident action is there for just a small number of people props up those in power and serves to keep power in the hands of the same groups that have most of it already. Though systemic change takes many decades, there are pressing questions for me and, I imagine, for some others like me, if we raise our daily consciousness on the perquisites of being light-skinned. What will we do with such knowledge? As we know from watching men, it is an open question whether we will choose to use unearned advantage to weaken hid- den systems of advantage, and whether we will use any of our arbitrarily awarded power to try to reconstruct power systems on a broader base.

notes

This paper was funded by the Anna Wilder Phelps Fund through the generosity of Anna Emery Hanson. I have appreciated commentary on this paper from the Working Papers Committee of the Wellesley College Center for Research on Women, from members of the Dodge seminar, and from many individuals, including Margaret Andersen, Sorel Berman, Joanne Braxton, Johnnella Butler, Sandra Dickerson, Marnie Evans, Beverly Guy-Sheftall, Sandra Harding, Eleanor Hinton Hoytt, Pauline Houston, Paul Lauter, Joyce Miller, Mary Norris, Gloria Oden, Beverly Smith, and John Walter.

1. This paper was presented at the Virginia Women's Studies Association conference in Richmond in April 1986 and the American Educational Research Association conference in Boston in October 1986 and discussed with two groups of participants in the Dodge Sem- inars for Secondary School Teachers in New York and Boston in the spring of 1987.

2. Andersen, Margaret, "Race and the Social Science Curriculum: A Teaching and Learn- ing Discussion," *Radical Teacher*, November 1984, pp. 17–20. Smith, Lillian, *Killers of the Dream*, New York, 1949.

3. "A Black Feminist Statement," The Combahee River Collective, pp. 13–22 in Hull, Scott, Smith, eds., *All the Women Are White, All the Blacks Are Men but Some of Us Are Brave: Black Women's Studies*, The Feminist Press, 1982.

2

the black male privileges checklist

Jewel Woods*

What does "privilege" have to do with black men?[1] We understand some kinds of privilege: The twentieth-century white privilege to call a black man "boy" even if that black man happened to be sixty years old or older. The white privilege to drive a car and never have to worry about racial profiling. These are privileges that have nothing to do with what a person has earned but rather are based entirely on race. As African Americans, we have the ability to critique and condemn these types of "unearned assets" because we recognize that these privileges come largely at our expense. We have also learned from social and political movements that have sought to redress these privileges and academic disciplines that have provided us with the tools to critically examine and explore them.

However, another type of privilege has caused untold harm to both black men and women, but our community has not had the benefit of that privilege being challenged by a social and political movement from within, nor has it been given adequate attention within our academic community. The privilege I am referring to is male privilege. Just as white privilege comes at the expense of African Americans and other people of color, black male privilege comes at the expense of women in general, and black women in particular.

Given the devastating history of racism in this country, it is understandable that getting black men to identify with the concept of male privilege isn't easy. For many of us, the phrase "black male privilege" seems like an oxymoron—three words that simply do not go together. Although it is understandable that some black men are hesitant or reluctant to examine the concept of male privilege, the African-American community will never be able to overcome the serious issues we face if we as black men do not confront our role in promoting and sustaining male supremacist attitudes and actions.

Inviting black men and boys into a conversation about male privilege does not deny centuries of discrimination or the burden of racism that we continue to suffer today. As long as a black man can be Tasered nine times in fourteen minutes,[2] arrested in his own home for "disorderly conduct,"[3] or receive fewer callbacks for a job than a white man with a felony record,[4] we know that racism that targets black men is alive and kicking.

But race is not the only factor. Examining black male privileges offers black men and boys an opportunity to go beyond old arguments of "personal responsibility" or "blaming the man" to gain a deeper level of insight into how issues of class and race are shaped by gender. *Often the focus on our experiences of racial oppression removes gender-based domination from the analytical—and the political—eye.*

The items presented on the Black Male Privileges Checklist reflect aspects of black men's lives we take for granted. I offer this checklist based on years of experience working with men and the profound influence of black woman activists and intellectuals such as bell hooks, Angela Davis, Patricia Hill-Collins, Kimberly Crenshaw, and numerous others. I have faith that we as African-American men have far more to gain than we have to lose by challenging our male privileges.

I also believe there are more similarities between men than there are differences. Therefore, many items on the Black Male Privileges Checklist apply to men generally, and others might apply to all men of color. However, because of the specific privileges black men possess in relationship to black women, certain items apply only to black men. *I will leave it up to the reader to determine which items apply only to black men and which items apply to all men of color or men in general.*

The Black Male Privileges Checklist

Leadership and Politics

1. I don't have to choose my race over my sex in political matters.
2. When I read African-American history textbooks, I will learn mainly about black men.
3. When I learn about the civil rights and Black Power movements, most of the leaders I will learn about will be black men.
4. I can rely on the fact that in the nearly one hundred–year history of national civil rights organizations, such as the NAACP and the Urban League, virtually all of the executive directors have been men.
5. I will be taken more seriously as a political leader than black women.
6. I can be pretty sure that all of the "race leaders" I see featured in the media will be men like me.
7. I can live my life without ever having read black feminist authors or knowing about black women's history or black women's issues.
8. I could be a member or an admirer of a black liberation organization, such as the Black Panther Party, where an "out" rapist like Eldridge Cleaver could assume a leadership position, without feeling threatened or demeaned because of my sex.
9. I will make more money than black women at equal levels of education and occupation.
10. I know that most of the national "opinion framers" in black America, including talk show hosts and politicians, are men.

Beauty

11. I have the ability to define black women's beauty by European standards in terms of skin tone, hair, and body size. In comparison, black women rarely define me by European standards of beauty in terms of skin tone, hair, or body size.
12. I do not have to worry about the daily hassles of having my hair conform to some standard image of beauty the way black women do.
13. I do not have to worry about the daily hassles of being terrorized by the fear of gaining weight. In fact, in many instances bigger is better for my sex.
14. My looks will not be the central standard by which my worth is valued by members of the opposite sex.

Sex and Sexuality

15. I can purchase pornography that typically shows men defiling women by the common practice of the "money shot."
16. I can believe that causing pain during sex is connected with a woman's pleasure without ever asking her.
17. When it comes to sex, if I say no, chances are that it will not be mistaken for yes.
18. If I am raped, no one will assume that "I should have known better" or suggest that my being raped had something to do with how I was dressed.
19. I can use sexist language like "bonin'," "laying the pipe," "hittin' it," and "banging" that convey images of sexual acts based on dominance and performance.
20. I live in a world where polygamy is still an option for men in some countries.
21. I can be involved with younger women socially and sexually and it will be considered normal.
22. In general, the more sexual partners I have, the more stature I receive among my peers.
23. I have easy access to pornography that involves virtually any category of sex where men degrade women, often young women.
24. When I consume pornography, I can gain pleasure from images and sounds of men causing women pain.

Popular Culture

25. I have the privilege of coming from a tradition of humor based largely on insulting and disrespecting women, especially mothers.
26. I have the privilege of not having black women dress up and play funny characters—often overweight—that are supposed to look like me, for the entire nation to laugh at.
27. When I go to the movies, I know that most of the leads in black films will be men. I can also be confident that all of the action heroes in black films will be men.
28. I can easily assume that most of the artists in hip-hop are members of my sex.
29. I can rest assured that most of the women that appear in hip-hop videos are there solely to please men.

30. Most of the lyrics I listen to in popular hip-hop perpetuate the ideas of men dominating women, sexually and socially.
31. I can consume and popularize the word "pimp," which is based on the exploitation of women, with virtually no opposition from other men.
32. I can hear and use language that refers to women as bitches and ho's, that demeans women, with virtually no opposition from men.
33. I can wear a shirt that others and I commonly refer to as a "wife beater" and never have the language challenged.
34. Many of my favorite movies include images of strength that do not include women and often are based on violence.
35. Many of my favorite genres of films, such as martial arts, are based on male violence.

Attitudes/Ideology

36. I have the privilege to define black women as having "an attitude" without referencing the range of attitudes that black women have.
37. I have the privilege of defining black women's attitudes without defining my attitudes as a black man.
38. I can believe that the success of the black family is dependent on men serving as the head of the family rather than in promoting policies that strengthen black women's independence or that provide social benefits to black children.
39. I have the privilege of believing that a black woman cannot raise a black son to be a man.
40. I have the privilege of believing that a woman must submit to her man.
41. I have the privilege of believing that before slavery, gender relationships between black men and women were perfect.
42. I have the privilege to define ideas such as feminism as being anti-black.
43. I have the privilege of believing that the failure of the black family is due in part to black women not allowing black men to be men.
44. I have the privilege of defining gender roles within the household.
45. I have the privilege of believing that black women are different sexually from other women and judging them negatively based on this belief.

Sports

46. I will make significantly more money as a professional athlete than women will.

47. My financial success or popularity as a professional athlete will not be associated with my looks.

48. I can talk about sports or spend large portions of the day playing video games while women are most likely tending to household chores or child care duties.

49. I have the privilege to restrict my displays of emotion to certain spheres, such as sports.

50. If I am a coach, I can motivate, punish, or embarrass a player by saying that the player plays like a girl.

51. Most sports talk show hosts that are members of my race are men.

52. I can rest assured that most of the coaches—even in predominantly female sports within my race—are male.

53. I am able to play sports outside without my shirt on and not worry it will be considered a problem.

54. I am essentially able to do anything inside or outside without my shirt on, whereas women are always required to cover up.

Diaspora/Global

55. I have the privilege of not being concerned that I am a member of a sex subjected to mutilation and disfigurement to deny our sexual sensations or to protect our virginity for males.

56. I have the privilege of not having rape be used as a primary tactic or tool to terrorize my sex during war and times of conflict.

57. I have the privilege of not being able to name one female leader in Africa or Asia, past or present, that I pay homage to the way I do male leaders in Africa and/or Asia.

58. I have the ability to travel around the world and have access to women in developing countries both sexually and socially.

59. I have the privilege of being a part of the sex that starts wars and that wields control of almost all the existing weapons of war and mass destruction.

College

60. In college I will have the opportunity to date outside of the race at a much higher rate than black women will.
61. I have the privilege of having the phrase "sowing my wild oats" apply to my sex as if it were natural.
62. I know that the further I go in education the more success I will have with women.
63. By the time I enter college, and even through college, I have the privilege of not having to worry whether I will be able to marry a black woman.
64. In college I will experience a level of status and prestige that is not offered to black women even though black women may outnumber me and outperform me academically.

Communication/Language

65. What is defined as "news" in black America is defined by men.
66. I can choose to be emotionally withdrawn and not communicate in a relationship and it may be considered unfortunate, yet normal.
67. I have the privilege of not knowing what words and concepts like patriarchy, misogyny, phallocentric, complicity, colluding, and obfuscation mean.

Relationships

68. I have the privilege of marrying outside my race at a much higher rate than black women.
69. My "strength" as a man is never connected with the failure of the black family, whereas the strength of black women is routinely associated with the failure of the black family.
70. If I am considering a divorce, I know that I have substantially more marriage and cohabitation options than my spouse.
71. Chances are I will be defined as a "good man" by things I do not do as much as what I do. If I don't beat, cheat, or lie, then I am considered a "good man." In comparison, women are rarely defined as "good women" based on what they do not do.
72. I have the privilege of not having to assume most of the household or child care responsibilities.

Church and Religious Traditions

73. In the black church, the majority of the pastoral leadership is male.
74. In the black church tradition, most of the theology has a male point of view. For example, most will assume that the man is the head of household.

Physical Safety

75. I do not have to worry about being considered a traitor to my race if I call the police on a member of the opposite sex.
76. I have the privilege of knowing men who are physically or sexually abusive to women and yet I still call them friends.
77. I can videotape women in public—often without their consent—with male complicity.
78. I can be courteous to a person of the opposite sex whom I do not know and say "hello" or "hi" and not fear that it will be taken as a come-on or fear being stalked because of it.
79. I can use physical violence or the threat of physical violence to get what I want when other tactics fail in a relationship.
80. If I get into a physical altercation with a person of the opposite sex, I will most likely be able to impose my will physically on that person.
81. I can go to parades or other public events and not worry about being physically and sexually molested by persons of the opposite sex.
82. I can touch and physically grope women's bodies in public—often without their consent—with male complicity.
83. In general, I have the freedom to travel in the night without fear of rape or sexual assault.
84. I am able to be out in public without fear of being sexually harassed by individuals or groups of the opposite sex.

Background

The Black Male Privileges Checklist was born out of years of organizing men's groups and the numerous—often heated—conversations I have had with men while using Barry Deutsch's Male Privilege Checklist.[5] In my experience, most men raise objections to at least some items on the Male Privilege Checklist. However, "men of color," especially African-American men, often have the sharpest criticisms of the Male Privilege Checklist and the greatest difficulty connecting to the idea of male privilege.

There are many reasons black men are reluctant to identify with the concept of male privilege. One of the most important reasons is that our experience with privilege has largely focused specifically on race, based on a history of political, economic, and military power that whites have historically exercised over black life. This conceptualization of privilege has not allowed us to see ourselves as privileged because the focus has been placed largely on white domination. Our inability to have a more expansive understanding of privilege and power has foreclosed important insights into virtually every aspect of black men's lives as well as the lives of other men of color. As black men, we have also been skeptical of profeminist males, most of whom were (and still are) white and middle class. Black men who fought for freedom during the civil rights and the Black Power movements were suspicious—to say the least—of the motives of white men requesting that black men give up the privileges they never felt they had. Given the timing of the profeminist male movement and the demographics of these men, it has not been easy to separate the message from the messenger. Black men had a similar reaction to the voices of black feminists, whom we viewed as being influenced by white middle-class feminism. In addition, many of the items on the Male Privilege Checklist simply did not apply to black men and other men of color. As a result, many black men argued that the list should have been called the White Male Privilege Checklist. In light of these considerations, the Black Male Privileges Checklist differs from the Male Privilege Checklist in several respects.

First, it departs from an "either/or" view of privilege that suggests that an individual or a group can only be placed into one category, isolating race or gender and ignoring the ways in which these traits interact in shaping our lives. Therefore, the focus is on privileges and not privilege. It also highlights belief systems that often serve as the basis for justifications and rationalizations of exploitation and discrimination. Second, the Black Male Privileges Checklist takes a life-course perspective, acknowledging that privilege takes on different forms at various points in men's lives. Third, it takes a global perspective to highlight the privilege that black males have as Americans, and the privileges black men share with other men of color worldwide. African-American men rarely acknowledge the privilege we have in relationship to people in developing countries—especially women. Too often, our conception of privilege is limited to white men and does not lead us to reflect on the power that men of color in Africa, Asia, and Latin America exercise over women. Finally, it calls for action, not just awareness. We need men of color to be actively involved in social-welfare and social-justice movements.

As men of color, we have a responsibility to acknowledge that we participate in this sex/gender system even though it offers us little reward. Most African Americans, for example, take for granted the system of capitalism that we all participate in, even though we know that it does not offer us the same rewards that it offers whites. The sex/gender system, which privileges men over women, operates in similar ways for all men. However, black men and other men of color participate in the sex/gender system without receiving the same material and nonmaterial rewards white men do. More important, the participation of black men and other men of color in the sex/gender system further weakens communities of color, which already suffer under the weight of racial and class oppression.

Finally, the Black Male Privileges Checklist is a tool that can be used by any individual, group, organization, family, or community interested in black males having greater insight into their individual lives and the collective lives of black women and girls. It is also a living tool that will grow and be amended as more discussion and dialogue occurs. This is the first edition of the Black Male Privileges Checklist, and it will be updated regularly. This checklist was created with black men in mind and does not necessarily capture the experiences and cultural references of other ethnic minority males. I welcome dialogue with others who are concerned about these constituencies as well.

notes

1. Please visit our website, http://renaissancemaleproject.com, to view our Teen and Male Youth Privileges Checklist, a historic tool for all young males, schools, community organizations, youth groups, sports teams, and families, that can be used to assist our young males in becoming the type of adult men we want them to be.

2. This case refers to twenty-one-year-old African-American male Baron Pikes, who, according to the officer's report, died in police custody after being Tasered while lying on the ground in handcuffs. www.chicagotribune.com/news/chi-taser_witt-web-jul19,0,2201847.story (retrieved August 1, 2009).

3. Henry Louis Gates Jr., a distinguished African-American scholar at Harvard University and editor in chief of the widely read and highly influential online African-American news journal TheRoot.com, was arrested at his home for disorderly conduct. www.theroot.com/views/roots-editor-chief-arrested (retrieved August 1, 2009).

4. According to research conducted by Princeton University sociologist Devah Pager, white males with criminal felony records received more callbacks for jobs than similarly qualified black males without criminal felony records; Devah Pager, "The Mark of a Criminal Record," *American Journal of Sociology* 108, no. 5 (2003): 937–975.

5. Barry Deutsch, www.amptoons.com/blog/the-male-privilege-checklist, September 15, 2004 (retrieved May 29, 2009). Deutsch's list was inspired by Peggy McIntosh's 1988 article "White Privilege and Male Privilege: A Personal Account of Coming to See Correspondences Through Work in Women's Studies" (Working Paper 189, Wellesley Center for Women, Wellesley, MA), available at mmcintosh@wellesley.edu.

3

the invisible crutch

Jessica Shea*

The Invisible Knapsack of White Privilege, conceived by Peggy McIntosh, discusses the many things a white person takes for granted, in list form. As a white person, I was uncomfortable reading many of these things, but I also saw reflected in them what men, wealthy people, and non-disabled people take for granted.

I've decided to build an invisible crutch from things that constitute abled privilege, without repeating too much of what is in McIntosh's list (so read her list, and substitute "disability" for "color" for many of those items).

1. I can, if I wish, arrange to attend social events without worrying if they are accessible to me.
2. If I am in the company of people who make me uncomfortable, I can easily choose to move elsewhere.
3. I can easily find housing that is accessible to me, with no barriers to my mobility.
4. I can go shopping alone most of the time and be able to reach and obtain all of the items without assistance, know that cashiers will notice I am there, and can easily see and use the credit card machines.
5. I can turn on the television and see people of my ability level widely and accurately represented.

*"The Invisible Crutch," by Jessica Shea. Copyright 2009, *She Dances on the Sand* blog, http://rioiriri.blogspot.com/2009/04/invisible-crutch.html. Reprinted by permission of the author.

6. I can be pretty sure of my voice being heard in a group where I am the only person of my ability level represented—and they will make eye contact with me.

7. I can advocate for my children in their schools without my ability level being blamed for my children's performance or behavior.

8. I can do well in a challenging situation without being told what an inspiration I am.

9. If I ask to speak to someone "in charge," I can be relatively assured that the person will make eye contact with me and not treat me like I am stupid.

10. I can belong to an organization and not feel that others resent my membership because of my ability level.

11. I do not have to fear being preyed upon because of my ability level.

12. I can be reasonably assured that I won't be late for meetings due to mobility barriers.

13. I can use most cosmetics and personal care products without worrying that they will cause a painful or dangerous reaction.

14. I can usually go about in public without other people's personal care products causing me painful or dangerous reactions.

15. My neighborhood allows me to move about on sidewalks, into stores, and into friends' homes without difficulty.

16. People do not tell me that my ability level means I should not have children.

17. I can be reasonably sure that I will be able to make it to a regular job every day.

18. I know that my income can increase based on my performance, and I can seek new and better employment if I choose; I do not have to face a court battle to get an increase in my income.

19. My daily routine does not have to be carefully planned to accommodate medication or therapy schedules.

20. I can share my life with an animal companion without my ability to care for it being called into question due to my financial and ability situations.

21. If I am not feeling well and decide to stay in bed, I will likely be believed and not told that I am lazy and worthless.

I am sure there are more I haven't thought of. Do keep in mind that I've tried *not* to copy Ms. McIntosh's work, because there's no need—most of what she says applies to this list as well.

4

10 myths about legacy preferences in college admissions

Richard D. Kahlenberg*

Legacy preferences, which provide a leg up in college admissions to applicants who are the offspring of alumni, are employed at almost three-quarters of selective research universities and virtually all elite liberal-arts colleges. Yet legacy preferences have received relatively little public attention, especially when compared with race-based affirmative-action programs, which have given rise to hundreds of books and law-review articles, numerous court decisions, and several state initiatives to ban the practice.

The secrecy surrounding legacy preferences has perpetuated a number of myths, including the following:

1. Legacy preferences are just a "tie breaker" in close calls.

While some colleges and universities try to play down the impact of legacy preferences, calling them "tie breakers," research from Princeton's Thomas Espenshade suggests that their weight is significant, on the order of adding 160 SAT points to a candidate's record (on a scale of 400–1600). Likewise, William Bowen, of the Andrew W. Mellon Foundation, and colleagues found that, within a given SAT-score range, being a legacy increased

---

one's chances of admission to a selective institution by 19.7 percentage points. That is to say, a given student whose academic record gave her a 40 percent chance of admission would have nearly a 60 percent chance if she were a legacy.

The children of alumni generally make up 10 to 25 percent of the student body at selective institutions. The proportion varies little from year to year, suggesting "an informal quota system," says the former *Wall Street Journal* reporter Daniel Golden. By contrast, at the California Institute of Technology, which does not use legacy preferences, only 1.5 percent of students are children of alumni.

2. Legacy preferences have an honorable history of fostering loyalty at America's great institutions of higher learning.

In fact, as Peter Schmidt, of *The Chronicle,* notes, legacies originated following World War I as a reaction to an influx of immigrant students, particularly Jews, into America's selective colleges. As Jews often outcompeted traditional constituencies on standard meritocratic criteria, universities adopted Jewish quotas. When explicit quotas became hard to defend, the universities began to use more indirect means to limit Jewish enrollment, including considerations of "character," geographic diversity, and legacy status.

3. Legacy preferences are a necessary evil to support the financial vitality of colleges and universities—including the ability to provide scholarships for low-income and working-class students.

While universities claim that legacy preferences are necessary to improve fund raising, there is little empirical evidence to support the contention. In fact, several colleges and universities that do not employ legacy preferences nevertheless do well financially. As Golden notes, Caltech raised $71 million in alumni donations in 2008, almost as much as the Massachusetts Institute of Technology ($77 million), even though MIT, which does provide legacy preferences, is five times the size and has many more alumni to tap. Berea College, in Kentucky, favors low-income students, not alumni, yet has a larger endowment than Middlebury, Oberlin, Vassar, and Bowdoin. And Cooper Union, in New York City, does not provide legacy preference but has an endowment larger than that of Bucknell, Haverford, and Davidson.

Moreover, a study included in our book, *Affirmative Action for the Rich,* finds no evidence that alumni preferences increase giving. Chad Coffman, of Winnemac Consulting, and his co-authors examined alumni giving from 1998 to 2007 at the top 100 national universities (as ranked by *U.S. News & World Report*) to test the relationship between giving and the existence of alumni preferences in admissions. They found that institutions with preferences for children of alumni did have higher annual giving per alumnus ($317 versus $201), but that the advantage resulted because the alumni in colleges with alumni preferences tended to be wealthier. Controlling for the wealth of alumni, they found "no evidence that legacy-preference policies themselves exert an influence on giving behavior." After controls, alumni of legacy-granting institutions gave only $15.39 more per year, on average, but even that slight advantage was uncertain from a statistical perspective. Coffman and his colleagues conclude: "After inclusion of appropriate controls, including wealth, there is no statistically significant evidence of a causal relationship between legacy-preference policies and total alumni giving at top universities."

The researchers also examined giving at seven institutions that dropped legacy preferences during the period of the study. They found "no short-term measurable reduction in alumni giving as a result of abolishing legacy preferences." For example, after Texas A&M eliminated the use of legacy preferences, in 2004, donations took a small hit, but then they increased substantially from 2005 to 2007.

Nor can legacy preferences be said to be necessary for colleges to maintain high standards of excellence. It is intriguing to note that, among the top 10 universities in the world in 2008, according to the widely cited Shanghai Jiao Tong University rankings, are four (Caltech, the University of California at Berkeley, the University of Oxford, and the University of Cambridge) that do not employ legacy preferences.

4. After a generation of affirmative action, legacy preferences are finally beginning to help families of color. Pulling the rug out now would hurt minority students.

In fact, legacy preferences continue to disproportionately hurt students of color. John Brittain, a former chief counsel at the Lawyers Committee for Civil Rights, and the attorney Eric Bloom note that underrepresented minorities make up 12.5 percent of the applicant pool at selective colleges and universities but only 6.7 percent of the legacy-applicant pool. At Texas A&M, 321 of the legacy admits in 2002 were white, while only three were black and 25 Hispanic. At Harvard, only 7.6 percent of legacy admits in

2002 were underrepresented minorities, compared with 17.8 percent of all students. At the University of Virginia, 91 percent of early-decision legacy admits in 2002 were white, 1.6 percent black, and 0.5 percent Hispanic.

Moreover, this disparate impact is likely to extend far into the future. In 2008, African-Americans and Latinos made up more than 30 percent of the traditional college-aged population but little more than 10 percent of the enrollees at the *U.S. News*'s top 50 national universities.

5. An attack on legacy preferences could indirectly hurt affirmative-action policies by suggesting that "merit" is the only permissible basis for admissions.

The elimination of legacy preferences would not threaten the future of affirmative action, because the justifications are entirely different. Affirmative-action policies to date have survived strict scrutiny because they enhance educational diversity. (For some members of the Supreme Court, though not a majority, affirmative action also has been justified as a remedy for centuries of brutal discrimination.) Legacy preferences, by contrast, have no such justification.

Because they disproportionately benefit whites, legacy preferences reduce, rather than enhance, racial and ethnic diversity in higher education. And rather than being a remedy for discrimination, they were born of discrimination. Affirmative action engenders enormous controversy because it pits two great principles against each other—the antidiscrimination principle, which says we should not classify people by ancestry, and the anti-subordination principle, which says we must make efforts to stamp out illegitimate hierarchies. Legacy preferences, by contrast, advance neither principle: They explicitly classify individuals by bloodline and do so in a way that compounds existing hierarchy.

6. Legacy preferences may be unfair, but they are not illegal. Unlike discrimination based on race, which is forbidden under the 14th Amendment, it is perfectly legal to discriminate based on legacy status, as the courts have held.

Remarkably, legacy preferences have been litigated only once in federal court, by an applicant to the University of North Carolina at Chapel Hill named Jane Cheryl Rosenstock, in the 1970s. A New York resident whose application was rejected, she claimed that her constitutional rights were violated by a variety of preferences, including those for in-state applicants, minorities, low-income students, athletes, and legacies. Rosenstock was not a particularly compelling candidate—her combined SAT score was about 850 on a 1600-point scale, substantially lower than most out-of-state applicants—and she was also a weak litigant. She never argued that, because legacy preferences are hereditary, they presented a "suspect" classification that should be judged by the "strict scrutiny" standard under the amendment's equal-protection clause.

The district court judge in the case, *Rosenstock v. Board of Governors of the University of North Carolina,* held that it was rational to believe that alumni preferences translate into additional revenue to universities, although absolutely no evidence was provided for that contention. The decision was never appealed. As Judge Boyce F. Martin Jr. of the US Court of Appeals for the Sixth Circuit notes, the 1976 opinion upholding legacy preferences in *Rosenstock* addressed the issue "in a scant five sentences" and is "neither binding nor persuasive to future courts."

A generation later, two new legal theories are available to challenge legacy preferences. First, Carlton Larson, a law professor at the University of California at Davis, lays out the case that legacy preferences at public universities violate a little-litigated constitutional provision that "no state shall . . . grant any Title of Nobility." Examining the early history of the country, Larson makes a compelling case that this prohibition should not be interpreted narrowly as simply prohibiting the naming of individuals as dukes or earls, but more broadly, to prohibit "government-sponsored hereditary privileges"—including legacy preferences at public universities. Reviewing debates in the Revolutionary era, he concludes: "Legacy preferences at exclusive public universities were precisely the type of hereditary privilege that the Revolutionary generation sought to destroy forever." The founders, Larson writes, would have resisted "with every fiber of their being" the idea of state-supported-university admissions based even in part on ancestry.

Second, the attorneys Steve Shadowen and Sozi Tulante argue that legacy preferences are a violation of the 14th Amendment's equal-protection clause. While the amendment was aimed primarily at stamping out discrimination against black Americans, it also extends more broadly to what Justice Potter Stewart called "preference based on lineage." Individuals are to be judged on their own merits, not by what their parents do, which is why the courts have applied heightened scrutiny to laws that punish children born out of wedlock, or whose parents came to this country illegally.

Shadowen and Tulante argue that legacy preferences at private universities, too, are illegal, under the Civil Rights Act of 1866. Unlike Title VI of the 1964 Civil Rights Act, which outlaws discrimination only on the basis of "race, color, or national origin," the 1866 law prohibits discrimination on the basis of both "race" and "ancestry."

7. Legacy preferences—like affirmative action, geographic preferences, and athletics preferences—are protected by academic freedom, especially at private universities and colleges.

It is true that the courts have recognized that colleges and universities should be given leeway in admissions in order to promote academic freedom. But that freedom is not unlimited, even at private institutions. As Peter Schmidt notes, the Supreme Court held, in *Runyon v. McCrary* (1976), that private schools could not engage in racial discrimination in admissions. In *Regents of the University of California v. Bakke* (1978), it struck down the use of racial quotas. And in the 2003 *Gratz v. Bollinger* decision, the court invalidated a policy that awarded bonus points to minority students. Ancestry discrimination—providing a leg up in admissions based not on merit but on whether a student's parents or grandparents attended a particular university or college—likewise falls outside the protected zone of academic freedom.

8. Legacy preferences have been around a long time and are unlikely to ever go away, because powerful political forces support them.

In fact, legacy preferences are not only legally vulnerable; they are politically vulnerable as well. Polls find that Americans oppose legacy preferences by 75 percent to 23 percent, and in the past decade or so, 16 leading institutions have abandoned them. As affirmative-action programs come under increasing attack, legacy preferences become even harder to justify politically.

Moreover, as a matter of tax law, legacy preferences are fundamentally unstable. Assuming it is true that they entice alumni to provide larger donations than they otherwise would—a claim that has not been empirically proven—then IRS regulations raise questions about whether those donations should be tax deductible. If universities and colleges are conferring a monetary benefit in exchange for donations, then the arrangement, writes the journalist Peter Sacks, "shatters the first principle underlying the charitable deduction, that donations to nonprofit organizations not 'enrich the giver.'" The IRS regulations place universities in a legal Catch-22: Either donations are not linked to legacy preferences, in which case the fundamental rationale for ancestry discrimination is flawed; or giving is linked to legacy preferences, in which case donations should not be tax deductible.

9. Legacy preferences don't keep nonlegacy applicants out of college entirely. They just reduce the chances of going to a particular selective college, so the stakes are low.

True, legacy preferences don't bar students from attending college at all. But the benefits of attending a selective institution are substantial. For one thing, wealthy selective colleges tend to spend a great deal more on students' education. Research finds that the least-selective colleges spend about $12,000 per student annually, compared with $92,000 per student at the most-selective ones. In addition, wealthy selective institutions provide much greater subsidies for families. At the wealthiest 10 percent of institutions, students pay, on average, just 20 cents in fees for every dollar the college spends on them, while at the poorest 10 percent of institutions, students pay 78 cents for every dollar spent on them. Furthermore, selective colleges are better than less-selective institutions at graduating equally qualified students. And future earnings are, on average, 45 percent higher for students who graduated from more-selective institutions than for those from less-selective ones, and the difference in earnings ends up being widest among low-income students. Finally, according to research by the political scientist Thomas Dye, 54 percent of America's corporate leaders and 42 percent of governmental leaders are graduates of just 12 institutions. For all those reasons, legacy preferences matter.

10. Everyone does it. Legacies are just an inherent reality in higher education throughout the world.

In fact, as Daniel Golden writes, legacy preferences are "virtually unknown in the rest of the world"; they are "an almost exclusively American custom." The irony, of course, is that while legacies are uniquely American, they are also deeply un-American, as Michael Lind, of the New America Foundation, has argued.

Thomas Jefferson famously sought to promote in America a "natural aristocracy" based on "virtue and talent," rather than an "artificial aristocracy" based on wealth. "By reserving places on campus for members of the pseudo-aristocracy of 'wealth and birth,'" Lind writes, "legacy preferences introduce an aristocratic snake into the democratic republican Garden of Eden."

For the most part, American higher education has sought to democratize, opening its doors to women, to people of color, and to the financially needy. Legacy preferences are an outlier in that trend, a relic that has no place in American society. In a fundamental sense, this nation's first two great wars—the Revolution and the Civil War—were fought to defeat different forms of aristocracy. That this remnant of ancestry-based discrimination still survives—in American higher education, of all places—is truly breathtaking.

5

the heterosexual questionnaire

M. Rochlin*

Purpose: The purpose of this exercise is to examine the manner in which the use of heterosexual norms may bias the study of gay men's and lesbians' lives.

Instructions: Heterosexism is a form of bias in which heterosexual norms are used in studies of homosexual relationships. Gay men and lesbians are seen as deviating from a heterosexual norm, and this often leads to marginalization and pathologizing of their behavior. Read the questionnaire below with this definition in mind. Then respond to the questions.

1. What do you think caused your heterosexuality?
2. When and how did you first decide you were a heterosexual?
3. Is it possible that your heterosexuality is just a phase you may grow out of?
4. Is it possible that your heterosexuality stems from a neurotic fear of others of the same sex?
5. If you have never slept with a person of the same sex, is it possible that all you need is a good gay lover?

---

* "The Heterosexual Questionnaire," by M. Rochlin. Reprinted by permission of the author.

6. Do your parents know that you are straight? Do your friends and/or roommate(s) know? How did they react?

7. Why do you insist on flaunting your heterosexuality? Can't you just be who you are and keep it quiet?

8. Why do heterosexuals place so much emphasis on sex?

9. Why do heterosexuals feel compelled to seduce others into their lifestyle?

10. A disproportionate majority of child molesters are heterosexual. Do you consider it safe to expose children to heterosexual teachers?

11. Just what do men and women *do* in bed together? How can they truly know how to please each other, being so anatomically different?

12. With all the societal support marriage receives, the divorce rate is spiraling. Why are there so few stable relationships among heterosexuals?

13. Statistics show that lesbians have the lowest incidence of sexually transmitted diseases. Is it really safe for a woman to maintain a heterosexual lifestyle and run the risk of disease and pregnancy?

14. How can you become a whole person if you limit yourself to compulsive, exclusive heterosexuality?

15. Considering the menace of overpopulation, how could the human race survive if everyone were heterosexual?

16. Could you trust a heterosexual therapist to be objective? Don't you feel s/he might be inclined to influence you in the direction of her/his own leanings?

17. There seem to be very few happy heterosexuals. Techniques have been developed that might enable you to change if you really want to. Have you considered trying aversion therapy?

18. Would you want your child to be heterosexual, knowing the problems that s/he would face?

19. What were your first reactions upon reading this questionnaire?

6

top ten differences between white terrorists and others

Juan Cole*

1. White terrorists are called "gunmen."[1] What does that even mean? A person with a gun? Wouldn't that be, like, everyone in the US? Other terrorists are called, like, "terrorists."
2. White terrorists are "troubled loners." Other terrorists are always suspected of being part of a global plot, even when they are obviously troubled loners.
3. Doing a study on the danger of white terrorists at the Department of Homeland Security will get you sidelined by angry white congressmen.[2] Doing studies on other kinds of terrorists is a guaranteed promotion.
4. The family of a white terrorist is interviewed, weeping as they wonder where he went wrong. The families of other terrorists are almost never interviewed.
5. White terrorists are part of a "fringe." Other terrorists are apparently mainstream.

*Juan Cole, "Top Ten Differences between White Terrorists and Others," *Informed Consent* blog, August 9, 2012, www.juancole.com/2012/08/top-ten-differences-between-white-terrorists-and-others.html. Copyright 2012, *Informed Consent*. Reprinted by permission of the author.

6. White terrorists are random events, like tornadoes. Other terrorists are long-running conspiracies.

7. White terrorists are never called "white." But other terrorists are given ethnic affiliations.

8. Nobody thinks white terrorists are typical of white people. But other terrorists are considered paragons of their societies.

9. White terrorists are alcoholics, addicts, or mentally ill. Other terrorists are apparently clean-living and perfectly sane.

10. There is nothing you can do about white terrorists. Gun control won't stop them. No policy you could make, no government program, could possibly have an impact on them. But hundreds of billions of dollars must be spent on police and on the Department of Defense, and on TSA, which must virtually strip-search 60 million people a year, to deal with other terrorists.

notes

1. www.latimes.com/news/nation/nationnow/la-na-nn-sikh-temple-gunman-201208 08,0,6572009.story.

2. www.wired.com/dangerroom/2012/08/dhs/all.

discussion questions & activities

Discussion Questions

1. What was most surprising/challenging/compelling for you in reading this section? Why?
2. When we study topics like race, gender, and sexuality, we often think first about the oppressed (people of color; women; LGBTQ people, etc.). Why is that?
3. Identify the various systems of privilege introduced in this section. Which system of privilege have you thought about least? Why?
4. Is it possible for someone to experience both oppression and privilege in his or her life? What factors make it difficult to recognize that?
5. McIntosh distinguishes between unearned advantage and conferred dominance. Does this distinction work when applied to other systems of privilege in addition to race and gender?

Personal Connections

The following questions and activities are designed to be completed either on your own or in class, and then discussed as a group with others. As you share your insights with others, think about the patterns and similarities that emerge, as well as the differences among your answers.

A. Identifying Yourself

Considering some of the most significant social identity categories examined in this text (race, gender, sexual orientation, class, religion, and ability), which of these have you thought about most in terms of their importance in *your* own life? Why? Has the relative importance of these identities in your life changed over time at all?

B. Examining Your Privilege

Part One provided a number of chapters that list privileges associated with specific social identities, such as race, masculinity, and ability. Select another category of privilege, if possible, one that you belong to, and create your own list. For example, you might select class, age, or nationality, then create a list of the often invisible privileges you gain.

C. Locating Yourself

Social Identity Development Theory describes the identity development process for members of privileged and oppressed identity groups. Identity is more complex than the overview (box, below) suggests. People may not move neatly from one stage to the next and may experience several stages simultaneously; some may even backslide. Nevertheless, reflecting upon these stages can be a useful tool for self-reflection. As you read about the developmental process, select two of your own social identities to examine, with at least one being a privileged social group identity (white, heterosexual, able-bodied, etc.). Write a two- to three-page discussion of where you see yourself in terms of these two identities and why.

Stages of Social Identity Development

Stage I: Naive

At this stage people are just becoming aware of differences between self and members of other social groups, are unaware of the complex codes of appropriate behavior for members of their social group, and are still learning what it means to be a member of their social identity group.

Numerous events transform children from naive (unsocialized) to accepting of their social dominance or subordination. Significant socializers include parents, education, religion, media, etc.

Stage II: Acceptance

The stage of acceptance represents some degree of internalization, whether conscious or unconscious, of the dominant culture's ideology. People at this stage see race, class, gender, and other hierarchical systems as natural, "the way things are." Codes of appropriate behavior are more or less internalized; he or she engages in blaming the victim, and may initially ignore or dismiss experiences that contradict the *acceptance* worldview.

Stage III: Resistance

People are likely to enter this stage by questioning previously accepted "truths" about the way things are, and gain increased awareness of the existence of privilege/oppression. As a result of experiences and information that challenge accepted ideology and self-definition, agents entering resistance begin formulating a new worldview and recognize that their identity has been shaped by social factors beyond their control. In resistance, people become more skilled at identifying oppression and inequality, may begin experiencing conflict with others who do not, and may experience strong emotions including anger, pain, rage, and shame. This stage represents a shift in paradigm.

Stage IV: Redefinition

The redefinition stage focuses on developing a liberated identity, independent of the hierarchical system of oppression and privilege. The person may be isolated from others in the same social identity group. He or she will begin developing a positive social identity and start identifying aspects of his or her culture and group that are affirming. The focus on defining oneself is independent of the perceived dominant culture. Members of oppressed identity groups may seek primary contact with members of their own social identity group who are at the same stage of consciousness, and may distance themselves from those in the privileged group.

Stage V: Internalization

This stage represents an ongoing process of internalizing and integrating the new social identity into other facets of one's life until it becomes a natural part of behavior so people act unconsciously, without external controls, and without having to think about what they are doing. It involves renegotiating interactions and relationships with significant people in one's life, and growing stronger and more secure in this new consciousness, even if the new social identity is not valued by those around the person. Empathy for oppressed groups increases. The process of refining identity can be ongoing; there is no end to this lifelong exploration.

(Adapted from Diane Goodman, *Promoting Diversity and Social Justice: Educating People from Privileged Groups,* 2nd ed. [New York: Routledge, 2011].)

part two

understanding privilege

7

privilege, power, difference, and us

Allan Johnson*

To do something about the trouble around difference, we have to talk about it, but most of the time we don't, because it feels too risky. This is true for just about everyone, but especially for members of privileged categories, for whites, for men, and for heterosexuals. As Paul Kivel writes, for example, "Rarely do we whites sit back and listen to people of color without interrupting, without being defensive, without trying to regain attention to ourselves, without criticizing or judging."

The discomfort, defensiveness, and fear come in part from not knowing how to talk about privilege without feeling vulnerable to anger and blame. They will continue until we find a way to reduce the risk of talking about privilege. The key to reducing the risk is to understand what makes talking about privilege *seem* risky. I don't mean that risk is an illusion. There is no way to do this work without the possibility that people will feel uncomfortable or frightened or threatened. But the risk isn't nearly as big as it seems, for like the proverbial (and mythical) human fear of the strange and unfamiliar, the problem begins with how people *think* about things and who they are in relation to them.

---

* "Privilege, Power, Difference, and Us," pp. 83–95 in *Privilege, Power, and Difference* by Allan Johnson. Copyright 2001 by McGraw-Hill. Reprinted with permission from the McGraw-Hill Companies.

Individualism, or the Myth that Everything Is Somebody's Fault

We live in a society that encourages us to think that the social world begins and ends with individuals. It's as if an organization or a society is just a collection of people, and everything that happens in it begins with what each one thinks, feels, and intends. If you understand people, the reasoning goes, then you also understand social life. It's an appealing way to think because it's grounded in our experience as individuals, which is what we know best. But it's also misleading, because it boxes us into a narrow and distorted view of reality. In other words, it isn't true.

If we use individualism to explain sexism, for example, it's hard to avoid the idea that sexism exists simply because men *are* sexist—men have sexist feelings, beliefs, needs, and motivations that lead them to behave in sexist ways. If sexism produces evil consequences, it's because men *are* evil, hostile, and malevolent toward women. In short, everything bad in the world is seen as somebody's fault, which is why talk about privilege so often turns into a game of hot potato.

Individualistic thinking keeps us stuck in the trouble by making it almost impossible to talk seriously about it. It encourages women, for example, to blame and distrust men. It sets men up to feel personally attacked if anyone mentions gender issues, and to define those issues as a "women's problem." It also encourages men who don't think or behave in overtly sexist ways— the ones most likely to become part of the solution—to conclude that sexism has nothing to do with them, that it's just a problem for "bad" men. The result is a kind of paralysis: people either talk about sexism in the most superficial, unthreatening, trivializing, and even stupid way ("The Battle of the Sexes," *Men Are from Mars, Women Are from Venus*) or they don't talk about it at all.

Breaking the paralysis begins with realizing that the social world consists of a lot more than individuals. We are always participating in something larger than ourselves—what sociologists call social systems—and systems are more than collections of people. A university, for example, is a social system, and people participate in it. But the people aren't the university and the university isn't the people. This means that to understand what happens in it, we have to look at both the university and how individual people participate in it. If patterns of racism exist in a society, for example, the reason is never just a matter of white people's personalities, feelings, or intentions. We also have to understand how they participate in particular kinds of behavior, and what consequences it produces.

Individuals, Systems, and Paths of Least Resistance

To see the difference between a system and the people who participate in it, consider a game like Monopoly. I used to play Monopoly, but I don't anymore because I don't like the way I behave when I do. Like everyone else, as a Monopoly player I try to take everything from the other players—all their money, all their property—which then forces them out of the game. The point of the game is to ruin everyone else and be the only one left in the end. When you win, you feel good, because you're *supposed* to feel good. Except that one day I realized that I felt good about winning—about taking everything from everyone else—even when I played with my children, who were pretty young at the time. But there didn't seem to be much point to playing without trying to win, because winning is what the game is *about*. Why land on a property and not buy it, or own a property and not improve it, or have other players land on your property and not collect the rent? So I stopped playing.

And it worked, because the fact is that I don't behave in such greedy ways when I'm not playing Monopoly, even though it's still me, Allan, in either case. So what's all this greedy behavior about? Do we behave in greedy ways simply because we *are* greedy? In a sense, the answer is yes, in that greed is part of the human repertoire of possible motivations, just like compassion, altruism, or fear. But how, then, do I explain the absence of such behavior when I'm not playing Monopoly? Clearly, the answer has to include both me as an individual human being who's capable of making all kinds of choices *and* something about the social situation in which I make those choices. It's not one or the other; it's both in relation to each other.

If we think of Monopoly as a social system—as "something larger than ourselves that we participate in"—then we can see how people and systems come together in a dynamic relationship that produces the patterns of social life, including problems around difference and privilege. People are indisputably the ones who make social systems happen. If no one plays Monopoly, it's just a box full of stuff with writing inside the cover. When people open it up and identify themselves as players, however, Monopoly starts to *happen.* This makes people very important, but we shouldn't confuse that with Monopoly itself. We aren't Monopoly and Monopoly isn't us. I can describe the game and how it works without saying anything about the personal characteristics of all the people who play it or might play it.

People make Monopoly happen, but *how*? How do we know what to do? How do we choose from the millions of things that, as human beings, we *could* do at any given moment? The answer is the other half of the dynamic relation between individuals and systems. As we sit around the table, we make Monopoly happen from one minute to the next. But our participation in the game also shapes how *we* happen as people—what we think and feel and do. This doesn't mean that systems control us in a rigid and predictable way. Instead, systems load the odds in certain directions by offering what I call "paths of least resistance" for us to follow.

In every social situation, we have an almost limitless number of choices we might make. Sitting in a movie theater, for example, we could go to sleep, sing, eat dinner, undress, dance, take out a flashlight and read the newspaper, carry on loud conversations, dribble a basketball up and down the aisles—these are just a handful of the millions of behaviors people are capable of. All of these possible paths vary in how much resistance we run into if we try to follow them. We discover this as soon as we choose paths we're not supposed to. Jump up and start singing, for example, and you'll quickly feel how much resistance the management and the rest of the audience offer up to discourage you from going any further. By comparison, the path of least resistance is far more appealing, which is why it's the one we're most likely to choose.

The odds are loaded toward a path of least resistance in several ways. We often choose a path because it's the only one we see. When I get on an elevator, for example, I turn and face front along with everyone else. It rarely occurs to me to do it another way, such as facing the rear. If I did, I'd soon feel how some paths have more resistance than others.

I once tested this idea by walking to the rear of an elevator and standing with my back toward the door. As the seconds ticked by, I could feel people looking at me, wondering what I was up to, and actually wanting me to turn around. I wasn't saying anything or doing anything to anyone. I was only standing there minding my own business. But that wasn't all that I was doing, for I was also violating a social norm that makes facing the door a path of least resistance. The path is there all the time—it's built in to riding the elevator as a social situation—but the path wasn't clear until I stepped onto a different one and felt the greater resistance rise up around it.

Similar dynamics operate around issues of difference and privilege. In many corporations, for example, the only way to get promoted is to have a mentor or sponsor pick you out as a promising person and bring you along by teaching you what you need to know and acting as an advocate who opens doors and creates opportunities. In a society that separates and privileges people by gender and race, there aren't many opportunities to get comfortable with people across difference. This means that senior managers will feel drawn to employees who resemble them, which usually means those who are white, straight, and male.

Managers who are white and/or male probably won't realize they're following a path of least resistance that shapes their choice until they're asked to mentor an African American woman or someone else they don't resemble. The greater resistance toward the path of mentoring across difference may result from something as subtle as feeling "uncomfortable" in the other person's presence. But that's all it takes to make the relationship ineffective or to ensure that it never happens in the first place. And as each manager follows the system's path to mentor and support those who most resemble them, the patterns of white dominance and male dominance in the system as a whole are perpetuated, regardless of what people consciously feel or intend.

In other cases, people know alternative paths exist but they stick to the path of least resistance anyway, because they're afraid of what will happen if they don't. Resistance can take many forms, ranging from mild disapproval to being fired from a job, beaten up, run out of town, imprisoned, tortured, or killed. When managers are told to lay off large numbers of workers, for example, they may hate the assignment and feel a huge amount of distress. But the path of *least* resistance is to do what they're told, because the alternative may be for them to lose their own jobs. To make it less unpleasant, they may use euphemisms like "downsizing" and "outplacement" to soften the painful reality of people losing their jobs. (Note in this example how the path of least resistance isn't necessarily an easy path to follow.)

In similar ways, a man may feel uncomfortable when he hears a friend tell a sexist joke, and feel compelled to object in some way. But the path of least resistance in that situation is to go along and avoid the risk of being ostracized or ridiculed for challenging his friend and making *him* feel uncomfortable. The path of least resistance is to smile or laugh or just remain silent.

What we experience as social life happens through a complex dynamic between all kinds of systems—families, schools, workplaces, communities, entire societies—and the choices people make as they participate in them and help make them happen. How we experience the world and ourselves, our sense of other people, and the ongoing reality of the systems themselves all arise, take shape, and happen through this dynamic. In this way, social life produces a variety of consequences, including privilege and oppression. To understand that and what we can do to change it, we have to see how systems are organized in ways that encourage people to follow paths of least resistance. The existence of those paths and the choice we make to follow them are keys to what creates and perpetuates all the forms that privilege and oppression can take in people's lives.

What It Means to Be Involved in Privilege and Oppression

Individuals and systems are connected to each other through a dynamic relationship. If we use this relationship as a model for thinking about the world and ourselves, it's easier to bring problems like racism, sexism, and heterosexism out into the open and talk about them. In particular, it's easier to see the problems in relation to us, and to see ourselves in relation to them.

If we think the world is just made up of individuals, then a white woman who's told she's "involved" in racism is going to think you're telling her she's a racist person who harbors ill will toward people of color. She's using an individualistic model of the world that limits her to interpreting words like *racist* as personal characteristics, personality flaws. Individualism divides the world up into different kinds of people—good people and bad, racists and nonracists, "good guys" and sexist pigs. It encourages us to think of racism, sexism, and heterosexism as diseases that infect people and make them sick. And so we look for a "cure" that will turn diseased, flawed individuals into healthy, "good" ones, or at least isolate them so that they can't infect others. And if we can't cure them, then we can at least try to control their behavior.

But what about everyone else? How do we see *them* in relation to the trouble around difference? What about the vast majority of whites, for example, who tell survey interviewers that they aren't racist and don't hate or even dislike people of color? Or what about the majority of men who say they favor an Equal Rights Amendment to the US Constitution? From an individualistic perspective, if you aren't consciously or openly prejudiced or hurtful, then you aren't part of the problem. You might show disapproval of "bad" people and even try to help out the people who are hurt by them. Beyond that, however, the trouble doesn't have anything to do with you so far as you can see. If your feelings and thoughts and outward behavior are good, then *you* are good, and that's all that matters.

Unfortunately, that isn't all that matters. There's more, because patterns of oppression and privilege are rooted in systems that we all participate in and make happen. Those patterns are built into paths of least resistance that people feel drawn to follow every day, regardless of whether they think about where they lead or the consequences they produce. When male professors take more seriously students who look like themselves, for example, they don't have to be self-consciously sexist in order to help perpetuate patterns of gender privilege. They don't have to be bad people in order to play a "game" that produces oppressive consequences. It's the same as when people play Monopoly—it always ends with someone winning and everyone else losing, *because that's how the game is set up to work as a system.* The only way to change the outcome is to change how we see and play the game and, eventually, the *system itself* and its paths of least resistance. If we have a vision of what we want social life to look like, we have to create paths that lead in that direction.

Of course there are people in the world who have hatred in their hearts—such as neo-Nazi skinheads who make a sport of harassing and killing blacks or homosexuals—and it's important not to minimize the damage they do. Paradoxically, however, even though they cause a lot of trouble, they aren't the key to understanding privilege or to doing something about it. They are participating in something larger than themselves that, among other things, steers them toward certain targets for their rage. It's no accident that their hatred is rarely directed at privileged groups, but instead those who are culturally devalued and excluded. Hate-crime perpetrators may have personality disorders that bend them toward victimizing *someone*, but their choice of whom to victimize isn't part of a mental illness. That's something they have to learn, and culture is everyone's most powerful teacher. In choosing their targets, they follow paths of least resistance built into a society that everyone participates in, that everyone makes happen, regardless of how they feel or what they intend.

So if I notice that someone plays Monopoly in a ruthless way, it's a mistake to explain that simply in terms of their personality. I also have to ask how a system like Monopoly rewards ruthless behavior more than other games we might play. I have to ask how it creates conditions that make such behavior appear to be the path of least resistance, normal and unremarkable. And since I'm playing the game, too, I'm one of the people who make it happen as a system, and its paths must affect me, too.

My first reaction might be to deny that I follow that path. I'm not a ruthless person or anything close to it. But this misses the key difference between systems and the people who participate in them: We don't have to be ruthless *people* in order to support or follow paths of least resistance that lead to behavior with ruthless *consequences*. After all, we're all trying to win, because that's the point of the game. However gentle and kind I am as I take your money when you land on my Boardwalk with its four houses, take it I will, and gladly, too. "Thank you," I say in my most sincerely unruthless tone, or even "Sorry," as I drive you out of the game by taking your last dollar and your mortgaged properties. Me, ruthless? Not at all. I'm just playing the game the way it's supposed to be played. And even if I don't try hard to win, the mere fact that I play the game supports its existence and makes it possible, especially if I remain silent about the consequences it produces. Just my going along makes the game appear normal and acceptable, which reinforces the paths of least resistance for everyone else.

This is how most systems work and how most people participate in them. It's also how systems of privilege work. Good people with good intentions make systems happen that produce all kinds of injustice and suffering for people in culturally devalued and excluded groups. Most of the time, people don't even know the paths are there in the first place, and this is why it's important to raise awareness that everyone is always following them in one way or another. If you weren't following a path of least resistance, you'd certainly know it, because you'd be on an alternative path with greater resistance that would make itself felt. In other words, if you're not going along with the system, it won't be long before people notice and let you know it. All you have to do is show up for work wearing "inappropriate" clothes to see how quickly resistance can form around alternative paths.

The trouble around difference is so pervasive, so long-standing, so huge in its consequences for so many millions of people that it can't be written off as the misguided doings of a small minority of people with personality problems. The people who get labeled as bigots, misogynists, or homophobes are all following racist, sexist, heterosexist paths of least resistance that are built into the entire society.

In a way, "bad people" are like ruthless Monopoly players who are doing just what the game calls for even if their "style" is a bit extreme. Such extremists may be the ones who grab the headlines, but they don't have enough power to create and sustain trouble of this magnitude. The trouble appears in the daily workings of every workplace, every school and university, every government agency, every community. It involves every major kind of social system, and since systems don't exist without the involvement of people, there's no way to escape being involved in the trouble that comes out of them. If we participate in systems the trouble comes out of, and if those systems exist only through our participation, then this is enough to involve us in the trouble itself.

Reminders of this reality are everywhere. I see it, for example, every time I look at the label in a piece of clothing. I just went upstairs to my closet and noted where each of my shirts was made. Although each carries a US brand name, only three were made here; the rest were made in the Philippines, Thailand, Mexico, Taiwan, Macao, Singapore, or Hong Kong. And although each cost me twenty to forty dollars, it's a good bet that the people who actually made them—primarily women—were paid pennies for their labor performed under terrible conditions that can sometimes be so extreme as to resemble slavery.

The only reason people exploit workers in such horrible ways is to make money in a capitalist system. To judge from the contents of my closet, that clearly includes *my* money. By itself, that fact doesn't make me a bad person, because I certainly don't intend that people suffer for the sake of my wardrobe. But it does mean that I'm involved in their suffering because I participate in a system that produces that suffering. As someone who helps make the system happen, however, I can also be a part of the solution.

But isn't the difference I could make a tiny one? The question makes me think of the devastating floods of 1993 along the Mississippi and Missouri rivers. The news was full of powerful images of people from all walks of life working feverishly side by side to build dikes to hold back the raging waters that threatened their communities. Together, they filled and placed thousands of sandbags. When the waters receded, much had been lost, but a great deal had been saved as well. I wonder how it felt to be one of those people. I imagine they were proud of their effort and experienced a satisfying sense of solidarity with the people they'd worked with. The sandbags each individual personally contributed were the tiniest fraction of the total, but each felt part of the group effort and was proud to identify with the consequences it produced. They didn't have to make a big or even measurable difference to feel involved.

It works that way with the good things that come out of people pulling together in all the systems that make up social life. It also works that way with the bad things, with each sandbag adding to the problem instead of the solution. To perpetuate privilege and oppression, we don't even have to do anything consciously to support it. Just our silence is crucial for ensuring its future, for the simple fact is that no system of social oppression can continue to exist without most people choosing to remain silent about it. If most whites spoke out about racism; if most men talked about sexism; if most heterosexuals came out of their closet of silence and stood openly against heterosexism, it would be a critical first step toward revolutionary change. But the vast majority of "good" people are silent on these issues, and it's easy for others to read their silence as support.

As long as we participate in social systems, we don't get to choose whether to be involved in the consequences they produce. We're involved simply through the fact that we're here. As such, we can only choose *how* to be involved, whether to be just part of the problem or also to be part of the solution. That's where our power lies, and also our responsibility.

8

hiring quotas for white males only

Eric Foner*

I graduated in 1965 from Columbia College. My class of 700 was all-male and virtually all-white. Most of us were young men of ability, yet had we been forced to compete for admission with women and racial minorities, fewer than half of us would have been at Columbia. None of us, to my knowledge, suffered debilitating self-doubt because we were the beneficiaries of affirmative action—that is, favored treatment on the basis of our race and gender.

Affirmative action has emerged as the latest "wedge issue" of American politics. The abrogation of California affirmative action programs by Governor Pete Wilson, and the Clinton Administration's halting efforts to re-evaluate federal policy, suggest the issue is now coming to a head. As a historian, I find the current debate dismaying not only because of the crass effort to set Americans against one another for partisan advantage but also because the entire discussion lacks a sense of history.

Opponents of affirmative action, for example, have tried to wrap themselves in the mantle of the civil rights movement, seizing upon the 1963 speech in which Martin Luther King Jr. looked forward to the time when his children would be judged not by the "color of their skin" but by the "content of their character." Rarely mentioned is that King came to be a strong supporter of affirmative action.

*"Hiring Quotas for White Males Only," by Eric Foner. Reprinted from *The Nation* 924, June 26, 1995. Reprinted with permission from *The Nation*.

In his last book, *Where Do We Go From Here?*, a brooding meditation on America's long history of racism, King acknowledged that "special treatment" for blacks seemed to conflict with the ideal of opportunity based on individual merit. But, he continued, "a society that has done something special *against* the Negro for hundreds of years must now do something special *for* him."

Our country, King realized, has never operated on a color-blind basis. From the beginning of the Republic, membership in American society was defined in racial terms. The first naturalization law, enacted in 1790, restricted citizenship for those emigrating from abroad to "free white persons." Free blacks, even in the North, were barred from juries, public schools, government employment and the militia and regular army. Not until after the Civil War were blacks deemed worthy to be American citizens, while Asians were barred from naturalization until the 1940s.

White immigrants certainly faced discrimination. But they had access to the political power, jobs, and residential neighborhoods denied to blacks. In the nineteenth century, the men among them enjoyed the right to vote even before they were naturalized. Until well into this century, however, the vast majority of black Americans were excluded from the suffrage except for a period immediately after the Civil War. White men, native and immigrant, could find well-paid craft and industrial jobs, while employers and unions limited nonwhites (and women) to unskilled and menial employment. The "American standard of living" was an entitlement of white men alone.

There is no point in dwelling morbidly on past injustices. But this record of unequal treatment cannot be dismissed as "vague or ancient wrongs" with no bearing on the present, as Republican strategist William Kristol claimed. Slavery may be gone and legal segregation dismantled, but the effects of past discrimination live on in seniority systems that preserve intact the results of a racially segmented job market, a black unemployment rate double that of whites, and pervasive housing segregation.

Past racism is embedded in the two-tier, racially divided system of social insurance still on the books today. Because key Congressional committees in the 1930s were controlled by Southerners with all-white electorates, they did not allow the supposedly universal entitlement of Social Security to cover the largest categories of black workers—agricultural laborers and domestics. Social Security excluded 80 percent of employed black women, who were forced to depend for a safety net on the much less generous "welfare" system.

The notion that affirmative action stigmatizes its recipients reflects not just belief in advancement according to individual merit but the older idea that the "normal" American is white. There are firemen and black firemen, construction workers and black construction workers: Nonwhites (and women) who obtain such jobs are still widely viewed as interlopers, depriving white men of positions or promotions to which they are historically entitled.

I have yet to meet the white male in whom special favoritism (getting a job, for example, through relatives or an old boys' network, or because of racial discrimination by a union or employer) fostered doubt about his own abilities. In a society where belief in black inferiority is still widespread (witness the success of *The Bell Curve*), many whites and some blacks may question the abilities of beneficiaries of affirmative action. But this social "cost" hardly counterbalances the enormous social benefits affirmative action has produced.

Nonwhites (and even more so, white women) have made deep inroads into the lower middle class and into professions once reserved for white males. Columbia College now admits women and minority students. Would these and other opportunities have opened as widely and as quickly without the pressure of affirmative action programs? American history suggests they would not.

It is certainly true, as critics charge, that affirmative action's benefits have not spread to the poorest members of the black community. The children of Harlem, regrettably, are not in a position to take advantage of the spots Columbia has opened to blacks. But rather than simply ratifying the advantages of already affluent blacks, who traditionally advanced by servicing the segregated black community, affirmative action has helped to create a *new* black middle class, resting on professional and managerial positions within white society.

This new class is much more vulnerable than its white counterpart to the shifting fortunes of the economy and politics. Far more middle-class blacks than whites depend on public employment—positions now threatened by the downsizing of federal, state, and municipal governments. That other actions are needed to address the problems of the "underclass" hardly negates the proven value of affirmative action in expanding black access to the middle class and skilled working class.

There is no harm in rethinking the ways affirmative action is effectuated—in reexamining, for example, the expansion to numerous other groups of a program originally intended to deal with the legacy of slavery and segregation. In principle, there may well be merit in redefining disadvantage to include poor whites. The present cry for affirmative action based on class rather than race, however, seems as much an evasion as a serious effort to rethink public policy. Efforts to uplift the poor, while indispensable in a just society, are neither a substitute for nor incompatible with programs that address the legacy of the race-based discrimination to which blacks have historically been subjected. Without a robust class politics, moreover, class policies are unlikely to get very far. The present Congress may well dismantle affirmative action, but it hardly seems sympathetic to broad "color-blind" programs to assist the poor.

At a time of deindustrialization and stagnant real wages, many whites have come to blame affirmative action for declining economic prospects. Let us not delude ourselves, however, into thinking that eliminating affirmative action will produce a society in which rewards are based on merit. Despite our rhetoric, equal opportunity has never been the American way. For nearly all our history, affirmative action has been a prerogative of white men.

9

becoming 100 percent straight

Michael A. Messner*

Many years ago I read some psychological studies that argued that even for self-identified heterosexuals it is a natural part of their development to have gone through "bisexual" or even "homosexual" stages of life. When I read this, it seemed theoretically reasonable, but did not ring true in my experience. I have always been, I told myself, 100 percent heterosexual! The group process of analyzing my own autobiographical stories challenged the concept I had developed of myself, and also shed light on the way in which the institutional context of sport provided a context for the development of my definition of myself as "100 percent straight." Here is one of the stories.

When I was in the ninth grade I played on a "D" basketball team, set up especially for the smallest of high school boys. Indeed, though I was pudgy with baby fat, I was a short 5'2," still prepubescent with no facial hair and a high voice that I artificially tried to lower. The first day of practice I was immediately attracted to a boy I'll call Timmy, because he looked like the boy who played in the *Lassie* TV show. Timmy was short, with a high voice, like me. And like me, he had no facial hair yet. Unlike me, he was very skinny. I liked Timmy right away, and soon we were together a lot. I noticed

*"Becoming 100 Percent Straight," by Michael A. Messner. Reprinted by permission of the author.

things about him that I didn't notice about other boys: he said some words a certain way, and it gave me pleasure to try to talk like him. I remember liking the way the light hit his boyish, nearly hairless body. I thought about him when we weren't together. He was in the school band, and at the football games I'd squint to see where he was in the mass of uniforms. In short, though I wasn't conscious of it at the time, I was infatuated with Timmy—I had a crush on him. Later that basketball season, I decided—for no reason that I could really articulate then—that I hated Timmy. I aggressively rejected him, began to make fun of him around other boys. He was, we all agreed, a geek. He was a faggot.

Three years later Timmy and I were both on the varsity basketball team, but had hardly spoken a word to each other since we were freshmen. Both of us now had lower voices, had grown to around 6 feet tall, and we both shaved, at least a bit. But Timmy was a skinny, somewhat stigmatized reserve on the team, while I was the team captain and starting point guard. But I wasn't so happy or secure about this. I'd always dreamed of dominating games, of being the hero. Halfway through my senior season, however, it became clear that I was not a star, and I figured I knew why. I was not aggressive enough.

I had always liked the beauty of the fast break, the perfectly executed pick and roll play between two players, and especially the long 20-foot shot that touched nothing but the bottom of the net. But I hated and feared the sometimes brutal contact under the basket. In fact, I stayed away from the rough fights for rebounds and was mostly a perimeter player, relying on my long shots or my passes to more aggressive teammates under the basket. But now it became apparent to me that time was running out in my quest for greatness: I needed to change my game, and fast. I decided one day before practice that I was gonna get aggressive. While practicing one of our standard plays, I passed the ball to a teammate, and then ran to the spot at which I was to set a pick on a defender. I knew that one could sometimes get away with setting a face-up screen on a player, and then as he makes contact with you, roll your back to him and plant your elbow hard in his stomach. The beauty of this move is that your own body "roll" makes the elbow look like an accident. So I decided to try this move. I approached the defensive player, Timmy, rolled, and planted my elbow deeply into his solar plexus. Air exploded audibly from Timmy's mouth, and he crumbled to the floor momentarily.

Play went on as though nothing had happened, but I felt bad about it. Rather than making me feel better, it made me feel guilty and weak. I had to admit to myself why I'd chosen Timmy as the target against whom to test out my new aggression. He was the skinniest and weakest player on the team.

At the time, I hardly thought about these incidents, other than to try to brush them off as incidents that made me feel extremely uncomfortable. Years later I can now interrogate this as a sexual story, and as a gender story unfolding within the context of the heterosexualized and masculinized institution of sport. Examining my story in light of research conducted by Alfred Kinsey a half century ago, I can recognize in myself what Kinsey saw as a very common fluidity and changeability of sexual desire over the life-course. Put simply, Kinsey found that large numbers of adult "heterosexual" men had previously, as adolescents and young adults, experienced sexual desire for males. A surprisingly large number of these men had experienced sexual contact to the point of orgasm with other males during adolescence or early adulthood. Similarly, my story invited me to consider what is commonly called the "Freudian theory of bisexuality." Sigmund Freud shocked the post-Victorian world by suggesting that all people go through a stage, early in life, when they are attracted to people of the same sex.[1] Adult experiences, Freud argued, eventually led most people to shift their sexual desire to what he called an appropriate "love object"—a person of the opposite sex. I also considered my experience in light of what lesbian feminist author Adrienne Rich called the institution of compulsory heterosexuality. Perhaps the extremely high levels of homophobia that are often endemic in boys' and men's organized sports led me to deny and repress my own homoerotic desire through a direct and overt rejection of Timmy, through homophobic banter with male peers, and the resultant stigmatization of the feminized Timmy. Eventually I considered my experience in the light of what radical theorist Herbert Marcuse called the sublimation of homoerotic desire into an aggressive, violent act as serving to construct a clear line of demarcation between self and other. Sublimation, according to Marcuse, involves the driving underground, into the unconscious, of sexual desires that might appear dangerous due to their socially stigmatized status. But sublimation involves more than simple repression into the unconscious. It involves a transformation of sexual desire into something else—often into aggressive and violent acting out toward others. These acts clarify the boundaries between oneself and others and therefore lessen any anxieties that might be attached to the repressed homoerotic desire.

Importantly, in our analysis of my story, the memory group went beyond simply discussing the events in psychological terms. The story did perhaps suggest some deep psychological processes at work, but it also revealed the importance of social context—in this case, the context of the athletic team. In short, my rejection of Timmy and the joining with teammates to stigmatize him in ninth grade stands as an example of what sociologist R. W. Connell calls a moment of engagement with hegemonic masculinity, where I actively took up the male group's task of constructing heterosexual/masculine identities in the context of sport. The elbow in Timmy's gut three years later can be seen as a punctuation mark that occurred precisely because of my fears that I might be failing in this goal.

It is helpful, I think, to compare my story with gay and lesbian "coming out" stories in sport. Though we have a few lesbian and bisexual coming out stories among women athletes, there are very few from gay males. Tom Waddell, who as a closeted gay man finished sixth in the decathlon in the 1968 Olympics, later came out and started the Gay Games, an athletic and cultural festival that draws tens of thousands of people every four years. When I interviewed Tom Waddell over a decade ago about his sexual identity and athletic career, he made it quite clear that for many years sports was his closet:

> When I was a kid, I was tall for my age, and was very thin and very strong. And I was usually faster than most other people. But I discovered rather early that I liked gymnastics and I liked dance. I was very interested in being a ballet dancer . . . [but] something became obvious to me right away—that male ballet dancers were effeminate, that they were what most people would call faggots. And I thought I just couldn't handle that. . . . I was totally closeted and very concerned about being male. This was the fifties, a terrible time to live, and everything was stacked against me. Anyway, I realized that I had to do something to protect my image of myself as a male—because at that time homosexuals were thought of primarily as men who wanted to be women. And so I threw myself into athletics—I played football, gymnastics, track and field. . . . I was a jock—that's how I was viewed, and I was comfortable with that.

Tom Waddell was fully conscious of entering sports and constructing a masculine/heterosexual athletic identity precisely because he feared being revealed as gay. It was clear to him, in the context of the 1950s, that being known as gay would undercut his claims to the status of manhood. Thus, though he described the athletic closet as "hot and stifling," he remained there until several years after his athletic retirement. He even knowingly played along with locker room discussions about sex and women as part of his "cover."

> I wanted to be viewed as male, otherwise I would be a dancer today. I wanted the male, macho image of an athlete. So I was protected by a very hard shell. I was clearly aware of what I was doing. . . . I often felt compelled to go along with a lot of locker room garbage because I wanted that image—and I know a lot of others who did too.

Like my story, Waddell's points to the importance of the athletic institution as a context in which peers mutually construct and reconstruct narrow definitions of masculinity. Heterosexuality is considered to be a rock-solid foundation of this concept of masculinity. But unlike my story, Waddell's may invoke a dramaturgical analysis.[2] He seemed to be consciously "acting" to control and regulate others' perceptions of him by constructing a public "front stage" persona that differed radically from what he believed to be his "true" inner self. My story, in contrast, suggests a deeper, less consciously strategic repression of my homoerotic attraction. Most likely, I was aware on some level of the dangers of such feelings, and was escaping the risks, disgrace, and rejection that would likely result from being different. For Waddell, the decision to construct his identity largely within sport was to step into a fiercely heterosexual/masculine closet that would hide what he saw as his "true" identity. In contrast, I was not so much stepping into a "closet" that would hide my identity; rather, I was stepping out into an entire world of heterosexual privilege. My story also suggests how a threat to the promised privileges of hegemonic masculinity—my failure as an athlete— might trigger a momentary sexual panic that can lay bare the constructed- ness, indeed, the instability of the heterosexual/masculine identity.

In either case, Waddell's or mine, we can see how, as young male athletes, heterosexuality and masculinity was not something we "were," but some- thing we were doing. It is significant, I think, that although each of us was "doing heterosexuality," neither of us was actually "having sex" with women (though one of us desperately wanted to). This underscores a point made by some recent theorists that heterosexuality should not be thought of simply as sexual acts between women and men. Rather, heterosexuality is a constructed identity, a performance, and an institution that is not necessarily linked to sexual acts. Though for one of us it was more conscious than for the other, we were both "doing heterosexuality" as an ongoing practice through which we sought to do two things:

- avoid stigma, embarrassment, ostracism, or perhaps worse if we were even suspected of being gay;
- link ourselves into systems of power, status, and privilege that appear to be the birthright of "real men" (i.e., males who are able to compete successfully with other males in sport, work, and sexual relations with women).

In other words, each of us actively scripted our own sexual and gender performances, but these scripts were constructed within the constraints of a socially organized (institutionalized) system of power and pleasure.

Questions for Future Research

As I prepared to tell this sexual story publicly to my colleagues at the sport studies conference, I felt extremely nervous. Part of the nervousness was due to the fact that I knew some of them would object to my claim that telling personal stories can be a source of sociological insights. But a larger part of the reason for my nervousness was due to the fact that I was revealing something very personal about my sexuality in such a public way. Most of us are not accustomed to doing this, especially in the context of a professional conference. But I had learned long ago, especially from feminist women scholars, and from gay and lesbian scholars, that biography is linked to history. Part of "normal" academic discourse has been to hide "the personal" (including the fact that the researchers are themselves people with values, feelings, and, yes, biases) behind a carefully constructed facade of "objectivity." Rather than trying to hide or be ashamed of one's subjective experience of the world, I was challenging myself to draw on my experience of the world as a resource. Not that I should trust my experience as the final word on "reality." White, heterosexual males like me have made the mistake for centuries of calling their own experience "objectivity," and then punishing anyone who does not share their worldview by casting them as "deviant."

Instead, I hope to use my experience as an example of how those of us who are in dominant sexual/racial/gender/class categories can get a new perspective on the "constructedness" of our identities by juxtaposing our subjective experiences against the emerging worldviews of gay men and lesbians, women, and people of color.

Finally, I want to stress that in juxtaposition neither my own nor Tom Waddell's story sheds much light on the question of why some individuals "become gay" while others "become" heterosexual or bisexual. Instead, I should like to suggest that this is a dead-end question, and that there are far more important and interesting questions to be asked:

- How has heterosexuality, as an institution and as an enforced group practice, constrained and limited all of us—gay, straight, and bi?
- How has the institution of sport been an especially salient institution for the social construction of heterosexual masculinity?
- Why is it that when men play sports they are almost always automatically granted masculine status, and thus assumed to be heterosexual, while when women play sports, questions are raised about their "femininity" and sexual orientation?

These kinds of questions aim us toward an analysis of the workings of power within institutions—including the ways that these workings of power shape and constrain our identities and relationships—and point us toward imagining alternative social arrangements that are less constraining for everyone.

references

Haug, Frigga. 1987. *Female Sexualization: A Collective Work of Memory*. London: Verso.

Lenskyj, Helen. 1986. *Out of Bounds: Women, Sport and Sexuality*. Toronto: Women's Press.

_____. 1997. "No Fear? Lesbians in Sport and Physical Education," *Women in Sport and Physical Activity Journal 6* (2): 7–22.

Messner, Michael A. 1992. *Power at Play: Sports and the Problem of Masculinity*. Boston: Beacon Press.

_____. 1994. "Gay Athletes and the Gay Games: An Interview with Tom Waddell," in M. A. Messner and D. F. Sabo (eds.), *Sex, Violence and Power in Sports: Rethinking Masculinity*. Freedom, CA: The Crossing Press, pp. 113–19.

Pronger, Brian. 1990. *The Arena of Masculinity: Sports, Homosexuality, and the Meaning of Sex*. New York: St. Martin's Press.

notes

1. The fluidity and changeability of sexual desire over the life-course is now more obvious in evidence from prison and military populations and single-sex boarding schools. The theory of bisexuality is evident, for example, in childhood crushes on same-sex primary schoolteachers.

2. Dramaturgical analysis, associated with Erving Goffman, uses the theater and performance to develop an analogy with everyday life.

10

white-blindness:
the dominant-group experience

Ashley "Woody" Doane*

What does it mean to be a member of the dominant group? My claimed ancestry is English American or "Yankee" (in the sense of a multigenerational inhabitant of New England). For many in my ethnic group, the strongest identity is simply "American." As Stanley Lieberson (1985) discovered in an analysis of US Census data, white Protestant Americans whose families have lived in the United States for many generations are most likely to self-identify as just "American." Indeed, as I will discuss later, the ability to claim "American" identity is an important marker of dominant-group status. More recently, since the 1950s, the label "'WASP" (White Anglo-Saxon Protestant) has often been applied to my group, reflecting the assimilation of other European ethnic groups into the Anglo-American core and the broadening of group boundaries (Glazer & Moynihan, 1963: 15). Whatever the label, the important point is, as John Myers (2003: 44) has put it, that "the White Anglo-Saxon Protestant group is the quintessential dominant group in our society."

Like many of the dominant-group students in my race and ethnic relations classes (for whom I assign an "ethnicity as personal experience" or

*Doane, Ashley. 2004. "White-Blindness: The Dominant Group Experience." Pp. 187–199 in *Minority Voices*, edited by J.P. Myers. Upper Saddle River, NJ: Pearson Education Inc.

"family background" project), I would have had difficulty writing this essay as a college student. Growing up, I never thought of myself as ethnic. I was "just like everyone else," an "American," as opposed to those who were "different" and could claim a specific ethnic affiliation. Most sociologists would not have seen me as ethnic either. The then-popular term "white ethnic," which was applied to such groups as Irish Americans, Italian Americans, or Jewish Americans, implied that there were white "nonethnics"—people who were just part of the "mainstream" or "larger society." Consequently, very little attention has been paid to the nature of dominant-group identity (Feagin & Feagin, 1996: 71–72; Doane, 1997a), as opposed to dominant-group treatment of racial and ethnic minorities. As I have argued elsewhere (Doane, 1997a), this "hidden" nature of dominant-group identity has assisted the dominant group in maintaining its position of power and influence. For me, developing an understanding of dominant-group identity has helped me to understand the history of my family.

Marking the Center: The Doane Family

On my father's side of the family, which is where I locate my ethnic identity, I am a twelfth-generation English American. Other branches of the family tree contain later immigrants from England and, on my mother's side, nineteenth-century immigrants from Scotland. All evidence, however, suggests that they assimilated rapidly into the Anglo-American group as what Charlotte Erickson (1972) has called "invisible immigrants." In any event, it is through my father's family that I take both my surname and my sense of heritage.

My first-generation ancestor, John Doane, migrated from England to the Plymouth Colony in Massachusetts around 1630 (Doane, 1960 [1902]; unless otherwise noted, all historical family information in this section is taken from this work). Interestingly, the family history refers to him as having "settled" in Plymouth, as opposed to more accurate terms such as *colonized* or even *invaded.* I do think that it is important to recognize that my ancestor, along with others of his time, were immigrants, even though their immigrant experience was different from that of other groups. While little is known as to where John Doane came from or why he migrated, I must assume that it was for economic opportunity, religious freedom, or both. Because he almost immediately came to occupy a position of relative prominence in Plymouth Colony (a 1633 document lists him as a member of the

Governor's Council, along with Myles Standish and William Bradford), he clearly did not experience life at the bottom of the stratification system (e.g., as a hired laborer or as an indentured servant). As a very early immigrant, he also would not have had the experience of having to adapt to a dominant group within the emerging colonial society.

In 1644 or 1645, dissatisfied with the lack of prosperity and economic opportunity in Plymouth, John Doane and many others relocated to Nauset (later Eastham) on Cape Cod. The land in Nauset is listed as being "purchased" from Native Americans for "moose skins, boats, wampum, and little knives." As we now know, Native American and English notions of land ownership and use were dramatically different. Native Americans viewed land as a resource to be used, while the English treated land as a "commodity" with perpetual ownership rights (Richter, 2001: 54). What is clear is that my ancestor (and his descendants) certainly benefited from the transaction. From all accounts, John Doane appeared to have at least a comfortable economic status after the move to Eastham, as his original land purchase was 200 acres. He also had considerable local influence as a deacon, selectman, and deputy to the Colony Court until his death in 1685 at the age of 95.

For the next five generations, my ancestors remained in Eastham, living as relatively prosperous farmers and frequently serving as town officials. Living on Cape Cod, my family was not on the front lines of armed conflict with Native Americans in New England, conflicts such as King Philip's War in 1675 and 1676. While it is difficult to say for certain, I suspect that they would have shared the prevailing attitude of New Englanders, which was to view Native Americans as inherently heathen, lazy, barbaric, and a threat to civilized Christian society. Historian Ronald Takaki (1993: 38) has termed this the "racialization of savagery," the perspective that Native Americans were incapable of civilization. These attitudes justified the conquest and taking of Native American land and enabled Europeans to view the devastating epidemics (probably smallpox) that decimated Native American communities as "God's divine intervention." Even though the "frontier" soon moved far away from my ancestors, the conflicts between English colonists and Native Americans set the stage for two centuries of conflict across the American continent. While my family was increasingly removed from later conflict with and the removal of Native Americans, they were members of a racial-ethnic group that clearly benefited from the territorial expansion of the United States.

Once Native American communities had been eliminated, evidence suggests that my ancestors would have encountered little ethnic or racial diversity during their first two centuries in the United States. As Vincent Parillo (1994: 528) has observed, the initial population of colonial America in 1689 was about 80 percent English. Even though the population of the colonies became more diverse (by the 1790 census English Americans were about 49 percent of the population) with the involuntary immigration of enslaved Africans and the immigration of non-English Europeans (e.g., Germans, Scots-Irish), New England remained the most English area and Massachusetts the most English state (Parillo, 1994). Out on Cape Cod, my ancestors probably would have had little exposure to the increasing diversity of the colonies; there would have been little to dissuade them from the belief that English culture and customs were universal.

What emerged from colonial America was what can be called the Anglo-Protestant "core" of American society (Feagin & Feagin, 1996). As the United States became an independent nation, its culture and institutions had a distinct English influence. More significantly, its ideologies and policies concerning race and ethnic relations have reflected the perspectives and interests of Anglo-Americans (Marger, 2003). Throughout US history, other ethnic and racial groups have been expected to adhere to these practices, a phenomenon Milton Gordon (1964) has referred to as "Anglo-conformity." As "old stock" Americans, my ancestors had the advantage of navigating in familiar social and cultural waters.

In the sixth generation, my ancestor Samuel Dill Doane died and was buried at sea during a voyage to the West Indies in 1809. While I cannot say for certain whether he participated in the slave trade, we do know that the growth of the Atlantic trade and the maritime industry in New England was due in large part to the economic activity generated by the slave trade. Vessels from New England participated in the "Triangle Trade," which involved bringing slaves from Africa to the Americas, raw materials to Europe, and finished goods to the American colonies. Ships from New England carried farm products and manufactured goods (bricks, candles, building materials) to the West Indies and returned with molasses, sugar, spices, and even a few enslaved Africans. This trade stimulated the New England economy and enabled the growth of farming, manufacturing, shipbuilding, and distilling—to the extent that New England in 1770 had perhaps the highest standard of living in the world (Bailyn, cited in Lang, 2002: 9). Thus, whether my ancestors participated in the slave trade is immaterial. All of New England (and the United States) profited either directly or indirectly.

While there is the temptation for white Americans with roots in New England or the North to seek to distance themselves from slavery, the historical reality is more complicated. Slavery did exist in the North; it was legalized in Massachusetts in 1641 (Feagin & Feagin, 1996: 239) and persisted in New England until after the Revolutionary War. According to the *Hartford Courant* (2002: 19), the first US Census in 1790 recorded 3,763 slaves in New England, the majority of whom were in Connecticut. I cannot say definitively whether any of my ancestors owned slaves, although higher status (e.g., a deacon or a more prosperous farmer) increased the likelihood of an individual being a slave owner. A recent listing of Connecticut slave owners in 1790 *(Hartford Courant,* 2002: 18) included a Seth Doan (*sic*) of Chatham as owning two slaves; he appears to be a descendant of John Doane and, hence, a relative (another part of my family tree, involving my maternal grandfather, disappears in Texas in the early twentieth century and I have no knowledge of what their involvement with slavery may have been). Ultimately, whether any of my direct ancestors owned slaves is almost beside the point. They participated in a society that condoned slavery and benefited from the economic contributions of slaves.

After the death of Samuel Dill Doane at sea, his widow remarried and moved to the small town of Dana in central Massachusetts. My great-great-great-grandfather, Leonard Doane, was a sailor and later a sea captain. Upon leaving the sea, he engaged in an unsuccessful business (with Charles Goodyear and others) to place rubber upon cloth. After losing all of his money in this venture, he returned to Dana and made his living by manufacturing palm leaf hats. According to the family history (Doane, 1960 [1902]: 279), Leonard Doane was an abolitionist, opposed to slavery, and an active member (a state representative) of the Free-Soil Party, which was against the expansion of slavery into the western territories acquired from Mexico (I think that it is also important to recognize antiracist traditions among white Americans). He was also described as an active supporter, along with his son, my great-great-grandfather George Wood Doane, of the Temperance movement and in favor of prohibition of alcohol. While I do not know what motivated them to support this movement, I do know that there was a historical relationship between Protestantism, antislavery, temperance, and nativism—negative attitudes toward immigrants (Roediger, 1991: 152). One of the forces that propelled the Temperance movement was the association (stereotype) in the minds of many Americans between drunkenness and immigrant groups, most notably the Germans and the Irish (Billington, 1963 [1938]: 195).

While my great-great-grandfather worked initially as a salesman (for patent medicines), he returned to Dana and made his living first as a manufacturer of palm leaf goods, and then later as a farmer and carpenter. Subsequent generations—my great-grandfather and my grandfather—also lived in Dana and worked as farmers and carpenters. In fact, my father was born while the family was still living in Dana. During this period, from the 1850s through the 1920s, my family members lived in relative isolation in a small, racially and ethnically homogeneous town in rural Massachusetts. It would be easy to describe them as removed from the ethnic and racial issues of this era: emancipation, reconstruction, and the emergence of formal racial segregation; increased European immigration (especially from Southern and Eastern Europe); the rise of anti-immigrant sentiment and the eventual imposition of immigration quotas; the debate over and eventual restriction of immigration from China and Japan; and the final conflicts with Native Americans in the western United States and the creation of the reservation system. At the same time, their lives were shaped by—and they directly or indirectly benefited from—the evolution of American society, including industrialization and economic growth facilitated by immigrant labor and by the exploitation of African American, Mexican American, and Chinese American labor. I do not know what my ancestors' opinions were on these questions; however, I suspect that, like most people, they were products of their times and either supported or did not oppose these developments. In any event, there is no record of strong advocacy on either side of these issues.

What is important to emphasize here is that generations upon generations of dominant-group members—including my family—have benefited from the social and institutional practices of American society. Exclusion, segregation, and the failure to enforce treaties and ensure equal protection under the law certainly reduced competition and created economic opportunities for dominant-group members. Political and social practices, from voting access to citizenship requirements to educational opportunities, all served to reproduce group power from generation to generation. Government policies, from fugitive slave laws to New Deal legislation to welfare policy to tax policy (e.g., the mortgage interest deduction), have generally given disproportionate benefits to dominant-group members.

In contemporary terms, the dominant-group has always enjoyed a home field advantage.

Following the flooding of Dana in the mid-1930s to create the Quabbin Reservoir (the water supply for metropolitan Boston), my grandfather moved his family to the mill town of Springfield, Vermont. There he worked in a variety of industrial positions, eventually rising to some sort of supervisory position in one of the factories. From my father's accounts, and my own research on ethnic relations in northern New England, Springfield would have been a much more ethnically diverse environment than any place in which my family had previously lived. I recall from my father's stories an awareness of the ethnic backgrounds of his high school classmates and some sense of low-level intergroup conflict. These decades (the 1930s and 1940s) would have been the time of the gradual but uneven incorporation and assimilation of European immigrant groups (Irish Americans, French Canadians, German Americans, Polish Americans, and so on) amidst the struggles of the Depression and World War II. I had limited contact with my grandparents' generation; however, I do recall hearing occasional ethnic or racial slurs in adult conversations. As I was to learn later in life, one dilemma for dominant-group members is how to respond when racist statements are made by family members or close friends.

My father left Springfield to attend a seminary in Maine, and then joined the Army near the end of World War II (he served with a medical unit in Alaska). After the war, aided by his veteran's benefits, he attended first the state university and then a theological seminary. I do not recall any specific discussion of the topic, yet I would assume that his environment was both mostly white, yet more diverse than that of previous generations. My mother, whom my father met while in college, had a broader range of intergroup experiences. She spent her early childhood in Texas, then, after her mother married her stepfather, who was a career army officer, moved with her parents through a variety of postings including Panama, a series of bases in the United States, and then high school experiences in postwar Beijing and Japan. Her classmates at the Peking American School came from a variety of nations, including local Chinese students. I would describe both of my parents as broadminded and antiracist, as evident in my father's ministry and my mother's work in community organizations. They certainly encouraged my siblings and me to be inclusive and to see diversity as positive.

Nevertheless, the world in which my siblings and I grew up was not a diverse one. The small New Hampshire towns in which we first lived and the

Maine coastal town in which I spent summers were extremely homoge-neous in terms of race and ethnicity. Even later, when my father's pastoral career led us to three different communities in suburban Boston in the 1960s and early 1970s (late elementary school through high school), race and ethnicity played a very limited role. There was no meaningful residential integration in any of these communities. I do vaguely recall identification and verbal jousting between Irish American and Italian American classmates, and ethnic slurs directed toward the latter group, but by the late 1960s, ethnic divisions among middle-class white Americans were becoming increasingly symbolic. In terms of my own ethnic identity, I only had a sense of just being present—of being "just like everybody else." This seemed also to be true for my Protestant European American classmates: They had either assimilated or were members of the dominant group to begin with.

Those intergroup experiences that I did have were somewhat unique in nature and linked to my father's work as a Congregational minister. We had missionaries and divinity students from sub-Saharan Africa and India stay with us at times, which certainly encouraged me to be aware of the diversity of the population of the world. I dimly recall my parents discussing events in the civil rights movement (I was only eight at the time of the March on Washington) or guest speakers coming to the church to talk about their role in the civil rights movement, but everything seemed very far away. Most of the events of the mid-and late 1960s (e.g., the later events in the civil rights movement, the urban rebellions) were merely headlines on the newspapers that I delivered on my afternoon paper route.

By high school, I began to become more aware of the scope of racial injustice in the United States. My parents' conversations began to have more impact. I remember, for example, their disgust upon moving to a new community and learning that some influential members of the church had been involved in discouraging a prominent African American athlete from purchasing a home in their neighborhood. I recall them successfully encouraging the church to provide office space for a former divinity school classmate of my father's who had left the ministry to work as an antiracist activist and consultant. Through the church, and at the encouragement of my mother, I spent a number of Saturdays in high school as a volunteer with a Boston community organization that rehabilitated housing in a low-income, predominantly African American neighborhood. This gave me first-hand exposure to the effects of residential segregation and concentrated poverty: It was clear that the neighborhood was very different from the suburban community in which we lived. I even recall coming home with copies of Nation of Islam and Black Panther Party newspapers that I picked up on the street. While I was becoming aware of some of the "costs" of being black in American society, I never really thought about the implications of being white.

One particular event does stand out in my memory. While volunteering with the community organization, I occasionally spent the lunch hour eating my bag lunch and answering the telephone while the office staff took a break. One day, a middle-aged African American man came into the office and inquired about employment possibilities. When I informed him that I had no knowledge of any openings and that he should return when the full-time staff members were available, I was shocked by his clear skepticism and repeated questioning of my statement. It was only later in the day that I realized that the communication gap between us was undoubtedly shaped by race. I think that it was the first time that I was ever aware that social interactions were affected by race. As a white American, I had the privilege of living for sixteen years before facing this reality.

After high school, new experiences continued to expand my awareness of ethnic and racial diversity. Before entering college, I spent six months working in one of the last textile mills (historically a significant employer of new immigrants) in Manchester, New Hampshire. Compared to my previous experiences in school and in my home communities, this was like entering the United Nations. My co-workers included, among others, Mexican Americans, French Canadians, Greek Americans, and Polish Americans. As I encountered linguistic barriers and cultural differences, and observed ethnic rivalry and conflict (verbal jousting), I began to appreciate the impact of group identities on everyday life. My own identity, however, remained unexamined as I focused upon the "differences" of others.

My undergraduate college experience did little to encourage examination of this issue, as the small liberal arts institution that I attended was not diverse. The first time that I ever recall thinking about my own ethnic identity in any concrete manner was near the end of my college career. By this time I had been exposed to "ethnic food," which was always the cuisine of "someone else." One week I happened to glance at the food section of the *Boston Globe* and saw an article on "Yankee food"—New England boiled dinner, codfish cakes, red flannel hash, smoked finnan haddie, "Indian pudding," and the like—dishes that regularly appeared on our family dinner table during my childhood. For the first time, I remember thinking, "I'm ethnic, too."

This insight also encouraged me to think about how other aspects of small-town New England life, the stuff of Norman Rockwell paintings, were not universal but represented a particular ethnic and cultural heritage. I began to appreciate the ways in which dominant-group experiences were embedded or hidden in what was presented as "American" traditions. We "see" St. Patrick's Day, Columbus Day, Cinco de Mayo, Kwanzaa, and Rosh Hashanah as "ethnic" holidays, but we generally fail to recognize the ethnic origins of Thanksgiving, even though the story and symbols are part of an Anglo-American origin myth (Loewen, 1992, 1995).

My first professional position after college, as a researcher on a one-year study of the occupational and educational status of Franco-Americans in New Hampshire, represented another step in my education. As part of this research, I delved into the literature on assimilation, the experiences of immigrant groups, issues of ethnic stratification, and the history of French Canadians and Franco-Americans (see Doane, 1979, 1983). This enabled me to begin to understand issues of ethnic change and assimilation, as well as the impact of pressures for assimilation, pressures that I realized emanated from my group. Through my interactions with Franco-American scholars and activists, I also came to appreciate the "costs" of assimilation, the struggle to preserve group customs and heritage, and the greater sense of solidarity that goes along with being part of a nondominant ethnic group. In contrast, I began to realize that my dominant-group status did not revolve around these types of experiences, but instead focused on the "differences" of others. To a significant degree, dominant-group identity is grounded in *not* being a member of a minority group.

Throughout my graduate studies in sociology and the early years of my teaching career, I continued to study issues of race and ethnicity. My doctoral dissertation (Doane, 1989) was an in-depth study of the historical evolution of ethnic and racial identities and inequality in the United States and South Africa. This work left me convinced that power and economic competition are at the core of race and ethnic relations and intergroup conflict, and that dominant groups use society's institutions in order to reinforce and maintain their advantages. On a personal level, I came to a fuller understanding of how the history of my group was inextricably connected to relations of domination and subordination—that much of our "success" had come at the expense of other groups. Since then, I have reexamined many of the cultural and historical images that I grew up with, from the "settling" of New England and the American West, to the realities of life in small-town or suburban middle-class white communities, to the redefinition of what it means to be an "American." This process has not always been easy, since being a member of a dominant group in many ways limits our ability to see the nuances of race and ethnic relations. It is much easier to see social and institutional practices as "normal" instead of examining them for ways in which they reflect and reinforce the position of the dominant group.

During the past decade, one major focus for my research and writing has been to analyze the social role of dominant-group ethnic and racial identities. I began with a paper titled "The Myth of WASP Non-Ethnicity" (Doane, 1992), in which I explored the ways dominant-group identities were different from nondominant identities and how these differences affected race and ethnic relations. Since then, I have written a number of pieces analyzing dominant-group ethnicity and "whiteness" (Doane, 1997a, 1997b, 2003). I have also incorporated these issues into my teaching, and over the years I have encouraged students to confront the nature of whiteness. Despite all of this work, however, I find that it still takes me additional effort to "see" racial issues and the role of whiteness. Being a member of the dominant group makes it that much more difficult to see race relations clearly. White-blindness continues to affect intergroup relations.

Over the past few decades, many things have changed. Part of my family has moved geographically from our northern New England base. We have married and adopted across ethnic and racial lines that would have been impermeable a couple of generations ago. The old ethnic divisions among European Americans appear to be largely irrelevant. Our workplaces are in some cases considerably more diverse than those of our ancestors. We have friendships or relationships with neighbors and co-workers that are more diverse than ever before. At the same time, we all live in predominantly white neighborhoods, work in predominantly white workplaces, and move in a largely white social environment. Our intergroup interactions are largely on "home fields," and we generally have the option of becoming involved or not in the racial issues of our community and our society. In a lot of ways, many things have not changed.

Dominant-Group Identity and the Twenty-First Century

So what does it mean to be a member of the dominant group in the United States at the beginning of the twenty-first century? In general, there is still a lower level of self-awareness when it comes to race and ethnicity. White Americans tend not to think about being white because they do not have to; Anglo-Americans still have a tendency to think of themselves as "American" when they consider issues of ethnicity. At the same time, I believe that there is an increasing debate about what it means to be an "American." Past assumptions that "American" is equivalent to white or Anglo-American are still prevalent, but they are being challenged by ideas such as multiculturalism, a rethinking of history, and a reevaluation of what constitutes "American" literature, art, or music. Perhaps this debate is particularly evident in the university environment where I work, but it is also making its way into the larger society.

The dominant group itself has undergone change. Over the centuries, the boundaries of the dominant group have expanded to include British Americans (Scots, Scots-Irish, Welsh), then Protestant European groups, and now to where it has become a generalized "white European American" identity. This has involved not only the assimilation of non-English groups, but also the evolution of the "Anglo core culture" into a more generalized European American culture. As I have argued elsewhere, this has been to the advantage of the dominant group, for by absorbing other European groups, it has been able to maintain its social, political, and economic advantages in the face of substantial immigration (Doane, 1997a: 388).

Dominant-group status has served to benefit its members over the years in a variety of ways. While some whites and English Americans have benefited more than others (social class *does* make a difference), as a group we have enjoyed easier access to social resources and less competition from groups who have been excluded from full participation. For example, my siblings and I have all attained middle- to upper-middle-class positions in society. On one hand, it would be easy to attribute our relative success to individual effort—our education was through our own efforts and we have all worked hard in our chosen fields. On the other hand, we have been beneficiaries of a system that for members of our group was more likely to reward effort. We were able to attend better than average schools; we had easier access to college, housing, and mortgage loans; and we benefited from assumptions of individuality and trustworthiness. While life has had its struggles, we never had to confront the kinds of obstacles faced by peoples of color in the United States. As Melvin Oliver and Thomas Shapiro have noted in their book *Black Wealth, White Wealth* (1995), this has translated into higher levels of wealth for white Americans, even when compared with

African Americans of the same income level. Higher levels of wealth in turn create more opportunities for the future—and for future generations.

What can we say about the present state of the dominant side of dominant-minority relations? In some, but not all, cases, there appears to be a greater sense of inclusiveness. According to survey researchers, attitudes of white Americans toward peoples of color have become more egalitarian and inclusive (e.g., Schuman et al., 1997). I see this when I look at my family—my parents' generation and my own generation. Yet we also know that behavior (and in-depth ideologies, as opposed to attitudes) are more problematic. For example, research shows that whites will still move out of neighborhoods once the percentage of black residents reaches a certain tipping point (Farley, Reynolds, & Frey, 1994). Follow-up interviews with white survey respondents find that initial inclusive attitudes (e.g., acceptance of interracial marriage) are qualified or contradicted when explored in depth (Bonilla-Silva, 2001). Racial stereotypes have evolved, often including more complex combinations of race and class. We are also becoming more aware that even unconscious attitudes may have an impact; for example, the response to "black-sounding" names on a resume (Associated Press, 2003).

Seemingly changing attitudes may be problematic in another sense. Dominant-group members may "talk the talk" of equality by supporting equal opportunity in the abstract, but fail to "walk the walk" by supporting specific measures to attain racial equality. It is hard to change a system from which one is the beneficiary. Recently, we have seen the emergence of a new dominant-group racial ideology, "color-blind racism" (Bonilla-Silva, 2001), one that claims that race no longer "matters" and that racism no longer exists save in individual acts of discrimination. It is too easy for whites as a group to claim that slavery was 140 years ago and that "the past is the past" (Bonilla-Silva, 2001: 158). When we say "not today" or "it wasn't me" (Myers, 2003: 538), we ignore the persistent racial inequality built into American institutions—what Joe Feagin (2000: 6) has termed "systemic racism." I do not say this as an exercise in white-bashing, but instead to assert that a realistic accounting of the past and examination of the present leads to the inescapable conclusion that dominant-group members (white European Americans) *continue* to benefit from existing social arrangements.

Unfortunately, the "color-blind" worldview makes change more difficult. If dominant-group members are relatively unaware of their group advantages, then it is even more difficult to see systemic racism and the obstacles facing peoples of color. This then makes it easier to say that racial inequality

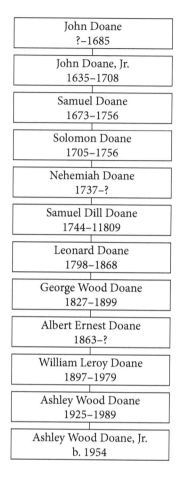

is the result of circumstance, or the lack of effort or ability on the part of subordinate groups. It even becomes possible to make the claim, as increasing numbers of dominant-group members are doing, that racism *against* whites (e.g., "reverse discrimination") is an emerging social problem and that dominant-group members are increasingly becoming the "victims" in race relations in the United States (Gallagher, 1995; Doane, 1996). To the extent that color-blind racism becomes a dominant racial ideology, I believe that it will become a significant obstacle to addressing racial inequality and pursuing racial justice.

What will be the nature of the dominant group in the future? We know that the United States is becoming more diverse. New immigration from Asia, Latin America, the Caribbean, Africa, the Middle East, and Eastern Europe is creating an even more complex ethnic and racial mosaic. US Census Bureau projections suggest that white European Americans will be a bare majority of the population by 2050. How will the dominant group respond to these changes? Will we see increased white assertion and defensiveness, as has happened in the past when the dominant group has felt itself to be threatened? Will we see, as some have predicted, a new expansion of the boundaries of the dominant group to include selected Latinos, Asian Americans, and multiracial persons, thereby once again increasing dominant-group numbers and power (Bonilla-Silva, 2003; Yancey, 2003)? Or will circumstances lead whites to become more willing to address systemic racism, share power, and work to make the American dream truly open to all? I do know that my son, my nieces, and my nephews will grow up and live their lives in a world that will be significantly different from the one that I experienced. What I do not know is what will be the nature of dominant-minority relations in this society.

references

Associated Press. 2003. "White-Sounding Names Open Job Search Doors." *Hartford Courant,* January 15. Available at www.ctnow.com/ business/hc-whitenames.art jan15.story.

Billington, Ray A. 1963 [1938]. *The Protestant Crusade, 1800–1860: A Study of the Origins of American Nativism.* Gloucester, MA: Peter Smith.

Bonilla-Silva, Eduardo. 2001. *White Supremacy and Racism in the Post–Civil Rights Era.* Boulder, CO: Lynne Rienner.

_____. 2003. "New Racism, Color-Blind Racism, and the Future of Whiteness in America." In *White Out: The Continuing Significance of Racism,* Ashley Doane and Eduardo Bonilla-Silva, eds. New York: Routledge.

Doane, Alfred Adler. 1960 [1902]. *The Doane Family,* 2nd ed. Boston: Doane Family Association.

Doane, Ashley W., Jr. 1979. "Occupational and Educational Patterns for New Hampshire's Franco-Americans." Report prepared for the New Hampshire Civil Liberties Union, Concord.

_____. 1983. "The Franco-Americans of New Hampshire: A Case Study of Ethnicity and Social Stratification." Master's Thesis, University of New Hampshire.

_____. 1989. "Ethnicity and Nationality: Towards a Class-Based Theoretical Framework." Ph.D. dissertation, University of New Hampshire.

_____. 1992. "The Myth of WASP Non-Ethnicity." Paper presented at the annual meeting of the Association for Humanist Sociology, Portland, ME, October 22–24, 1992.

_____. 1996. "Contested Terrain: Negotiating Racial Understanding in Public Discourse." *Humanity and Society* 20(4): 32–51.

_____. 1997a. "Dominant Group Ethnic Identity in the United States: The Role of 'Hidden' Ethnicity in Intergroup Relations." *Sociological Quarterly* 38: 375–397.

_____. 1997b. "White Identity and Race Relations in the 1990s." In *Perspectives on Current Social Problems,* Gregg Lee Carter, ed. Boston: Allyn and Bacon, pp. 151–159.

_____. 2003. "Rethinking Whiteness Studies." In *White Out: The Continuing Significance of Racism,* Ashley Doane and Eduardo Bonilla-Silva, eds. New York: Routledge.

Erickson, Charlotte. 1972. *Invisible Immigrants: The Adaptation of English and Scottish Immigrants in Contemporary America.* Coral Gables, FL: University of Miami Press.

Farley, Reynolds, & William H. Frey. 1994. "Changes in the Segregation of Whites from Blacks in the 1980s: Small Steps Toward a More Integrated Society." *American Sociological Review* 59: 23–45.

Feagin, Joe. 2000. *Racist America: Roots, Current Realities, and Future Reparations.* New York: Routledge.

Feagin, Joe, & Clairece Booher Feagin. 1996. *Racial and Ethnic Relations,* 5th ed. Upper Saddle River, NJ: Prentice Hall.

Gallagher, Charles A. 1995. "White Reconstruction in the University." *Socialist Review* 94(1–2): 165–187.

Glazer, Nathan, & Daniel Patrick Moynihan. 1963. *Beyond the Melting Pot: The Negroes, Puerto Ricans, Jews, Italians, and Irish of New York City.* Cambridge, MA: MIT Press.

Gordon, Milton M. 1964. *Assimilation in American Life: The Role of Race, Religion, and National Origins.* New York: Oxford University Press.

Hartford Courant. September 29, 2002. "Connecticut Slave Owners in 1790." pp. 16–19.

Lang, Joel. September 29, 2002. "The Plantation Next Door: How Salem Slaves, Wethersfield Onions, and West Indies Sugar Made Connecticut Rich." *Hartford Courant,* pp. 6–13.

Lieberson, Stanley. 1985. "Unhyphenated Whites in the United States." *Ethnic and Racial Studies* 8: 159–180.

Loewen, James W. 1992. "The Truth About the First Thanksgiving." *Monthly Review* 44(6): 12–25.

_____. *Lies My Teacher Told Me: Everything Your American History Textbook Got Wrong.* New York: New Press.

Marger, Martin N. 2003. *Race and Ethnic Relations: American and Global Perspectives,* 6th ed. Belmont, CA: Wadsworth.

Myers, John P. 2003. *Dominant-Minority Relations in America.* Boston: Allyn and Bacon.

Oliver, Melvin L., & Thomas M. Shapiro. 1995. *Black Wealth, White Wealth: A New Perspective on Racial Inequality.* New York: Routledge.

Parillo, Vincent. 1994. "Diversity in America: A Socio-historical Analysis." *Sociological Forum* 9: 523–546.

Richter, Daniel K. 2001. *Facing East from Indian Country: A Native History of Early America.* Cambridge, MA: Harvard University Press.

Roediger, David R. 1991. *Wages of Whiteness: Race and the Making of the American Working Class.* London: Verso.

Schuman, Howard, Charlotte Steeh, Lawrence Bobo, & Maria Krysan. 1997. *Racial Attitudes in America: Trends and Interpretations.* Cambridge, MA: Harvard University Press.

Takaki, Ronald. 1993. *A Different Mirror: A History of Multicultural America.* Boston: Little, Brown.

Yancey, George. 2003. *Who Is White? Latinos, Asians, and the New Black/Nonblack Divide.* Boulder, CO: Lynne Rienner.

11

class

Still Alive and Reproducing in the United States

Diana Kendall*

Elites are elites not because of who they are but because of who they
are in relation to other social actors and institutions. Elites are made.

—SHAMUS RAHMAN KHAN (2011)

Many of us are fascinated by elites and how they fit into the United States
class structure. My larger research has focused on members of the upper
class and documented how this top class possesses a distinct demographic
identity and routinely engages in boundary maintenance activities that help
preserve their elite status. In this article, I describe how elites maintain and
perpetuate their social location in society through their relations to other
social actors and institutions in the US class hierarchy.

Although the concept of class is employed in a variety of ways by social
scientists, it is most frequently applied in an economic context which refers
to levels of income and/or wealth that an individual or family has accumu-
lated. From this approach, in the twenty-first century, income inequality

* "Class: Still Alive and Reproducing in the United States." Adapted from "Class in the United
States: Not Only Alive but Reproducing" by Diana Kendall, originally published in *Research
in Social Stratification and Mobility* 24, no. 1 (2006): 89–104. Reprinted by permission of the
author.

and class divisions have intensified. The rising standard of living in the West basically concealed increasing inequality until the 1980s when the most affluent US households began earning a larger and larger share of overall income to the extent the top 1 percent earns about one-sixth of all income and the top 10 percent earns about half, leaving the bottom 90 percent with about half of all earned income. Similarly, the distribution of wealth has become more concentrated as well. Wealth refers to the value of a person's or family's economic assets, including income, personal property, and income-producing property (Kendall, 2013). Today in the United States, the top 20 percent own at least 85 percent of all privately held wealth, leaving the bottom 80 percent with less than 15 percent of such wealth.

However, class is not always used as a strictly objective criteria based on measurable amounts of money or other financial resources: Class can also be used to identify a person's more subjective location in a "social pecking order" based on factors such as one's family background, level of prestige, and social networks. As such, all classes, from the highest to the lowest, are constantly being socially reproduced. Although social reproduction of class occurs across class lines, this process is particularly found among elites who desire to maintain their privilege and pass it on to their children and grandchildren. A key point highlighted is that the US upper class not only exists economically but also socially and in terms of identity and class consciousness. My study of social reproduction shows that many people in local and regional upper classes form stable identities in class terms and that these identities remain features of contemporary life.

Class exists as a salient factor when people think in terms of "us" and "them" in society. The us-versus-them mentality of class-based relations in the local community has been a topic of sociological interest for many years. In the 1950s, scholars showed how members of the upper class created a set of exclusive clubs, luxury residential enclaves, and private social occasions unique to the upper class to ensure that many elites had a protective inner social circle that provided them with proximity to each other and a shield against having to deal with those who were "not our kind of people." There was also elaboration on how the upper-class debutante presentation served as a mechanism by which elites not only introduced their daughters to eligible bachelors but also introduced the young women to high society. This "coming out" ritual indicated that the daughters of privileged families were not full-fledged members of a restricted and exclusive group for which they and their families had fulfilled certain class-based prerequisites. This is an example of stratification by status based on a positive or negative social estimation of honor that is associated with a particular lifestyle expected of people in a specific social circle (Gerth and Mills, 1958). Implicit in these early studies of the upper class was the idea that elites were in the "inner circle," whereas people in other classes were outsiders, not only socially but also in the opportunity structure of the community and perhaps the larger society. In addition to these earlier studies of the upper class, a number of well-known community-based studies have addressed the issue of how class is reproduced not only biologically, but socially.

My research took place over a ten-year period in which I interviewed and observed privileged women in Texas (see Kendall, 2002). The participants generally are from wealthy, old-guard families who share not only an interest in the arts but also an interest—whether or not openly acknowledged—in the social reproduction of the upper class. Almost all of the women in the groups I studied are members of households with an annual income that would place them in the top 1–5 percent of households in this nation. I found that social elites across cities typically engage in similar behavior and have somewhat similar outlooks.

Maintenance and Social Reproduction of the Upper Class

Long-established elite families are in a unique economic and social position to perpetuate the advantages they hold because they have possessed wealth and privilege for several generations. They are not newcomers to privilege and exclusivity, and, for many of them, their primary goal is to maintain the boundaries that protect their elite position and that make it possible for them to pass their advantages on to their children.

My study focused on privileged women because, throughout the history of elite social reproduction, women have played a significant role in maintaining class-based boundaries and fostering cohesion among members of the upper class (Daniels, 1988; Domhoff, 1970, 1998; Odendahl, 1990; Ostrander, 1984; Ostrower, 1995, 2002). Boundary maintenance involves both geographic and social dimensions. In Texas, there is a distinct social geography of the upper class that is reflected in residential housing patterns, exclusive private schools many privileged children attend, by-invitation-only clubs and organizations, and seemingly archaic rituals such as debutante presentations that bring members of the upper class (and some who aspire to the inner circles of the upper class) together as a class-conscious, socially cohesive group.

The Upper-Class Residence, Children's Peer Groups, and "The Bubble"

One of the most significant ways that social class boundary maintenance occurs is through the selection of the family residence, an activity in which privileged women play a major role. The establishment of an upper-class home within a proper upper-class neighborhood is one key way in which both visible and invisible barriers can be created to keep others out and to provide the right social environment for the socialization of the next generation. Another mechanism of boundary maintenance is the highly selective nature of children's peer groups, which I also examine.

Whether stay-at-home moms, full-time community volunteers, or professional women, the women in my study typically indicated that they had been actively involved in the choice of residential location and style for their families. Based on location, type, and quality, an elite family's residence may be both a showplace of conspicuous consumption and a part of the social "bubble": a safe haven that provides the family with comfort, safety, and isolation from those of other social classes. Geographic isolation and exclusivity may be seen by elite parents as related to safety issues and often are described to the children as such. A number of women in my study recalled being repeatedly told during their childhood not to stray outside their own residential area without the protection and supervision of their own or a friend's parents or household employees. For example, "Nancy," a white woman in her mid-30s from a wealthy family, learned the importance of remaining in the "bubble" at an early age:

> We lived in a large brick house on a tree-lined street, but several blocks away there were smaller, wood-frame houses with families living in them. I wanted to play with a child who lived in one of those houses, but my mother repeatedly said, "We don't play with the children who live on [name of street]." When I asked, "Why?" I always got the same answer, "Well, they are different from you and me, and there are plenty of children that you can be friends with on our own street." When I pressed her further, one day Mother blurted out, "Nancy, I wish you'd quit asking me about that. I've told you time after

time that 'They are not our kind of people,' so will you kindly hush up about that?" (Kendall, 2006: 95)

Patterns of residential selection and segregation are found among elites in all major cities: Elite residences tend to be in exclusive urban enclaves, affluent suburbs, and multi-million-dollar gated communities where housing costs prohibit all but the wealthiest families from acquiring a home. As a result, no middle- or lower-income families and few families of color will be the neighbors of elite white families.

Although anyone with sufficient financial resources can acquire a residence in one of the affluent neighborhoods, the goal of elites—particularly those with children—is sufficient social distance and geographical isolation to separate themselves from people of other classes, races, or ethnic groupings and to be in the proximity of others from their own social group. This separation becomes part of the social reproduction of the upper class; whether parents explicitly use such terms or not, elite children quickly learn that some people are "our kind of people" and all others are not. Members of the upper class and the more affluent members of the upper-middle class seek, perhaps above all else, to purchase a home in a prestigious urban neighborhood or a wealthy suburban enclave. Social science literature affirms that residential choice patterns of elites and others are not strictly individual choices: Other practices are also at work at the macro, social structural, level of society that keep people in divergent class groupings segregated.

Residential boundary maintenance is a powerful force in perpetuating class distinctions because upper-class children are taught to have pride in their neighborhoods, and they do not realize that these neighborhoods are not representative of the larger social world. For the most part, elite children are surrounded by others (except for household help) who are similar to themselves. As one respondent stated, "When I was a kid, I thought everybody lived like we did." Preserving the social bubble for children in settings such as these is especially important to elite women because it provides a safe and protective environment from which the children only emerge in supervised and special circumstances.

To further insulate and isolate children in the "bubble," privileged women are careful about their children's play groups. Building social networks and controlling outsiders' access to these networks begins in early childhood for the typical upper-class child, and one early manifestation of such net-works is the play group. Consider, for example, why one elite woman in my study believed it was extremely important for her to help her children choose their friends and play groups:

> My children don't really select their own friends. They decide who they like most or have the most fun with in playgroups that we set up for them. Young children don't really know how to go out and find friends of their own, but they enjoy doing activities together that the mothers have set up or that are like playday in the summer at the country club. . . . There are so many sad things that happen to children today, and as a parent, I have a responsibility to keep my kids away from anyone who might harm them. Sometimes I think children with nice things are victimized by other children, like those who come from the "wrong side of the tracks" [holding up the index and third finger of each hand to make visual quotation marks], if you know what I mean. (Kendall, 2006: 96)

Although play groups and play dates are popular ideas among middle- and upper-middle class parents, elite mothers appear to be uniquely fond of this approach for building their children's social networks. For most of these women, the intended function of the play group has nothing to do with ex-cluding outsiders but rather is based on the belief that children should in-teract with "others like us who share our family values and act like we want our kids to behave." However, the result of parental play-group management is largely one of promoting upper-class segregation.

Taking control of play groups is also a mechanism used by upper-class parents to ensure that their children will receive the appropriate socialization for an upper-class lifestyle and will not come to question their family's wealth or social position. For upper-class parents, careful selection of members of their child's play group is the key to building social networks for the child, but also has the effect of instilling notions of entitlement in the children. When upper-class children interact only with other privileged children, they compare themselves to others on a within-economic-class basis rather than looking across class lines where invidious distinctions in wealth and oppor-tunity are highly visible. For example, children come to assume that the own-ership of multiple luxury vehicles or possession of extravagant amenities in their homes is not unusual.

Prep Schools, Universities, and Upper-Class Reproduction

Children of the upper classes typically attend either private preparatory schools or even highly regarded public schools located within wealthy residential enclaves. The importance of elite private schools in the lives of the privileged is shown by the fact that women like "Gay," an upper-class white woman who was in her mid-20s at the time of these remarks, often seek to secure a position for their offspring in such schools even before the children are born:

> After the obstetrician told me I was pregnant, the first phone call I made was to my husband to tell him. The second call I made was to [an elite private school] to put my [unborn] child on the school's waiting list for four years down the road. I've been extremely happy with my choice and have enrolled my other children in the same school because they learn values that are in keeping with what we try to teach the children at home, and they develop playgroups and friendships with other children like themselves. (Kendall, 2002: 81)

As Gay's statement suggests, upper-class beliefs and values initially taught at home are strengthened in elite private schools and prestigious public schools primarily populated by elites, where students are encouraged to develop a sense of collective identity that involves school, peers, and one's place within the larger society.

As privileged young people create a web of affiliations in dormitories, sporting events, classrooms, and other settings within their schools, they establish ties that, because they are interwoven in such a way as to become indistinguishable from the students' individual identity, will grow and become even more important after graduation. Consequently, to develop solidarity with one's classmates is to develop a form of class solidarity because of the commonalities in beliefs and lived experiences shared over a period of time, frequently without the students being exposed to countervailing belief systems or social networks. Over time, identity with others in the same class is a stronger link than merely some vague perception that they share similar values. Additionally, and most importantly, elite schools convey to students the idea that their privilege is justified (Cookson and Persell,

1985; Gaztambide-Fernández, 2009; Khan, 2011); this attitude is essential for maintaining an upper-class outlook.

Do Upper-Class Mechanisms of Social Reproduction Work?

Because of the need to socially (as well as biologically) reproduce the upper class in each new generation, elite women use the mechanisms set forth in this article to maintain class-based boundaries and to convey to their children social and cultural capital not as easily available to those in other classes. Do the class reproduction strategies described in this article actually work? I believe the answer is "yes." The social reproduction processes engaged in by privileged women do, in fact, help elite young people become class actors who support upper-class ideologies, and those same processes deny many other children the opportunities that might be available for them in a true democracy.

Do the advantages of the upper class disadvantage other people? Any form of exclusionary practice based on class (or race/ethnicity and gender), even in voluntary organizations and charitable activities, reproduces inequality in the United States. Exclusionary practices provide an unfair advantage to those elites who assume that it is their *right* to possess the most wealth in society, to hold the top positions, and to create a world of advantage for their children while showing little concern for those in the bottom tiers of society, whose labor often helps privileged elites to maintain their dominant position in a capitalist economy where they enjoy a consumer-oriented, leisure-class lifestyle.

references

Cookson, Peter W., Jr., and Caroline Hodges Persell. 1985. *Preparing for Power: America's Elite Boarding Schools.* New York: Basic Books.
Daniels, Arlene Kaplan. 1988. *Invisible Careers.* Chicago: University of Chicago Press.
Domhoff, G. William. 1970. *The Higher Circles.* New York: Random House.
———. 1998. *Who Rules America? Power and Politics in the Year 2000.* Mountain View, CA: Mayfield.
Gaztambide-Fernández, Rubén A. 2009. *The Best of the Best: Becoming Elite at an American Boarding School.* Cambridge, MA: Harvard University Press.
Gerth, H. H., and C. Wright Mills. 1958. *From Max Weber: Essays in Sociology.* New York: Oxford University Press.
Kendall, Diana. 2002. *The Power of Good Deeds: Privileged Women and the Social Reproduction of the Upper Class.* Lanham, MD: Rowman & Littlefield.

_____. 2006. "Class in the United States: Not Only Alive but Reproducing." *Research in Social Stratification and Mobility* 24: 89–104.

_____. 2013. *Sociology in Our Times,* 9th ed. Belmont, CA: Wadsworth/Cengage.

Khan, Shamus Rahman. 2011. *Privilege: The Making of an Adolescent Elite at St. Paul's School.* Princeton, NJ: Princeton University Press.

Odendahl, Teresa. 1990. *Charity Begins at Home: Generosity and Self-Interest Among the Philanthropic Elite.* New York: Basic Books.

Ostrander, Susan. 1984. *Women of the Upper Class.* Philadelphia: Temple University Press.

Ostrower, Francie. 1995. *Why the Wealthy Give: The Culture of Elite Philanthropy.* Princeton, NJ: Princeton University Press.

_____. 2002. *Trustees of Culture: Power, Wealth, and Status on Elite Arts Boards.* Chicago: University of Chicago Press.

12

the everyday impact of christian hegemony

Paul Kivel*

There is no country in the world where the Christian religion retains a greater influence over the souls of men than in America.

—ALEXIS DE TOCQUEVILLE (1831)[1]

Introduction

Historically, there is no shortage of evidence of Christian power and influence. Though Christianity often portrays itself as benign, as a force for good in the world, the actual story is much more complex than that. What is at stake here is not just the impact of Christianity but also the role of Christianity as a determinant of institutions, culture, and behavior through its centralizing and hierarchical authority structures, its alignment with political elites, and its militant values.

For the last seventeen centuries ruling elites have used Christian institutions and values to control, exploit, and violate people in many regions

---

*"Living in the Shadow of the Cross: Understanding and Resisting the Power and Privilege of Christian Hegemony," by Paul Kivel. Copyright © 2005. www.christianhegemony.org.

throughout the world. Claiming Christianity to be the only true source of spiritual salvation, Christian leaders used their religion to sanction and to justify participation in genocide, colonialism, slavery, cultural appropriation, and other forms of violence and exploitation. Today, in the twenty-first century, can we really speak about Christianity as a dominant force in our lives?

Buried even deeper than the political, military, and economic policies and actions of Christian institutions and individuals there seems to be a dominant Christian worldview which has shaped western culture so profoundly that it is difficult to delineate fully. The dominant form of western Christianity calls for a transcendence of the material world. It gives suffering and death a particular meaning and proclaims that salvation and eternal life are possible, contingent, and exclusively available to some and not to others based on God's judgment. A single person, Jesus, suffered and died to redeem humankind and make this possible. This western Christian story of transcendence, salvation, the purpose of suffering, and the possibility of redemption, as well as a number of related concepts and beliefs, have provided some of the core framework for western languages, art, music, and literature, philosophy, architecture, politics, and ritual.

Within this framework there has been a thousand years of crusades against evil, terrorism, and Islam, including US wars in Iraq, Afghanistan, and Pakistan. Within this framework multinational corporate capitalism, colonialism, slavery, and various forms of genocide have ravaged the world, leading us to the brink of ecological destruction. Within this framework women, men and women of color, people who are queer, people who have disabilities, immigrants, and everyone who is not Christian—all those labeled "Other" by dominant Christianity—have been and remain marginalized, exploited, and vulnerable to violence.

What Is Christian Hegemony?

I define Christian hegemony as the everyday, pervasive, and systematic set of Christian values and beliefs, individuals, and institutions that dominate all aspects of our society through the social, political, economic, and cultural power they wield. Nothing is unaffected by Christian hegemony including our personal beliefs and values, our relationships to other people and to the natural environment, and our economic, political, education, health care, criminal/legal, housing, and other social systems.

Christian hegemony as a system of domination is complex, shifting, and operates through the agency of individuals, families, church communities, denominations, parachurch organizations, civil institutions, and through decisions made by members of the ruling class and power elite.

Christian hegemony benefits all Christians, all those raised Christian, and those passing as Christian. However, the concentration of power, wealth, and privilege under Christian hegemony accumulates to the ruling class and the predominantly white male Christian power elite that serve its interests.

At one level Christian hegemony operates through the internalization of dominant western Christian beliefs and values by individuals. Concepts such as original sin, manifest destiny, there is only one truth and Christianity holds it, and man (*sic*) was given dominion over the earth influence the behavior and voting patterns of tens of millions, of people in the US.

The power that individual preachers, ministers, and priests have on people's lives is another level of influence. This influence often condones US expansionism abroad, missionary activity towards those who are not Christian, and exclusion and marginalization for groups or behaviors deemed sinful or dangerous by Christians.

Particular churches and some Christian denominations wield very significant political and economic power in our country. For example, the Mormon and Catholic churches and many individual religious leaders and particular churches raised millions of dollars, organized public campaigns, and mobilized constituents to vote for Proposition 8 on the California ballot—a ballot measure that would have made gay marriage illegal.[2]

There is a vast network of parachurch organizations, general tax-supported non-profits such as hospitals, broadcasting networks, publishing houses, lobbying groups, and organizations like Focus on the Family, Prison Fellowship, The Family, World Mission, and thousands of others which wield influence in particular spheres of US society and throughout the world. As just one example, the Child Evangelism Fellowship runs Good News Clubs in *public* schools across the country teaching hundreds of thousands of children to find Jesus and to proselytize to other children.[3]

Another level of Christian dominance is within the power elite, the network of 7,000 to 10,000 predominantly white Christian men who control the largest and most powerful social, political, economic, and cultural institutions in the country. The Koch brothers, Rupert Murdoch, and Bill Gates are examples of power elite members who wield this kind of power.

And finally there is the level that provides the foundation for all the others—the long and deep legacy of Christian ideas, values, practices, policies, icons, and texts that have been produced within dominant western Christianity over the centuries. That legacy continues to shape our language, culture, and beliefs, and to frame public and foreign policy decisions.

These levels of Christian dominance have substantial personal, interpersonal, institutional, and structural effects in our society. The personal impact shows up in beliefs about heaven and hell, the apocalypse, sin and salvation, and the way that many Christians internalize feelings of superiority, entitlement, judgment, and narrow-mindedness while those who are not Christian may internalize feelings of inferiority, inadequacy, and low self-worth.

The interpersonal effects include the specific acts of discrimination, harassment, and violence directed at those who are not Christian or Christian of the wrong sort, e.g., Muslims or lesbians and gays.

The institutional effects show up in the ways that the policies, practices, and procedures of the health care, educational, and criminal/legal systems favor Christians and Christian values and treat those who are not Christian as abnormal, dangerous, and outside society's circle of caring. The interweaving and cumulative impact of Christian dominance in our institutions creates an overall *structure* that is dense, pervasive, and devastating to our society.

The pervasive nature of Christian dominance can be seen in the way that, regardless of our awareness, certain words, symbols, and practices have resonances that influence our thinking and behavior. Words such as "crusade," "inquisition," or even "Christian," symbols like the cross, concepts like evil or hell, practices like public prayer, the torture of prisoners, or the public shaming of women—these and so many more can be triggered and manipulated by ruling elites because of our history of Christian dominance.

Frequently, discussions of Christian power or Christian values focus on the Christian right or other extreme versions of Christianity that are both visible and explicitly Christian. Evangelicals and fundamentalists constitute a powerful force. However, focusing on Christian Evangelicals and fundamentalists without reference to mainstream Christian dominance is similar to talking about the KKK and neo-Nazi groups without talking about institutional racism and white power. Defining the extremists and extreme versions of Christianity as aberrations leaves unexamined the institutions, policies, and practices of mainstream forms of Christianity and gives dominant Christianity itself a deceptively benign status.

Although it may seem confusing, in this discussion we are not talking about Christianity but about western Christian dominance. Christians and Christian institutions have done many beneficial things over the centuries. For example, some Christians and Christian institutions have fed the hungry, set up housing programs, provided medical care, and fought for social justice.

Nor are we talking about individual Christian beliefs and spiritual practices. If you are Christian you might feel a need to defend your religion or religious practice. You might want to say that "that" Christianity is not "my" Christianity. Just as I, as a man who respects women, works to end male violence, and challenges male dominance, might be tempted to say that I have rejected patriarchy and now stand against it. But I still benefit from male privilege, I still (often unwittingly) collude with the exploitation of women (Who made my clothes? Who made my computer?), and I still have to continually challenge internalized forms of male entitlement and superiority in myself. As social justice educator Mamta Motwani Accapadi wrote, "Christians cannot willingly dissolve and disown their Christian privilege because of their individual relationship with their Christian identity."[4]

A hegemonic system provides a worldview—an intellectual framework, a language, and a set of values—that is promoted as common sense, as just the way things are, as unchallengeable. Many of the everyday manifestations of Christian hegemony are often mistaken as non-Christian or secular. See the checklist at the end of the article for many examples of how it plays out in our lives.

Original Christians

The original Christians were West Asian and North African Jews, predominantly Arab. Jesus, Mary, the Apostles, and all of the early leaders in the church were Jewish Arabs of varying ethnic and cultural identities, and with diverse but certainly not white skin tones.

Since then, dominant western Christianity has produced another kind of "original" Christian—one who is white, male, European, and contrasted with and juxtaposed with *Others* such as Jews, pagans, Muslims, white Christian women, heretics, homosexuals, heathens, and people who were lepers, people with disabilities, and those with other physical "conditions." Women, people of color, and many others could become Christians of a sort but they were inferior imitations of the "real" thing because they were contaminated by their difference from the white, male, physically and morally perfect images of God, Adam, Jesus, the Apostles, and a long line of church leaders continuing into the current day. A person from any of these groups was considered more likely to revert to non-Christian ways, more likely to tempt good, i.e., white Christian men and women away from virtue, and more likely to subvert Christian community norms and thus be a danger to community health and safety in their very being. On the other hand, as a group and taking into account differences in class, this system accords straight, white, male Christians power, prestige, political and economic representation, respect, protection, and credibility.

Key Concepts

There are six key concepts that have come to dominate Christian institutions and shape western culture. Christianity is based on a *binary framework* with a belief in a *cosmic battle between good and evil*. It embraces *love within a theology of hierarchy, dominance, and obedience*. It has a core belief that *people are innately sinful individuals who need to be saved* and they have available to them *one truth, one way to God*. There is *a linear, temporal focus*—God set things going in the beginning, gave us guidelines and a timeline in the Bible, revealed his plan in the natural world, and history is the unfolding of that plan. These powerful concepts frame our foreign and domestic policy—how we think about the world.

Foreign and Domestic Policy

The belief that "You're either with us or against us"[5] is the foundation of a Christian-based foreign policy. Early Christians offered pagans and Jews a choice: "convert or die."[6] Centuries later, Crusaders offered Jews and Muslims the same choice. Later still, indigenous peoples in the Western Hemisphere were told to convert and give up their land or be killed. Today US crusaders for freedom and "free" markets offer similar conditions to countries like Vietnam, Cuba, Iraq, or Afghanistan.

Manifest destiny is the belief that God has a plan for the world moving forward in time towards the final judgment and that the Christian-inspired United States has a special role in the unfolding of that plan. Along with a crusader mentality, belief in the manifest destiny of the US keeps the public supporting the invasion of other countries and a vast network of missionary organizations involving tens of thousands of individuals and billions of dollars of support for proselytizing around the world as well as in our local communities.

Examples of Christian dominance in the public policy arena are everywhere and include:

- Good News Clubs, athletic prayer programs, and other proselytizing efforts in our public schools
- The lack of reproductive rights for women, such as limits on access to conception alternatives, severe limitations on access to safe abortion options
- Government funding for purity-based programs, such as abstinence-only sex education, zero tolerance, and prohibition campaigns instead of for the proven effectiveness of safer sex, needle-sharing, and other harm-reduction programs
- An economic system based on the invisible hand (whose hand?) of the market
- A criminal/legal morality system that rewards the wealthy (considered to be virtuous) and punishes those who are poor, are sexually active, or use substances deemed to be illegal (considered to be sinful)
- Lack of civil, worker, and human rights in Christian institutions and organizations
- Large-scale Christian Zionist support for the Israeli occupation of Palestine
- Intervention by groups such as The Family in the internal affairs of other countries
- Widespread ecological destruction based on the belief that God gave humans dominion over the earth
- Lack of full civil and human rights for lesbians, gays, bisexuals, and people who are transgender
- Widespread support and use of corporal punishment by parents and school personnel

Christian Allies

An ally is someone who uses their privilege and their resources to stand with those under attack and to dismantle systems of oppression. There have always been Christian dissidents—those individuals and groups who rejected dominant interpretations of the meaning of Christianity or the political, economic, and social role of the church.

There is also a long and honorable social justice tradition in Christianity, derived from the Jewish prophetic tradition in the Bible, which has challenged injustice in its many manifestations. This resistance has continued in the role of black churches, the development of the social gospel, and the liberation theology movement. There are many Christians today working for peace and justice.

In contemporary times, some Christian churches have challenged US wars of aggression, supported majority world liberation struggles, worked for economic, racial, and gender justice, fought for civil and human rights, and worked diligently to challenge Christian hegemony within Christian organizations. They have also created alternative feminist-, black-, Native American–, Latino-, gay-, and social justice–focused churches and organizations. Christian dissidents and liberation theologians[7] continue to try to reclaim Christianity.

What's a Christian Ally to Do?

If you are Christian or were raised Christian, there are many concrete things you can do to counter Christian hegemony.

- Learn the history of Christianity and its impact on other peoples.
- Learn the history of the denomination that you belong to and/or grew up in.
- Understand and acknowledge the benefits you gain from being Christian in the United States.
- Use your privilege to support the struggles of non-Christian peoples throughout the world for land, autonomy, independence, reparations, and justice.
- Notice the operation of Christian hegemony in your everyday life.
- Learn how to raise these issues with other Christians.
- Challenge organizational and institutional policies that perpetuate Christian hegemony.
- Challenge public exhibitions of Christianity.
- Respect other peoples' sacred places, rituals, sacred objects, and culture—don't appropriate them in any way.

- Support the First Amendment separation of church and state and work for religious pluralism.
- Challenge missionary programs.
- Challenge attempts to justify US imperialism by appeals to the special, superior, or righteous role that the US should play as a Christian, civilized, democratic, free-market, or human rights–based society.
- Examine the ways that you may have internalized feelings of superiority or negative judgment of others, especially those from marginalized or non-Christian groups based on Christian teachings.
- Examine the ways that you may have internalized judgments about yourself based on Christian teachings.
- Examine the ways that you may have cut yourself off from your body, from natural expressions of your sexuality or spirituality, from connections to the natural world, or from particular groups, ethnicities, behaviors, or cultures because of Christian teachings.
- Avoid excusing hurtful behavior or policies because of the good intent of their perpetrators.
- Look for the complexity in situations and people and avoid reducing things to an artificial either/or dynamic.
- Don't assume that other people you meet are Christian—or should be.

No living Christian created the system of Christian hegemony that we live within. In that sense none is guilty. But Christians are responsible for their response to it, for the way that they show up as allies in the struggle to build a just society.

All of us, Christian or not, working to create a world without hate, terror, exploitation, and violence must identify the internalization of Christian ideology in our thinking and eliminate its negative consequences from our behavior. In addition, we must learn effective techniques for educating people about Christian hegemony and for organizing to challenge its power.

Finally, we must free ourselves from the restraints it has imposed on our imaginations so that we can establish relationships with ourselves, other people, and all living things built on values of mutuality, cooperation, sustainability, and interdependence with all life.

Living in a Christian Dominant Culture Checklist[8]

Please check the following that apply to you:

1. You have ever attended church regularly.
2. You ever attended Sunday school as a child, or attended church periodically, e.g., during Christian holidays.
3. You ever attended a Christian-based recreational organization as a young person, such as the YMCA or YWCA, or church-based summer camp, or participated in a program of a nonreligious youth organization that was based in Christian beliefs, such as the Girl Scouts and Boy Scouts.
4. You were ever told or instructed by a Christian or by a Christian authority figure, such as a minister, priest, teacher, parent, public official, or counselor, that things that you do with your body, sex with others, or sex by yourself was sinful or unclean.
5. You were ever told by a Christian or Christian authority figure that sexual acts other than intercourse between a man and a woman, or sexual orientations other than heterosexual, are sinful or unclean.
6. You were ever told or instructed by a Christian or Christian authority figure that women are unclean, that women are the source of temptation, or that they are the source of sin or evil.
7. You have ever heard heaven and good described as light or white and hell and evil described as dark or black.
8. You have ever been told something you did was sinful or evil, or that you were sinful or evil.
9. You have ever noticed that a Christian theological either/or framework of good/evil, black/white, sinner/saved is used by you, people around you, or is prominent in mainstream culture.
10. You have ever been approached by family members, friends, or strangers trying to convince you to become Christian or a Christian of a particular kind.
11. You have ever been rejected in any way by family or community members because you were not Christian or were not Christian enough.
12. You have ever found that, in your community, the church is a major center of social life that influences those around you and is difficult to avoid.
13. You have ever taken Christian holidays such as Christmas or Easter off, whether you practice them as Christian holidays or not, or have taken Sunday off or think of it, in any way, as a day of rest.
14. You have ever been given a school vacation or paid holiday related to Christmas or Easter when school vacations or paid holidays for

non-Christian religious celebrations, such as Ramadan or the Jewish High Holidays, were not observed.

15. The public institutions you use, such as offices, buildings, banks, parking meters, the post office, libraries, and stores, are open on Fridays and Saturdays but closed on Sundays.

16. When you write the date, the calendar of time you use calculates the year from the birth of Jesus and is divided into two segments, one before his birth and one after it.

17. You have ever seen a public institution in your community, such as a school, hospital, or city hall, decorated with Christian symbols, e.g., Christmas trees, wreathes, Jesus, nativity scenes, or crosses.

18. If you wanted to, you could easily find Christian music, TV shows, movies, and places of worship.

19. You can easily access Christmas- or Easter-related music, stories, greeting cards, films, and TV shows at the appropriate times of the year.

20. You have ever received public services—medical care, family planning, food, shelter, or substance-abuse treatment—from a Christian-based organization or public services that were marked by Christian beliefs and practices, e.g., Alcoholics Anonymous or other 12-step programs, pro-life family planning, hospitals, etc.

21. You daily use currency that includes Christian words or symbols, such as the phrase "in God we trust" (the "god" in this phrase does not refer to Allah, Ogun, Shiva, the goddess, or the great spirit).

22. You have ever received an educational, job training, job, housing, or other opportunity where Jews, Muslims, Buddhists, or other non-Christians were screened out or discriminated against.

23. You have ever been told that a war or invasion, historical or current, was justified because those who were attacked were heathens, infidels, unbelievers, pagans, terrorists, evil, sinners, or fundamentalists of a non-Christian religion.

24. Your foreparents or ancestors were ever subject to invasion, forced conversion, or the use of missionaries as part of a colonization process either in the US or in another part of the world.

25. In your community or metropolitan area, there have been hate crimes against Jews, Muslims, gays, people who are transgender, women, or others based on the perpetrator's Christian beliefs.

26. You have ever attended public nonreligious functions, such as civic or governmental meetings, which were convened with Christian blessings, references, or prayers.

27. You have ever been asked or commanded to sing or recite, in public, material which had Christian references, such as the Pledge of Allegiance, "The Battle Hymn of the Republic," or "America, the Beautiful."
28. You have ever heard the US referred to as a Christian or God-fearing country.
29. As a young person you were ever read or told to read Christian-themed stories that were not identified as such, for example, *The Chronicles of Narnia*, *The Last of the Mohicans*, *Little House on the Prairie*, *Doctor Doolittle*, *Charlie and the Chocolate Factory*, *Babar*, *Indian in the Cupboard*, or the Grimm Brothers' fairy tales.
30. You or young people you know have ever played video games in which white people colonized, attacked, killed, or "converted" darker skinned people, games in which women were physically brutalized or sexually assaulted, or games where there were "implicit stereotypes of colonial domination."[9]
31. You have ever viewed Christian-themed movies that were not identified as such, for example, *Star Wars*, *The Matrix*, *The Lion, the Witch, and the Wardrobe*, *Tarzan*.
32. You have ever thought of yourself as non-Christian or not religious, but when you think about it have had a Christian upbringing or have been influenced by Christian rituals and values.
33. You have any feelings of discomfort, reluctance, fear, or defensiveness in talking about the major impact Christianity has had on you and on our society.

notes

1. Tocqueville, Alexis de. "Democracy in America" (trans. Henry Reeve; Longdon: Saunders and Otley, 1835), chapter 17. quoted in Prothero, Stephen. *American Jesus: How the Son of God Became a National Icon*. New York: Farrar, Straus and Giroux, 2003, p. 6.

2. ProtectMarriage, the official proponent of Proposition 8, estimates that about half the donations it received came from Mormon sources, and that LDS church members made up somewhere between 80% and 90% of the volunteers for early door-to-door canvassing. McKinley, Jesse; Johnson, Kirk (2008-11-14). "Mormons Tipped Scale in Ban on Gay Marriage." *The New York Times*. Retrieved 7-8-12. http://www.nytimes.com/2008/11/15/us/politics/15marriage.html?_r=3&pagewanted=1&hp&oref=slogin.

3. Katherine Stewart. *The Good News Club: The Christian Right's Stealth Assault on America's Children*. New York: PublicAffairs, 2012, p. 45.

4. Accapadi, Mamta Motwani. "Christmas in a Cultural Center," in Blumenfeld, Warren, et al., *Investigating Christian Privilege and Religious Oppression in the United States*. Sense Publishers, 2008, p. 126.

5. This is a phrase that George W. Bush used just days after the 9/11 attacks.

6. Conversion did not mean acceptance or safety but was simply less life-threatening.

7. Such as Cornel West, Matthew Fox, Rita Nakashima Brock, Mary Radford Reuther, James Cone, Howard Thurmond, Tricia West, Karen Armstrong, Catherine Keller, and thousands of others, as well as the multitude of majority world cohorts.

8. © 2004. Adapted from Allan Creighton by Paul Kivel with input by Luz Guerra, Nell Myhand, Hugh Vasquez, and Shirley Yee.

9. The phrase is from Sardar, Ziauddin. *Postmodernism and the Other: The New Imperialism of Western Culture.* London: Pluto Press, 1998, p. 116.

discussion questions & activities

Discussion Questions

1. In the first section, you examined some of the forms of privilege you benefit from. We all share the experience of benefiting from some form of privilege. Is it possible to opt out? To refuse to benefit from your privilege?
2. What is intersectionality? How does examining intersectionality change our understanding of our privilege?
3. Re-read and respond to the three questions posed by Messner at the end of his chapter.
4. Each chapter in this section examines examples of the ways in which privilege is reproduced and maintained. Identify examples of how this occurs at the individual level as well as at the level of social systems.
5 Individual behaviors both shape and are shaped by social systems. Identify examples in this section of how this occurs in terms of the maintenance of privilege.
6. We have been examining various forms of privilege based on social identity. Do you find some forms easier to acknowledge than others? Are some forms more visible than others?
7. Kendall examines the reproduction of class privilege. How does gender shape the ways in which women are involved in perpetuating class privilege?
8. Select another social identity, and examine some of the ways in which it is reproduced and maintained over generations.

Personal Connections

The following questions and activities are designed to be completed either on your own or in class, and then discussed as a group with others. As you share your insights, think about the patterns and similarities that emerge, as well as the differences among your answers.

A. The Messages We Learn

- Identify three of the most significant socializing institutions in your life, such as family, education, religion, media, sports, law, criminal justice, etc. For each institution, list the key messages you received about the following: race, gender, class, sexual orientation, religion, and ability. Have the messages been consistent? Have you heard more about some classifications than others?
- Next, consider the category of race more closely. Create a list of the major racial/ethnic groups in the United States, and consider and write down the messages you received about each one of these groups from each of these social institutions. Then do the same for at least two other social identity classifications (gender, class, sexual identity, etc.), considering the subsets we assign people to in each classification system. What messages did you receive? What did you learn? Whom did you learn about, and who was invisible?
- As you examine the messages identified above, what are some of the ways in which you have experienced or witnessed the reproduction and maintenance of privilege? Discuss one example for each of the institutions you examined.

B. Abandoning the Path of Least Resistance

- Identify at least five specific moments/examples throughout your life when you have taken the path of least resistance, and why.
- Now identify one specific example in your life today where you see yourself taking the path of least resistance and how it contributes to the status quo of inequality.
- What makes it difficult to *not* choose the path of least resistance? What are we afraid of? What are the risks? What can we do to make alternative paths more visible? More appealing or compelling?
- Try *not* taking the path of least resistance. How will you change your behavior in one specific case? Select an example where you can change

your behavior right now (for example, if you hang out with a group of friends who make racist or anti-Semitic jokes, and you usually just ignore it, choose to say something about it next time).

- After making this change, discuss the experience and describe what it felt like. What were the results? Did it have any immediate impact on you or others? Depending upon what you have changed, is this a change you think you can continue to embrace? Work on responding to this question as you work through the next two sections of this text.

part three

intersections:
the complicated reality

13

seeing privilege where it isn't

Marginalized Masculinities and the Intersectionality of Privilege

Bethany M. Coston and Michael S. Kimmel*

"Privilege is invisible to those who have it" has become a touchstone epigram for work on the "super-ordinate"—that is, white people, men, heterosexuals, and the middle class. When one is privileged by class, or race or gender or sexuality, one rarely sees exactly how the dynamics of privilege work. Thus, pedagogical tools such as Peggy McIntosh's (1988) "invisible knapsack" and the Male Privilege Checklist or the "heterosexual questionnaire" have become staples in college classes.

Yet sometimes these efforts posit a universal and dichotomous understanding of privilege: one either has it or one does not. The notion of intersectionality complicates this binary understanding. Occasionally a document breaks through those tight containers, such as Jewel Woods's (2010) Black Male Privileges Checklist, but such examples are rare.

We propose to investigate sites of inequality within an overall structure of privilege. Specifically, we look at three groups of men—disabled men,

*"Seeing Privilege Where It Isn't: Marginalized Masculinities and the Intersectionality of Privilege," by Michael Kimmel and Bethany Coston. Article first published online: March 19, 2012; DOI: 10.1111/j.1540–4560.2011.01738.x Volume 68, Issue 1 March 2012, pp. 97–111.

gay men, and working-class men—to explore the dynamics of having privilege in one sphere but being unprivileged in another arena. What does it mean to be privileged by gender and simultaneously marginalized by class, sexuality, or bodily status?

This is especially important, we argue, because for men, the dynamics of removing privilege involve assumptions of emasculation—exclusion from that category that would confer privilege. Gender is the mechanism by which the marginalized are marginalized. That is, gay, working-class, or disabled men are seen as "not-men" in the popular discourse of their marginalization. It is their masculinity—the site of privilege—that is specifically targeted as the grounds for exclusion from the site of privilege. Thus, though men, they often see themselves as reaping few, if any, of the benefits of their privileged status as men.

And yet, of course, they do reap those benefits. But often such benefits are less visible, since marginalized men are less likely to see a reduced masculinity dividend as much compensation for their marginalization. This chapter will explore these complex dynamics.

Doing Gender and the Matrix of Oppression

In the United States, there is a set of idealized standards for men. These standards include being brave, dependable, and strong, emotionally stable, as well as critical, logical, and rational. The ideal male is supposed to be not only wealthy, but also in a position of power over others. Two words sum up the expectations for men: hegemonic masculinity (cf. Connell, 1995)—that is, the predominant, overpowering concept of what it is to be a "real man."

The idealized notion of masculinity operates as both an ideology and a set of normative constraints. It offers a set of traits, attitudes, and behaviors (the "male role"), as well as organizing institutional relationships among groups of women and men. Gender operates at the level of interaction (one can be said to "do" gender through interaction) as well as an identity (one can be said to "have" gender, as in the sum total of socialized attitudes and traits). Gender can also be observed within the institutionally organized sets of practices at the macro-level—states, markets, and the like all express and reproduce gender arrangements. One of the more popular ways to see gender is as an accomplishment; an everyday, interactional activity that reinforces itself via our activities and relationships. "Doing gender involves a complex of socially guided perceptual, interactional, and micropolitical activities that cast particular pursuits as expressions of masculine and feminine 'natures'" (West & Zimmerman, 1987).

These "natures," or social *norms* for a particular gender, are largely internalized by the men and women who live in a society, consciously and otherwise. In other words, these social norms become personal identities. Moreover, it is through the intimate and intricate process of daily interaction with others that we fully achieve our gender, and are seen as valid and appropriate gendered beings. For men, masculinity often includes preoccupation with *proving* gender to others. Indeed, "in presenting ourselves as a gendered person, we are making ourselves accountable—we are purposefully acting in such a way as to be able to be recognized as gendered" (West & Fenstermaker, 1995).

Society is full of men who have embraced traditional gender ideologies—even those who might otherwise be marginalized. While the men we discuss below may operate within oppression in one aspect of their lives, they have access to alternate sites of privilege via the rest of their demographics. A working-class man, for example, may also be white and have access to white privilege and male privilege. What is interesting is how these men choose to navigate and access their privilege within the confines of a particular social role that limits, devalues, and often stigmatizes them as "not-men."

Marginalization requires the problematization of the category (in this case masculinity) so that privilege is rendered invisible. And yet, at the same time, marginalization also frames power and privilege from an interesting vantage point; it offers a seemingly existential choice: to overconform to the dominant view of masculinity as a way to stake a claim to it or to resist the hegemonic and develop a masculinity of resistance.

The commonalities within the somewhat arbitrary categories (race, class, sexuality, etc.) are often exaggerated and the behavior of the most dominant group within the category (e.g., rich, straight, white men) becomes idealized as the only appropriate way to fulfill one social role. "This conceptualization is then employed as a means of excluding and stigmatizing those who do not or cannot live up to these standards. This process of 'doing difference' is realized in constant interpersonal interactions that reaffirm and reproduce social structure" (West & Fenstermaker, 1995).

It is important to realize that masculinity is extremely diverse, not homogenous, unchanging, fixed, or undifferentiated. Different versions of masculinities coexist at any given historical period and can even coexist within different groups. However, it is this diversity and coexistence that creates a space for marginalization. "The dominant group needs a way to justify its dominance—that difference is inferior" (Cheng, 2008).

Dynamics of Marginalization and Stigma

Marginalization is both gendered and dynamic. How marginalized groups respond to the problematization of masculinity as the dynamic of their marginalization is the central interest of this chapter. How do marginalized men respond to the problematization of their masculinity as they are marginalized by class, sexuality, or disability status?

Goffman's (1963) understanding of stigma may be of use to explicate this dynamic. Stigma is a stain, a mark, and "spoiled identity," Goffman writes, an attribute that changes you "from a whole and usual person to a tainted and discounted one." People with stigmatized attributes are constantly practicing various strategies to ensure minimal damage. Since being stigmatized will "spoil" your identity, you are likely to attempt to alleviate it.

Goffman identified three strategies to neutralize stigma and revive a spoiled identity. He listed them in order of increased social power—the more power you have, the more you can try to redefine the situation (these terms reflect the era in which he was writing, since he obviously uses the civil rights movement as the reference). They are:

Minstrelization: If you're virtually alone and have very little power, you can overconform to the stereotypes that others have about you. To act like a minstrel, Goffman says, is to *exaggerate* the differences between the stigmatized and the dominant group. Thus, for example, did African Americans overact as happy-go-lucky entertainers when they had no other recourse. Contemporary examples might be women who act "ultrafeminine"—helpless and dependent—in potentially harassing situations, or gay men who really "camp it up," like Carson Kressley on *Queer Eye for the Straight Guy*. Note that minstrels exaggerate difference in the face of those with more power; when they are with other stigmatized people, they may laugh about the fact that the powerful "actually think we're like this!" That's often the only sort of power that they feel they have.

Normification: If you have even a small amount of power, you might try to *minimize* the differences between the stigmatized groups. "Look," you'll say, "we're the same as you are, so there is no difference to discriminate against us." Normification is the strategy that the stigmatized use to enter institutions formerly closed to them, like when women entered the military or when black people ran for public office. Normification is the process that gays and lesbians refer to when they argue for same-sex marriage, or that women use when they say they want to be engineers or physicists. Normification involves exaggerating the similarities and downplaying the differences.

Militant chauvinism: When your group's level of power and organization is highest, you may decide to again *maximize* differences with the dominant group. But militant chauvinists don't just say "we're different," they say "we're also better." For example, there are groups of African Americans ("Afrocentrists" or even some members of the Nation of Islam) who proclaim black superiority. Some feminist women proclaim that women's ways are better than the dominant "male" way. These trends try to turn the tables on the dominant group. (Warning: Do not attempt this if you are the only member of your group in a confrontation with members of the dominant group.)

These three responses depend on the size and strength of the stigmatized group. If you're alone, minstrelizing may be a lifesaving technique. If there are many of you and you are strong, you might try to militantly turn the tables.

However, we might see these three strategic responses to stigma through a somewhat different lens. It's clear that normification is a strategy of conformity, a strategy that minimizes the differences between the dominant group and the stigmatized group. Normifiers, therefore, are likely to accept the dominant group's definition of the situation; their only strategy is to demonstrate that there is no reason for them to be excluded from the dominant category. By contrast, both minstrels and militant chauvinists can be said to be resisters. Minstrelizing exaggerates the differences between the dominant and marginalized groups, by seeming to accept the terms of marginalization as legitimate. Minstrels say, in effect, "Yes, you are right to marginalize us. We are not real men as you define masculinity." However, behind the scenes, with other similarly marginalized men, they may also critique the criteria by which they are judged and found wanting. Militant chauvinists likewise resist dominant conceptions by exaggerating the differences between the dominant group and the marginalized group. However, with greater resources, the marginalized can also assert that the dominant group cannot actually approximate the traits and behaviors of the marginalized; indeed, the marginalized may be so precisely because the dominant group fears the marginalized's power.

In this sense, the overconformity of normification accepts the criteria that the dominant group uses to maintain its power; normifiers simply want to be included. By contrast, both minstrelizers and militant chauvinists resist their marginalization by rejecting the criteria by which they are marginalized.

We realize that it might also seem to be arguable in the exact opposite frame—that, for example, normifiers may be seen to be resisting their own marginalization, while minstrelizers and militant chauvinists accept their marginalization and overconform to those stereotypic characterizations that the dominant culture may hold about them. However, we argue that resistance comes in the posture toward those criteria themselves: normifiers accept the criteria and make efforts to demonstrate their legitimate claim for inclusion. Minstrelizers and militant chauvinists turn the criteria on their head, play with them paradoxically, and even suggest that the dominant culture is impoverished for being unable to express those traits.

In this way, marginalized men may present to us overconformity to hegemonic masculinity and resistance to it.

Disabled Men

Discrimination against men with disabilities is pervasive in American society, and issues of power, dominance, and hegemonic masculinity are the basis. Over time, hegemonic masculinity has grown to encompass all aspects of social and cultural power, and the discrimination that arises can have an alarmingly negative effect on a man and his identity. Disabled men do not meet the unquestioned and idealized standard of appearance, behavior, and emotion for men. The values of capitalist societies based on male dominance are dedicated to warrior values, and to a frantic able-bodiedness represented through aggressive sports and risk-taking activities that do not make room for those with disabilities.

For example, one man interviewed by Robertson (2011) tells the story of his confrontations with those who discriminate against him. Frank says,

If somebody doesn't want to speak to me 'cause I'm in a chair, or they shout at me 'cause I'm in a chair, I wanna know why, why they feel they have to shout. I'm not deaf you know. If they did it once and I told them and they didn't do it again, that'd be fair enough. But if they keep doing it then that would annoy me and if they didn't know that I could stand up then I'd put my brakes on and I'd stand up and I'd tell them face-to-face. If they won't listen, then I'll intimidate them, so they will listen, because it's important. (p. 12)

Scholars seem to agree that terms such as "disability" and "impairment" refer to limitations in function resulting from physiological, psychological, and anatomical dysfunction of bodies (including minds), causing restrictions in a person's ability to perform culturally defined normal human activities (World Health Organization, 1980). Normal life activities are defined as walking, talking, using any of the senses, working, and/or caring for oneself.

Men with physical disabilities have to find ways to express themselves within the role of "disabled." Emotional expression is not compatible with the aforementioned traits because it signifies vulnerability; in this way, men, especially disabled men, must avoid emotional expression. If they fail in stoicism, discrimination in the form of pejorative words ("cripple," "wimp," "retard") is sometimes used to suppress or condemn the outward expressions of vulnerability.

But men with disabilities don't need verbal reminders of their "not-men" status. Even without words, their social position, their lack of power over themselves (let alone others), leads them to understand more fully their lacking masculinity. One man, Vernon, detailed these feelings specifically:

Yeah, 'cause though you know you're still a man, I've ended up in a chair, and I don't feel like a red-blooded man. I don't feel I can handle 10 pints and get a woman and just do the business with them and forget it, like most young people do. You feel compromised and still sort of feeling like "will I be able to satisfy my partner." Not just sexually, other ways, like DIY, jobs round the house and all sorts. (Robertson, 2011, pp. 8–9)

It seems that in the presence of their disability, these men are often left with three coping strategies: they can reformulate their ideas of masculinity (minstrelize); rely on and promote certain hegemonic ideals of masculinity (normify); or reject the mass societal norms and deny the norms' importance, creating another set of standards for themselves (militant chauvinism) (Gerschick & Miller, 1995).

When reformulating ideas of masculinity, these men usually focus on personal strengths and abilities, regardless of the ideal standards. This can include maneuvering an electric wheelchair or driving a specially equipped vehicle, tasks that would be very difficult for other people. Men who rely on hegemonic ideals are typically very aware of others' opinions of masculinity. These men internalize ideals such as physical and sexual prowess, and athleticism, even though it can be nearly impossible for them to meet these standards. Then there are men who reject hegemonic masculinity. These men believe that masculine norms are wrong; they sometimes form their own standards for masculinity, which often go against what society thinks is right for men. Some men even try devaluing masculinity's importance altogether. The operative word is "try," because despite men's best efforts to reformulate or reject hegemonic masculinity, the expectations and ideals for men are far more pervasive than can be controlled. Many men trying to reformulate and reject masculine standards often end up "doing" gender appropriately in one aspect of life or another.

Indeed, some men find that hypermasculinity is the best strategy. Wedgwood (2011) interviewed disabled men and Carlos was certainly one who appreciated gender conformity:

> The thrill you get out of doing it [playing contact sports] because I'm an adrenaline junkie! [laughs] Contact for me, gets your adrenaline going, gets your blood going and it's a rush. . . . If I have a really hard match and I'm getting bruised and getting smashed in there and I'm still trying to go for the ball and I keep getting hit—that's what I love about contact sports—I keep getting hit and everything and still getting up. (p. 14)

Scott Hogsett, a wheelchair rugby player, detailed this feeling as well in the movie *Murderball* when he discussed some people's perceptions that their Special Olympics sport wasn't difficult or a "real" sport. He said, "We're not going for a hug. We're going for a fucking gold medal."

However, as Erving Goffman (1963) writes, "The stigmatized individual tends to hold the same beliefs about identity that we do. . . . His deepest feelings about what he is may be his sense of being a 'normal person,' a human being like anyone else" (p. 116). Failing to maintain the hegemonic norms for masculinity has a direct, sometimes negative psychological effect. People tend to judge themselves and measure their worth based upon an intersubjective, sometimes impossible reality. Goffman (1963) goes on to say any man who fails to meet the social standards for masculinity is "likely to view himself—during moments at least—as unworthy, incomplete, and inferior" (p. 128). Identity, self-worth, and confidence depend on whether he accepts, conforms to, or relies on the social norms.

Men with disabilities are no strangers to accepting and relying upon social norms of masculinity. Despite their sometimes stigmatized status, they do have access to sites of privilege. For instance, disability has emerged as an important niche for expansion by prostitution industries. In some countries, giving the disabled access to open and free sexual rights has been argued as a way to make prostitution respectable and to suggest that it serves a noble purpose. As a matter of fact, in February 2008 the sex-industry lobby group Sexual Freedom Coalition, in the UK, staged a demonstration of disabled men against proposed legislation that would have restricted men's rights to access prostituted women.

Another example of the normification of disabled men has been around sexuality. Recently narratives of how disabled men utilize prostitutes as sex tourists and within their own countries have emerged. For example, a 2008 documentary, *Real Life: For One Night Only,* aired in the UK and Australia, is described in an Australian newspaper review as a "charming documentary on the sexuality of disabled people" (Jeffreys, 2008). Here, a disabled man is taken on a trip to Spain by his parents to access prostituted women in a special brothel for "people with various disabilities" (Schwartz, 2008). In this way, he claims male privilege—the ability to use economic resources to gain access to women's bodies—and we, the viewers, see his masculinity—his sexual needs, rights, and entitlements—as validated.

This normalization of prostitution in the interests of servicing disabled men's "sexual rights" is supported by the rhetoric about the sexual rights of people with disabilities that is common to much academic and practitioner literature on disability (Earle, 2001). Much of the material on sexuality and disability is composed of reasonable arguments for information and training to be supplied to persons with disabilities so that they may understand sexuality, pleasure themselves, develop relationships, and, in the case of men and boys, learn not to engage in unacceptable behaviors such as masturbation in public.

But the sexual-rights argument goes further and leads to demands that men with disabilities, though gender is never referred to in this literature, which is carefully neutral, should not only be able to access pornography and prostitution, but be helped by their caregivers, including nurses, to do so. The argument has gone so far, under the title of "facilitated sexuality" that it appears that nurses may be expected to become adjuncts to the sex industry or even a part of it, by directly "sexually facilitating" men with disabilities themselves (Earle, 2001).

Yet, the desire to maintain a disabled man's masculinity does not just stem from within that man. The model of rehabilitation of people with disabilities, the medical model of disability, has a male body and male sexuality in mind. "Rehabilitation programs seek to cultivate 'competitive attitudes' and address 'concerns about male sexuality'" (Jeffreys, 2008). They are about "enabling men to aspire to dominant notions of masculinity" (Begum, 1992).

In today's world, men with disabilities fight an uphill battle against hegemonic masculinity—their position in the social order—and its many enforcers. Men with disabilities seem to scream, "I AM STILL A MAN!" They try to make up for their shortcoming by exaggerating the masculine qualities they still have, and society accommodates this via support of disabled men's sexual rights and the sexist nature of medical rehabilitation programs and standards.

Robert David Hall is an actor on the hit television show *CSI* and walks on two artificial legs due to having both of his legs amputated in 1978 after an eighteen-wheeler crushed his car. His character is not defined by his disability. "I used to hate the word 'disability,'" he says. "But I've come to embrace the fact that I'm one of more than 58 million Americans with some kind of physical or learning disability. After the accident, I realized I had more strength than I knew," he says. "I was forced to face up to reality, but facing such a reality helped me face any fears I had of taking risks" (Skrhak, 2008, p. 1).

Gay Men

Male homosexuality has long been associated with effeminacy (i.e., not being a real man) throughout the history of Western societies; the English language is fraught with examples equating men's sexual desire for other men with femininity: "molly" and "nancy-boy" in eighteenth-century England; "buttercup," "pansy," and "she-man" of early twentieth-century America; and the present-day "sissy," "fairy," "queen," and "faggot" (Edwards,

1994). Moreover, the pathologization of male homosexuality in the early twentieth century led to a rhetoric of de-masculinization. By the 1970s, a number of psychiatric theorists referred to male homosexuality as "impaired masculine self-image" (Bieber, 1965), "a flight from masculinity" (Kardiner, 1963), "a search for masculinity" (Socarides, 1968), and "masculine failure" (Ovesey & Person, 1973).

Today in the United States, gay men continue to be marginalized by gender—that is, their masculinity is seen as problematic. In a survey of over 3,000 American adults (Levitt & Klassen, 1976), 69 percent believed homosexuals acted like the opposite sex and that homosexual men were suitable only to the "unmasculine" careers of artist, beautician, and florist, but not the "masculine" careers of judges, doctors, and ministers. Recent studies have found similar results, despite the changing nature of gay rights in America (Blashill & Powlishta, 2009; Wright & Canetto, 2009; Wylie, Corliss, Boulanger, Prokop, & Austin, 2010).

The popular belief that gay men are not real men is established by the links among sexism (the systematic devaluation of women and "the feminine"), homophobia (the deep-seated cultural discomfort and hatred toward same-sex sexuality), and compulsory heterosexuality. Since heterosexuality is integral to the way a society is organized, it becomes a naturalized, "learned" behavior. When a man decides he is gay (if this "deciding" even occurs), he is rejecting the *compulsion* toward a heterosexual lifestyle and orientation (Rich, 1980).

More than this, though, compulsory heterosexuality is a mandate; society demands heterosexuality. And in response, men find that one of the key ways to prove masculinity is to demonstrate sexual prowess. Thus, a normifying process can be discerned among gay men of the pre-HIV, post-Stonewall era.

The ideological turn in the 1970s made by gay men, away from camp and drag, and toward a more hypermasculine affective style, dominated mainstream gay male culture through the 1980s. Hypermasculine men began to emerge in many major Western cities in the 1970s (Levine, 1995; Messner, 1997). "Like the less visible queer movement of the early 1900s, the hypermasculine appearance and sensibility announced a new masculine gay identity to replace the 'limp-wristed swish' stereotype of the previous eras" (Taywaditep, 2001).

Levine's classic ethnography of clone culture makes clear that among gay men, hypermasculine display—clothing, affective styles, fashion, and above all, sexual promiscuity—consisted of a large promissory note to the larger culture—a culture that was both heterosexist and sexist in its anti-gay sentiments (Levine, 1995). "We are real men!" that note read. "We not only perform masculinity successfully, but we embrace the criteria that denote and confer masculinity. And so we want you, the larger dominant culture, to confer masculinity on us."

But larger dominant culture has not, generally, conferred masculinity on gay men. Indeed, one study found that "the stereotype of gay men as more feminine and less masculine than other men appears robust" (Mitchell & Ellis, 2011). This research found that simply labeling a man gay, despite the man's presenting as gender-typical, made the man more likely to be rated as effeminate. Gender-nonconforming gay men may often feel marginalized *within gay culture itself* from other gay men, who are most likely to have experienced stigmatization and may have been effeminate earlier in their lives. Writing about gay men's feminine stereotype, Lehne (1989) notes that "effeminacy itself is highly stigmatized in the homosexual subculture" (p. 417).

In the wake of the liberation movement, gay men seemed to rely on similar coping strategies as the disabled men detailed earlier: they reformulated their ideas of masculinity; relied on and promoted certain hegemonic ideals of masculinity; or rejected the mass societal norms and denied the norms' importance, creating another set of standards for themselves (Gerschick & Miller, 1995). But such a move also opened up an oppositional culture within the gay community—a culture of resistance to masculinist overconformity. It consisted in reclaiming the nelly queen, the camp and drag affective styles that the mainstream had discarded.

Sociologist Tim Edwards detailed this type of rejection and reliance: on one hand, there are the *effeminists,* who express gender nonconformity and/or seek to denounce traditional masculinity because of their personal style or a commitment to feminism—in other words, they reject mass social norms and deny their importance or very foundation. On the other hand, there are the *masculinists,* who are proponents of gay male "machismo" and seek to challenge the long-held effeminate stereotype of gay men—they rely heavily on the hegemonic ideals.

This reliance is, interestingly, the main site of access to privilege for these gay men. Gay men's misogyny in humor and argot, as well as some politico-ideological departures from feminism, have been well documented (Goodwin, 1989). As noted by Astrachan (1993), though it would seem beneficial for gay men and women to unite under their common experiences within the oppressive gender system, some gay men oppress and dominate women by "searching for people they can define as inferior—and finding women. A gay man told me, 'We want to be the equals of straight men, and if that means screwing women—figuratively—we'll do it'" (p. 70).

The gay men who conform to hegemonic norms secure their position in the power hierarchy by adopting the heterosexual masculine role and subordinating both women and effeminate gay men. Having noted that hypermasculine gay men have been accused of being "collaborators with patriarchy," Messner (1997) points out the prominence of hegemonic masculinity in gay culture: "It appears that the dominant tendency in gay culture eventually became an attempt to claim, eroticize, and display the dominant symbols of hegemonic masculinity" (p. 83).

Historically, camp and drag were associated with minstrelizers, those who exaggeratedly expressed stereotypic constructions of homosexual masculinity. The 1950s hairdresser, interior decorator, and florist of classic cultural stereotype were embraced as lifestyle choices, if not yet a political position. Minstrelizers embraced the stereotypes; their effeminacy asked the question "who wants to be butch all the time anyway? It's too much work."

On the other hand, there was a group of effeminists who were explicitly political. As a political movement, effeminism emerged in the first years of the modern post-Stonewall gay liberation movement, but unlike their normifying brethren, effeminists explicitly and politically rejected mainstream heterosexual masculinity. Largely associated with the work of Steve Dansky, effeminists published a magazine, *Double F*, and three men issued "The Effeminist Manifesto" (Dansky, Knoebel, & Pitchford, 1977).

The effeminists thrilled to the possibilities for a liberated masculinity offered by feminism. Effeminism, they argued, is a positive political position, aligning anti-sexist gay men with women, instead of claiming male privilege by asserting their difference from women. Since, as Dansky et al. (1977) argued, male supremacy is the root of all other oppressions, the only politically defensible position was to renounce manhood itself, to refuse privilege. Dansky and his effeminist colleagues were as critical of mainstream gay male culture (and the denigration of effeminacy by the normifiers) as was the hegemonic dominant culture.

This position was also taken up by John Stoltenberg, in his book *Refusing to Be a Man* (1989). Refusing manhood meant refusing privilege out of solidarity with women and in opposition to women's oppression. Though little observed today in mainstream gay male culture's uncritical embrace of mainstream masculinity, effeminacy was a most politicized form of gendered resistance to male privilege.

Working-Class Men

Working-class men are, perhaps, an interesting reference group when compared to disabled men and gay men. The way(s) in which they are discriminated against or stigmatized seem very different. These men, in fact, are often seen as incredibly masculine; strong, stoic, hard workers—there is something particularly masculine about what they have to do day in and day out. Indeed, the masculine virtues of the working class are celebrated as the physical embodiment of what all men should embrace (Gagnon & Simon, 1973).

Working-class white males may work in a system of male privilege, but they are not the main beneficiaries; they are in fact expendable. The working class is set apart from the middle and upper classes in that the working class is defined by jobs that require less formal education, sometimes (not always) less skill, and often low pay. For men, these jobs often include manual labor, such as construction, automotive work, or factory work. The jobs these men hold are typically men-dominant.

If the stereotypic construction of masculinity among the working class celebrates their physical virtues, it also problematizes their masculinity by imagining them as dumb brutes. Working-class men are the male equivalent of the "dumb blonde"—endowed with physical virtues, but problematized by intellectual shortcomings. Minstrelizing might be the sort of self-effacing comments such as "I'm just a working stiff." It can be a minstrelizing strategy of low-level resistance because these behaviors actually let the working-class man off the hook when it comes to accountability or responsibility. He exempts himself from scrutiny because he clearly isn't capable of such deep analytic thought.

We can also see this type of minstrelization in men who overemphasize their adherence to strict gender roles—being rough, uncivilized, brave, or brutish. Like Oliver Mellors in *Lady Chatterly's Lover*, these men want it to be known that they are the epitome of masculinity. By some standards, though, Mellors is the ultimate nightmare boyfriend: socially isolated and isolating; highly critical of others; the type to spitefully pick fights with others; with an attitude problem, making him highly likely to quit jobs or be fired. And yet Connie Chatterley is obsessed with him. She finds his vulnerabilities entrancing; she can't wait to have his child.

Here is a sociological example of minstrelizing. In their classic work, *The Hidden Injuries of Class*, Sennett and Cobb (1993) document a difference between working-class and middle-class men as they view the relationships between fathers and sons. Middle-class men see themselves as role models, Sennett and Cobb found. They want their sons to grow up to be "just like me." Such a posture requires a certain accountability and probity on the part of the middle-class father. Being a role model is a responsibility.

However, by contrast, the working-class fathers saw themselves as *negative* role models.

"If you grow up to be like me," they said, "I'll feel like a failure." "Don't make the same mistakes I made." Or as one of the chapter authors' own father used to say all the time: "If a son does not surpass his father, then both are failures." Such sentiments remove responsibility and actually place the onus for acting responsibly on the son, not the father. "It's too late for me, but not for thee." Thus, working-class men, by conforming to the dumb-brute stereotype, offer a modest resistance to the dominant mode of masculinity as upwardly mobile striver. Giving up can also imply not actually giving in.

Of course, there are elements of militant chauvinism in the proclamation of those stereotypes as well. For men in these positions, sexism and patriarchy are key features of their masculine dominance. When the workforce is all or mostly male, relationships are often "built through a decidedly male idiom of physical jousting, sexual boasting, sports talk, and shared sexual activities" (Freeman, 1993). Here, what is key for men is how they can effectively "compensate" for being underlings in the eyes of the managers who rule over them and the families they go home to. Using physical endurance and tolerance of discomfort, required by their manual labor, they signify a truer masculinity than even their office-working bosses can embody. They somehow signify a truer masculinity than their effeminate, "yes-men," paper-pushing managers can lay claim to (Collinson, 1992).

Moreover, those in the working, or blue-collar, class form a network of relationships with other blue-collar workers that serves to support them and give them a sense of status and worth, regardless of actual status or worth in the outside world (Cohen & Hodges Jr., 1963). In fact, because those in the working class cannot normally exercise a great amount of power in their jobs or in many other formal relationships, they tend to do so in their relationships with other working-class members. "To a greater extent than other classes, [the lower-lower class] will tend to measure status by power, and to validate his own claim to status, where he feels entitled to it, by asserting a claim to power" (Cohen & Hodges Jr., 1962).

However, for those who want to minimize the apparent differences between them and the more dominant masculine ideal, a site of normification could be the focus on all men's general relationship to women and the family. Those involved in the union movement, for example, stake claims to manhood and masculinity by organizing around the principal of men as breadwinners. The basic job that all "real men" should share is to provide for their wives and children. This would explain the initial opposition to women's entry into the workplace, and also now the opposition to gay men's and lesbian women's entrance. There is a type of white, male, working-class solidarity that these men have constructed and maintained, that promotes and perpetuates racism, sexism, and homophobia—the nexus of beliefs that all men are supposed to value (Embrick, Walther, & Wickens, 2007).

This power in the workplace translates directly to the home, as well. In the absence of legitimated hierarchical benefits and status, working-class husbands and partners are more likely to "produce hypermasculinity by relying on blatant, brutal, and relentless power strategies in their marriages, including spousal abuse" (Pyke, 1996). However, violence can also extend outside the home. As Pyke (1996) points out, "The hypermasculinity found in certain lower-status male locales, such as on shop floors, in pool halls, motorcycle clubs, and urban gangs, can be understood as both a response to ascendant masculinity and its unintentional booster." Willis (1977) details how working-class boys refuse to submit to the "upper-class" imperatives of social mobility, knowledge, and skill acquisition, instead choosing to reproduce themselves as working class, despite the social and financial consequences. These students become agentic, rebellious even, but in doing so also become "uneducated" workers of manual labor.

Conclusion

Privilege is not monolithic; it is unevenly distributed. Even among members of one privileged class, other mechanisms of marginalization may mute or reduce privilege based on another status. Thus, a white gay man might receive race and gender privilege, but will be marginalized by sexuality. In his paper, we described these processes for three groups of men—men with disabilities, gay men, and working-class men—who see their gender privilege reduced and their masculinity questioned, not confirmed, through their other marginalized status. We described strategies these men might use to restore, retrieve, or resist that loss. Using Goffman's discussion of stigma, we described three patterns of response. It is through these strategies—minstrelization, normification, and militant chauvinism—that their attempts to access privilege can be viewed and, we argue, that we can better see the standards, ideals, and norms by which society measures a man and his masculinity, and the benefits or consequences of his adherence or deviance.

references

Astrachan, A. 1993. "Dividing Lines: Experiencing Race, Class, and Gender in the United States." In M. S. Kimmel and M. A. Messner, eds., *Men's Lives* (pp. 63–73). New York: Macmillan.

Begum, N. 1992. "Disabled Women and the Feminist Agenda." *Feminist Review* 40: 70–84.

Bieber, I. 1965. "Clinical Aspects of Male Homosexuality." In J. Marmor, ed., *Sexual Inversion: The Multiple Roots of Homosexuality* (pp. 248–267). New York: Basic Books.

Blashill, A. J., and K. K. Powlishta. 2009. "The Impact of Sexual Orientation and Gender Role on Evaluations of Men." *Psychology of Men & Masculinity* 10, no. 2: 160. doi:10.1037/a0014583

Cheng, C. 2008. "Marginalized Masculinities and Hegemonic Masculinity: An Introduction." *Journal of Men's Studies* 7, no. 3: 295–315.

Cohen, A. K., and H. M. Hodges Jr. 1963. "Characteristics of the Lower-blue-collar Class." *Social Problems* 10, no. 4: 303–334.

Collinson, D. 1992. *Managing the Shopfloor: Subjectivity, Masculinity, and Workplace Culture.* New York: Walter de Gruyter.

Connell, R. W. 1995. *Masculinities.* Berkeley: University of California Press.

Dansky, S., J. Knoebel, and K. Pitchford. 1977. "The Effeminist Manifesto." In J. Snodgrass, ed., *A Book of Readings: For Men Against Sexism* (pp. 116–120). Albion, CA: Times Change Press.

Earle, S. 2001. "Disability, Facilitated Sex, and the Role of the Nurse." *Journal of Advanced Nursing* 36, no. 3: 433–440. doi:10.1046/j.1365–2648.2001.01991.x

Edwards, T. 1994. *Erotics & Politics: Gay Male Sexuality, Masculinity, and Feminism.* New York: Routledge .

Embrick, D. G., C. S. Walther, and C. M. Wickens. 2007. "Working-class Masculinity: Keeping Gay Men and Lesbians Out of the Workplace." *Sex Roles* 56, no. 11: 757–766.

Freeman, J. B. 1993. "Hardhats: Construction Workers, Manliness, and the 1970 Prowar Demonstrations." *Journal of Social History* 26, no. 4: 725–744; www.jstor.org.libproxy.cc.stonybrook.edu/stable/pdfplus/3788778.pdf.

Gagnon, J. H., and W. Simon. 1973. *Sexual Conduct: The Social Origins of Human Sexuality.* Chicago: Aldine.

Gerschick, T. J., and A. S. Miller. 1995. "Coming to Terms: Masculinity and Physical

Disability." In D. Sabo and D. F. Gordon, eds., *Men's Health and Illness: Gender, Power, and the Body, Research on Men and Masculinities Series*, vol. 8 (pp. 183–204). Thousand Oaks, CA: Sage.

Goffman, E. 1963. *Stigma*. Englewood Cliffs, NJ: Prentice-Hall.

Goodwin, J. P. 1989. *More Man than You'll Ever Be: Gay Folklore and Acculturation in Middle America*. Bloomington: Indiana University Press.

Jeffreys, S. 2008. "Disability and the Male Sex Right." *Women's Studies International Forum* 31, no. 5: 327–335. doi:10.1016/j.wsif.2008.08.001

Kardiner, A. 1963. "The Flight from Masculinity." In H. M. Ruisenbeck, ed., *The Problem of Homosexuality in Modern Society* (pp. 17–39). New York: Dutton.

Lehne, G. K. 1989. "Homophobia Among Men: Supporting and Defining the Male Role." In M. Kimmel and M. Messner, eds., *Men's Lives* (pp. 416–429). New York: Macmillan.

Levine, M. 1995. *Gay Macho*. New York: New York University Press.

Levitt, E. E., and A. D. Klassen. 1976. "Public Attitudes Toward Homosexuality." *Journal of Homosexuality* 1, no. 1: 29–43. doi:10.1300/J082v01n01_03

Mcintosh, P. 1988. "White Privilege and Male Privilege: A Personal Account of Coming to See Correspondences Through Work in Women's Studies." Working paper no. 189, Wellesley College Center for Research on Women, Wellesley, MA.

Messner, M. A. 1997. *Politics of Masculinities: Men in Movements*. New York: Sage.

Mitchell, R. W., and A. L. Ellis. 2011. "In the Eye of the Beholder: Knowledge that a Man Is Gay Promotes American College Students' Attributions of Cross-gender Characteristics." *Sexuality & Culture* 15, no. 1: 80–100.

Ovesey, L., and E. Person. 1973. "Gender Identity and Sexual Psychopathology in Men: A Psychodynamic Analysis of Homosexuality, Transsexualism, and Transvestism." *Journal of the American Academy of Psychoanalysis and Dynamic Psychiatry* 1, no. 1: 53–72.

Pyke, K. D. 1996. "Class-based Masculinities: The Interdependence of Gender, Class, and Interpersonal Power." *Gender and Society* 10, no. 5: 527–549.

Rich, A. 1980. "Compulsory Heterosexuality and Lesbian Existence." *Signs* 5, no. 4: 631–660.

Schwartz, L. 2008. *For One Night Only*. Melbourne, Australia: The Age.

Sennett, R., and J. Cobb. 1993. *The Hidden Injuries of Class*. New York: W. W. Norton.

Skrhak, K. S. 2008. "*CSI*'s Robert David Hall Is Still Standing." *Success Magazine*; www.successmagazine.com/csi-robert-david-hall-is-still-standing/PARAMS/article/1134/channel/22.

Stoltenberg, J. 1989. *Refusing to Be a Man*. Portland, OR: Breitenbush Books.

Taywaditep, K. J. 2001. "Marginalization Among the Marginalized: Gay Men's Anti-effeminacy Attitudes." *Journal of Homosexuality* 42, no. 1: 1–28.

West, C., and S. Fenstermaker. 1995. "Doing Difference." *Gender and Society* 9, no. 1: 8–37.

West, C., and D. Zimmerman. 1987. "Doing Gender." *Gender and Society* 1, no. 2: 125–151.

Willis, P. E. 1977. *Learning to Labor: How Working-class Kids Get Working-class Jobs*. New York: Columbia University Press.

World Health Organization. 1980. *International Classification of Impairments, Disabilities, and Handicaps*, pp. 27–28.

Wright, S. L., and S. Canetto. 2009. Stereotypes of Older Lesbians and Gay Men. *Educational Gerontology* 35, no. 5: 424–452. doi:10.1080/03601270802505640

14

class and race

The New Black Elite

bell hooks*

Collectively, black folks in the United States have never wanted to highlight the issue of class and class exploitation, even though there have always been diverse caste and class groups among African-Americans. Racist biases shaped historical scholarship so that the information about African explorers who came to the Americas before Columbus was suppressed along with elementary knowledge of the black folks who came as explorers and immigrants who were never slaves. Indeed, until recently most black people telling the story of our presence here in the so-called New World would begin that narrative with slavery. They would not talk about the Africans who came here bringing gifts of cotton seed, or the small numbers of black immigrants who came seeking the same freedom as their white counterparts.

While a few white Americans are willing to acknowledge that a large majority of the European colonizers who came to these shores were indigents and working-class folks seeking to improve their lot, mostly they tell the story of their arrival on these shores by calling attention to the journeys of the privileged. Like their black counterparts, those whites who could count themselves among the privileged were few. The vast majority of whites who entered states of indentured servitude were working class and poor. Yet the journeys of the privileged have come to constitute the normative "white" colonizer and/or immigrant experience, whereas the norm for black people continues to be slavery.

Annals of history do let us know that there was caste and class division between the small number of free blacks and the majority of the enslaved black population. More often than not racial solidarity forged a bond between black-skinned folks even if they did not share the same caste or class standing. They were bonded by the knowledge that at any moment, whether free or enslaved, they could share the same fate.

This did not mean that free blacks did not at times "lord" it over their enslaved counterparts. Nor did enslavement keep some black folks from emulating white colonizers by embracing a color caste hierarchy wherein fair-skinned individuals had higher rank than their darker counterparts. This hierarchy based on color would later be reflected in postslavery class divisions. Since racially mixed slaves often received greater material benefits from their slaveholding white relatives even when those relatives did not publicly acknowledge these blood ties, they often had more resources than their darker counterparts.

Despite segregation and legal racial apartheid, by the onset of the twentieth century distinct class divisions were emerging in segregated black communities. Still, racial solidarity became even more the norm as postslavery white exploitation and oppression intensified. The logic of racial uplift meant that black folks on the bottom of the class hierarchy were encouraged to regard with admiration and respect peers who were gaining class power. In those days, the tiny privileged black middle class was not seen as the enemy of the working poor and indigent. They were examples that it was possible for everyone to rise. It was this belief that informed W. E. B. DuBois's vision of a talented tenth that would lead efforts to uplift the race and change the collective lot of African-Americans. In 1903 he emphasized this point, insisting that it was important to develop "the Best of this race that they may guide the Mass away from the contamination and death of the Worst, in their own and other races." By 1948 he critiqued this earlier supposition, stating: "When I came out of college into the world of work, I realized that it was quite possible that my plan of training a talented tenth might put in control and power, a group of selfish, self-indulgent, well-to-do men, whose basic interest in solving the Negro Problem was personal; personal freedom and unhampered enjoyment and use of the world, without any real care, or certainly no arousing care, as to what became of the mass of American Negroes, or of the mass of any people." Growing up in the fifties, I was acutely aware of the contempt black folks with class privilege directed toward the masses.

In our segregated town, the black folks with relative class power, whom group sociologist E. Franklin Frazier would later identify as the black bourgeoisie, enjoyed their role as mediators between the black masses and the white folks who were really in charge. They openly espoused contempt for less-privileged black folks even as they needed that group to stay on the bottom so they could measure how far up they had gotten by how far down the black masses remained. At the end of the day, no matter our class, all black folks lived together in segregated neighborhoods. The surrounding white supremacist world reminded all of us through exploitation and domination that even the richest black person could be crushed by racism's heavy weight.

That sense of solidarity was altered by a class-based civil rights struggle whose ultimate goal was to acquire more freedom for those black folks who already had a degree of class privilege, however relative. By the late 1960s class-based racial integration disrupted the racial solidarity that often held black folks together despite class difference. Pressured to assimilate into mainstream white culture to increase their class power and status, privileged black individuals began to leave the underprivileged behind, moving into predominantly white neighborhoods, taking their money and their industry out of the segregated black world. Historically, white colleges and universities had not yet hired the best and the brightest of black thinkers. Anti-racist sentiment was not the reason for racial integration. Strategically, white politicians recognized the threat that a decolonized militant self-determined black population could pose to the existing status quo.

Desegregation was the way to weaken the collective radicalization of black people that had been generated by militant civil rights and Black Power movements. It was better to give privileged black people greater access to the existing social structure than to have a radical talented tenth that would lead the black masses to revolt and cultural revolution. Concurrently, a shift in global politics had made it apparent that white people would have to do business with people of color globally to maintain US imperialist economic domination. The old colonialism could not form the basis of contemporary economic exchanges globally. It was vital that new generations of white people learn to relate in new and different ways to people of color globally if the ruling class power of the United States was to remain intact. Given these concerns racial integration was useful. It diffused politics of racial uplift and black radicalization and simultaneously produced a new class of privileged, upwardly mobile black folks who would see their interests as more allied with the existing white power structure than with any group of black people. After years of collective struggle, by the end of the sixties liberal individualism had become more the norm for black folks, particularly the black bourgeoisie, more so than the previous politics of communalism, which emphasized racial uplift and sharing resources.

In the community of my growing up it was not difficult to distinguish those black folks with class privilege who were committed to racial uplift, to sharing resources, from those who were eager to exploit the community solely for their own individual gain. The latter were fixated on making money, on flaunting their status and power. They were not respected or revered. That, however, began to change as market values wiped out core beliefs in the integrity of communalism and shared resources, replacing them with the edict that every woman and man "live for yoself, for yoself and nobody else."

Traditional black communities, like the one I grew up in, which had always included everyone, all classes, were changed by the end of the seventies. Folks with money took their money out of the community. Local black-owned business all but ceased with the exception of the undertakers. Exercising their equal rights as citizens, black folks began to live, and most importantly, to shop, everywhere, seemingly not noticing the changes in predominantly black communities. These changes happened all over the United States. By the early nineties, the black poor and underclass were fast becoming isolated, segregated communities. Big business, in the form of a booming drug trade, infiltrated these communities and let addiction and the violence it breeds and sustains chip away and ultimately erode the overall well-being of the poor, and working-class black folks left.

Militant Black Power advocates of the sixties (many of whom were from privileged class backgrounds) successfully working to end racism, to feed the poor, and raise the consciousness of all would no doubt be shocked to see gates walling off indigent black communities all around this nation. The black middle and upper classes in no way protest these modern-day concentration camps. Historical amnesia sets in and they conveniently forget that the fascists who engineered the Nazi holocaust did not begin with gas chambers but rather began their genocidal agenda by herding people together and depriving them of the basic necessities of life—adequate food, shelter, health care, etc. Lethal drugs like crack cocaine make gas chambers unnecessary in these modern times. Without outright naming, concentration camp–like conditions now exist in this nation in all major urban communities. Like their uncaring counterparts in other racial groups, most black privileged folks need never enter these communities, need never see the slow genocide that takes place there. They can choose to stand at a distance and blame the victims.

A thriving, corrupt "talented tenth" have not only emerged as the power brokers preaching individual liberalism and black capitalism to everyone (especially the black masses), their biggest commodity is "selling blackness." They make sure they mask their agenda so black capitalism looks like black self-determination. Whether it is movies made by black filmmakers that glamorize and celebrate black-on-black predatory violence while placing blame on the victims, or literature produced by black academics and/or writers that does the same, it is evident that the vast majority of privileged-class black folks feel they have nothing in common with the black poor. Whenever well-to-do black persons justly complain about the ways racism operates to keep them from reaching the highest pinnacle of career success or the way everyday racism makes it hard for them to get a taxi or does not exempt them from being treated unjustly by the police, if these complaints are not linked to an acknowledgment of how their class power mediates racial injustice in a way that it does not for the poor and underprivileged, they collude in the nation's refusal to acknowledge the solace and protection that class privilege affords them.

Prior to civil rights and the militant black power struggle, class privilege did little to help upwardly mobile black folks if white folks wanted to exploit and oppress them with impunity. This is no longer the case. This does not mean that racism does not daily assault black people with class privilege; it does. The pain of the privileged is linked to the pain of the indigent who also daily suffer racial assault, just as anti-racist struggle to end that suffering promises liberation to all classes. However, as the gap between privileged blacks and the black poor widens, all who are truly committed to justice and an end to racial domination must break through the denial that allows the haves to disavow the myriad ways class privilege mediates the pain of racial assault. The black working class, poor, and underclass cannot use class status and privilege to escape racial assault or to pacify wounds when they are inflicted.

In large and small ways, middle-class, upper-class, and wealthy black people can create lifestyles that enable them to minimize contact with harsh racism. Numerous privileged black folks hire white underlings to interface between them and a racist white world. Assimilation is yet another strategy they deploy to deflect harsh racism away from them and onto "other" blacks. Ellis Cose's book *The Rage of the Black Middle Class* reminded everyone that class privilege does not mean that well-off blacks will not suffer racial assault, and it enrages them. Yet he did not link their rage with a rage against the conditions imposed upon the black poor and indigent by white supremacist exploitation and oppression. While all our rage at racism is justifiable, it undermines anti-racist struggle and the call for social justice when well-off black folks attempt to create a social context where they will be exempt from racist assault even as the underprivileged remain daily victimized.

Nowadays, practically every public representation of blackness is created by black folks who are materially privileged. More often than not, they speak about the black poor and working class but not with them, or on their behalf. The presence of a small number of privileged black folks who continue to work for justice, who work to change this culture so that all black people can live fully and well, is often obscured by the dominant white culture's focus on those who are fundamentally opportunistic and/or corrupt. These conservative black elites, chosen and appointed to positions of authority by the mainstream, not only take charge of interrupting and shaping public policy that will affect the lives of underprivileged black folks, they police black folks who do not agree with them or support their agendas. That policing may take the form of preventing folks from getting jobs or getting heard if they speak and/or write publicly, or deploying various forms of psychological terrorism.

When possible they use their class power to censor and silence, deploying their greater access to white mainstream media, and all other avenues of power, in ways that discredit dissenting black voices. They censor and isolate these voices to diffuse the power of those lone individuals who care for justice enough to link word and deed, theory and practice. Ideologically, they perpetuate the false assumption that everyone is really corrupt, that all privileged-class blacks by virtue of their achievements and status betray those without privilege. As this thinking gains widespread acceptance they need not worry about critique or exposure. They take advantage of the fact that the poor and underclass masses know nothing about their lives and have no power to expose their contradictions or their betrayals. They isolate and ignore dissenting voices whether they come from progressive visionary underprivileged sources or their more radical privileged-class counterparts.

More individual black folks than ever before are entering the ranks of the rich and upper class. Allegiance to their class interests usually supersedes racial solidarity. They are not only leaving the underprivileged black masses behind, they collude in the systems of domination that ensure the continued exploitation and oppression of the poor. Unlike many of their middle-class peers who may be bonded with lower-class and poor people, who are compelled by kinship ties to share resources, they refuse identification with the black poor, unless it serves their interests to act concerned. Michael Jordan, one of the richest men in the world, epitomizes this perspective. His commitment to capitalist profit at any cost has characterized his economic success. For mainstream culture he is the global example that colonized mind can strengthen one's class power. There are many wealthy and upper-class black people who "think like Mike" but they are not in the public eye, or if they are visible they do not openly reveal their identification with the values of a ruling class elite.

When Harvard academic Henry Louis Gates Jr. deemed by mainstream white culture to be one of the most powerful black spokespersons in this society, did a program for public television where he candidly challenged the notion that black people across class share common perspectives, he was subject to forms of critique that had not previously characterized black folks' response to his success. Even so, he and many folks like him live in and conduct business in a world where black people's response, whether positive or negative, is not perceived as influential or important. Black people do not have the power to invite the black elite to the White House and do not reward them with unprecedented fame, status, and financial remuneration.

The miseducation of all underprivileged black groups strengthens the class power of the nonprogressive black elite. Without anti-racist reparations, a central one being affirmative action programs, which once offered financial aid to the poor and working class, these groups are not allowed entry into the ranks of the talented tenth. Since they are the individuals who are best situated to experientially understand the dynamics of class among black folks, who may retain allegiance to their class of origins and breed dissent in the world of the privileged, denying them access to higher education is a strategic act of repression. Without quality education, which broadens the mind and strengthens one's capacity to think critically, they are less likely to threaten the status quo. Increasingly, there are few black folks from poor and working-class backgrounds being educated in elite settings. They simply do not have the means. Those select few who receive aid are far more likely to share the conservative perspectives of their well-to-do counterparts.

Unlike my generation (poor and working-class children of the late sixties and seventies), who were able to receive college educations because of financial aid but were not seduced by the fantasy of becoming rich or entering the ranks of the mainstream black elite, as that elite was not yet in place, the underprivileged today are more tempted by the goodies offered by the status quo. Since they have no organized visionary radical movement for social justice to make them more conscious and to sustain them should they rebel, they fear dissent. They are more likely than not to claim that racism has ended or that if it exists it does not affect them. They are more likely to believe that the economic plight of the black masses is caused by a lack of skills, will, and know-how and not by systemic exploitation and oppression. They have learned to think this way from the lessons mainstream culture teaches them about what they must do to succeed. They stand ready to ascend to the heights of class privilege by any means necessary. And now more than ever, there is a corrupt talented tenth in place to guide them along the way.

Significantly, even though a growing majority of privileged-class black folks condemn and betray the black poor and underclass, they avoid critique and confrontation themselves by not focusing on their class power. In the nineties they prefer to talk about race and ignore class. All black people know that no matter your class you will suffer wounds inflicted by racism, however relative. Fewer black people know intimately the concrete everyday ways class power and privilege mediate this pain, allowing some black folks to live luxuriously despite racism. Sadly, to escape this pain or to shield themselves from the genocide that is assaulting black masses, they surrender all transformative forms of racial solidarity in anti-racist struggle to protect their class interests. They betray their people even as they maintain their status and public image by pretending that they know best and are best positioned to protect the collective public good of all black people irrespective of class.

The black masses are encouraged by an empowered privileged few to believe that any critique they or anyone makes of the class power of black elites is merely sour grapes. Or they are made to feel they are interfering with racial uplift and racial solidarity if they want to talk about class. They live the reality of class divisions among black people. Unlike the black elite, they are not ashamed or afraid to talk about class; they simply have few or no public venues in which to air their views. Radical black voices, especially those with some degree of class privilege, must have the courage to talk about class. Racial solidarity in anti-racist struggle can, sometimes does, and must coexist with a recognition of the importance of ending class elitism.

Vigilant critique of the politics of class in diverse black communities is and should be a dynamic dimension of all progressive struggles for black self-determination. Being upwardly mobile need not mean that one betrays the people on the bottom. Yet we need to know more about the concrete ways we can have a degree of class privilege without abandoning allegiance to those who are underprivileged or accountability for their fate. Progressive black folks who have class privilege must intervene when our more conservative and liberal counterparts seek to deny the reality of black-on-black class cruelty and exploitation.

We must courageously challenge the privileged who aggressively seek to deny the disadvantaged a chance to change their lot. Privileged people are the individuals who create representations of blackness where education is deemed valueless, where violence is glamorous, where the poor are dehumanized. These images are not just produced by white folks. Understanding that many black people seeking success in the existing white supremacist capitalist patriarchy embrace white supremacist thought and action, we need sophisticated strategies to challenge and resist their exploitation and oppression of the masses. Saying that they are not "black" or that they are "Uncle Toms" is a shallow critique that does not address in any meaningful way the reality that any viable anti-racist movement for social justice must have a program aimed at decolonizing and converting those black folks who act in collusion with the status quo. Conversion empowers; judgmental assaults alienate.

Until visionary black thinkers, from all walks of life, can create strategies and lifestyles that embrace the idea of empowerment without domination for all classes, all efforts toward black self-determination will fail. Were the black poor and underclass able to create constructive class solidarity, there would be hope that their needs would be articulated and addressed. Progressive black "elites" must humanely confront and challenge conservative peers. It is our task to forge a vision of solidarity in ending domination, which includes anti-racist struggle that realistically confronts class difference and constructively intervenes on the growing class antagonism between black folks with class privilege and the black masses who are daily being stripped of class power. While we need not return to the notion of leadership by a talented tenth, we do need to draw on the legacy of constant radical commitment to social justice for all, which undergirds the dream of liberatory black self-determination that was at the heart of DuBois's vision.

15

how gay stays white and what kind of white it stays

Allan Bérubé*

The Stereotype

When I teach college courses on queer history or queer working-class studies, I encourage students to explore the many ways that homosexuality is
shaped by race, class, and gender. I know that racialized phantom figures
hover over our classroom and inhabit our consciousness. I try to name these
figures out loud to bring them down to earth so we can begin to resist their
stranglehold on our intelligence. One by one, I recite the social categories
that students have already used in our discussions—immigrant, worker, corporate executive, welfare recipient, student on financial aid, lesbian mother—
and ask students first to imagine the stereotypical figure associated with the
category and then to call out the figure's race, gender, class, and sexuality. As
we watch each other conjure up and name these phantoms, we are stunned
at how well each of us has learned by heart the same fearful chorus.

*"How Gay Stays White and What Kind of White It Stays," by Alan Bérubé. From *The Making
and Unmaking of Whiteness*, Brander Rasmussen, et al., eds., pp. 234–265. Copyright 2001,
Duke University Press. All rights reserved. Republished by permission of the copyright
holder. www.dukeupress.edu.

Whenever I get to the social category "gay man," the students' response is always the same: "white and well-to-do." In the United States today, the dominant image of the typical gay man is a white man who is financially better off than most everyone else.

My White Desires

Since the day I came out to my best friend in 1968, I have inhabited the social category "gay white man." As a historian, writer, and activist, I've examined the gay and the male parts of that identity, and more recently I've explored my working-class background and the Franco-American ethnicity that is so intertwined with it. But only recently have I identified with or seriously examined my gay male whiteness.[1]

Several years ago I made the decision to put race and class at the center of my gay writing and activism. I was frustrated at how my own gay social and activist circles reproduced larger patterns of racial separation by remaining almost entirely white. And I felt abandoned as the vision of the national gay movement and media narrowed from fighting for liberation, freedom, and social justice to expressing personal pride, achieving visibility, and lobbying for individual equality within existing institutions. What emerged was too often an exclusively gay rights agenda isolated from supposedly nongay issues, such as homelessness, unemployment, welfare, universal health care, union organizing, affirmative action, and abortion rights. To gain recognition and credibility, some gay organizations and media began to aggressively promote the so-called positive image of a generic gay community that is an upscale, mostly male, and mostly white consumer market with mainstream, even traditional, values. Such a strategy derives its power from an unexamined investment in whiteness and middle-class identification. As a result, its practitioners seemed not to take seriously or even notice how their gay visibility successes at times exploited and reinforced a racialized class divide that continues to tear our nation apart, including our lesbian and gay communities.

My decision to put race and class at the center of my gay work led me as a historian to pursue the history of a multiracial maritime union that in the 1930s and 1940s fought for racial equality and the dignity of openly gay workers.[2] And my decision opened doors that enabled me as an activist to join multiracial lesbian, gay, bisexual, and transgender groups whose members have been doing antiracist work for a long time and in which gay white men are not the majority—groups that included the Lesbian, Gay, Bisexual, and Transgender Advisory Committee to the San Francisco Human Rights Commission and the editorial board of the now-defunct national lesbian and gay quarterly journal *Out/Look*.

But doing this work also created new and ongoing conflicts in my relationships with other white men. I want to figure out how to handle these conflicts as I extend my antiracist work into those areas of my life where I still find myself among gay white men—especially when we form new activist and intellectual groups that once again turn out to be white. To do this I need "to clarify something for myself," as James Baldwin put it, when he gave his reason for writing his homosexual novel *Giovanni's Room* in the 1950s.[3]

I wanted to know how gay gets white, how it stays that way, and how whiteness is used both to win and attack gay rights campaigns.

I want to learn how to see my own whiteness when I am with gay white men and to understand what happens among us when one of us calls attention to our whiteness.

I want to know why I and other gay white men would want to challenge the racist structures of whiteness, what happens to us when we try, what makes me keep running away from the task, sometimes in silent despair, and what makes me want to go back to take up the task again.

I want to pursue these questions by drawing on a gay ability, developed over decades of figuring out how to "come out of the closet," to bring our hidden lives out into the open. But I want to do this without encouraging anyone to assign a greater degree of racism to gay white men, thus exposed, than to other white men more protected from exposure, and without inviting white men who are not gay to more safely see gay men's white racism rather than their own.

I want to know these things because gay white men have been among the men I have loved and will continue to love. I need them in my life and at my side as I try to make fighting racism a more central part of my work. And when students call out "white" to describe the typical gay man, and they see me standing right there in front of them, I want to figure out how, from where I am standing, I can intelligently fight the racist hierarchies that I and my students differently inhabit.

Gay Whitening Practices

Despite the stereotype, the gay male population is not as white as it appears to be in the images of gay men projected by the mainstream and gay media, or among the "out" men (including myself) who move into the public spotlight as representative gay activists, writers, commentators, and spokesmen. Gay men of color, working against the stereotype, have engaged in long, difficult struggles to gain some public recognition of their cultural heritages, political activism, and everyday existence. To educate gay white men, they've had to get our attention by interrupting our business as usual, then convince us that we don't speak for them or represent them or know enough about either their realities or our own racial assumptions and privileges. And when I and other gay white men don't educate ourselves, gay men of color have done the face-to-face work of educating us about their cultures, histories, oppression, and particular needs—the kind of personal work that tires us out when heterosexuals ask us to explain to them what it's like to be gay. Also working against their ability to put "gay" and "men of color" together in the broader white imagination are a great many other powerful *whitening practices* that daily construct, maintain, and fortify the idea that gay male means white.

How does the category "gay man" become white? What are the whitening practices that perpetuate this stereotype, often without awareness or comment by gay white men? How do these practices operate, and what racial work do they perform?

I begin by mining my own experience for clues.[4] I know that if I go where I'm surrounded by other gay white men, or if I'm having sex with a white man, it's unlikely that our race will come up in conversation. Such racially comfortable, racially familiar situations can make us mistakenly believe that there are such things as gay issues, spaces, culture, and relationships that are not "lived through" race, and that white gay life, so long as it is not named as such, is not about race.[5] These lived assumptions, and the privileges on which they are based, form a powerful camouflage woven from a web of unquestioned beliefs—that gay whiteness is unmarked and unremarkable, universal and representative, powerful and protective, a cohesive bond. The markings of this camouflage are pale—a characteristic that the wearer sees neither as entirely invisible nor as a racial "color," a shade that allows the wearer to blend into the seemingly neutral background of white worlds. When we wear this everyday camouflage into a gay political arena that white men already dominate, our activism comes wrapped in a *pale protective coloring* that we may not notice but which is clearly visible to those who don't enjoy its protection.

I start to remember specific situations in which I caught glimpses of how other gay whitening practices work.

One night, arriving at my favorite gay disco bar in San Francisco, I discovered outside a picket line of people protesting the triple-carding (requiring three photo IDs) of gay men of color at the door. This practice was a form of racial *exclusion*—policing the borders of white gay institutions to prevent people of color from entering. The management was using this discriminatory practice to keep the bar from "turning," as it's called—a process by which a "generically gay" bar (meaning a predominantly white bar) changes into a bar that loses status and income (meaning gay white men with money won't go there) because it has been "taken over" by black, Latino, or Asian gay men. For many white owners, managers, and patrons of gay bars, only a white gay bar can be *just* gay; a bar where men of color go is seen as racialized. As I joined the picket line, I felt the fears of a white man who has the privilege to choose on which side of a color line he will stand. I wanted to support my gay brothers of color who were being harassed at the door, yet I was afraid that the doorman might recognize me as a regular and refuse to let me back in. That night, I saw a gay bar's doorway become a racialized border, where a battle to preserve or challenge the whiteness of the clientele inside was fought among dozens of gay men who were either standing guard at the door, allowed to walk through it, or shouting and marching outside. (The protests eventually made the bar stop the triple-carding.)

I remember seeing how another gay whitening practice works when I watched, with other members of a sexual politics study group, an antigay video, "Gay Rights, Special Rights," produced in 1993 by The Report, a religious right organization. This practice was the *selling* of gay whiteness— the marketing of gays as white and wealthy to make money and increase political capital, either to raise funds for campaigns (in both progay and antigay benefits, advertising, and direct-mail appeals) or to gain economic power (by promoting or appealing to a gay consumer market). The antigay video we watched used racialized class to undermine alliances between a gay rights movement portrayed as white and movements of people of color portrayed as heterosexual. It showed charts comparing mutually exclusive categories of "homosexuals" and "African Americans," telling us that homosexuals are wealthy, college-educated white men who vacation more than anyone else and who demand even more "special rights and privileges" by taking civil rights away from low-income African Americans.[6] In this zero-sum, racialized world of the religious right, gay men are white; gay, lesbian, and bisexual people of color, along with poor or working-class white gay men, bisexuals, and lesbians, simply do not exist. The recently vigorous gay media promotion of the high-income, brand-loyal gay consumer market—which is typically portrayed as a population of white, well-to-do, college-educated young men—only widens the racialized class divisions that the religious right so eagerly exploits.

During the 1993 Senate hearings on gays in the military, I saw how these and other whitening practices were used in concentrated form by another gay institution, the Campaign for Military Service (CMS).

The Campaign for Military Service was an ad hoc organization formed in Washington, D.C., by a group composed primarily of well-to-do, well-connected, professional men, including billionaires David Geffen and Barry Diller, corporate consultant and former antiwar activist David Mixner (a personal friend of Bill Clinton's), and several gay and lesbian civil rights attorneys. Their mission was to work with the Clinton White House and sympathetic senators by coordinating the gay response to hearings held by the Senate Armed Services Committee, chaired by Sam Nunn. Their power was derived from their legal expertise, their access to wealthy donors, and their contacts with high-level personnel inside the White House, Senate, and Pentagon. The challenge they faced was to make strategic, pragmatic decisions in the heat of a rapidly changing national battle over what President Clinton called "our nation's policy toward homosexuals in the military."[7]

The world in and around the CMS that David Mixner describes in his memoir, *Stranger Among Friends,* is a network of professionals passionately dedicated to gay rights who communicated with Washington insiders via telephone calls, memos, and meetings in the White House, the Pentagon, and private homes. Wearing the protective coloring of this predominantly white gay world, these professionals entered the similarly white and male but heterosexual world of the US Senate, where their shared whiteness became a common ground on which the battle to lift the military's ban on homosexuals was fought—and lost.

The CMS used a set of arguments they called the *race analogy* to persuade senators and military officials to lift the military's antigay ban. The strategy was to get these powerful men to take antigay discrimination as seriously as they supposedly took racial discrimination, so they would lift the military ban on homosexuals as they had eliminated official policies requiring racial segregation. During the Senate hearings, the race analogy projected a set of comparisons that led to heated disputes over whether sexual orientation was analogous to race, whether sexual desire and conduct were like "skin color," or, most specifically, whether being homosexual was like being African American. (Rarely was "race" explicitly discussed as anything other than African American.) On their side, the CMS argued for a qualified analogy—what they called "haunting parallels" between "the words, rationale and rhetoric invoked in favor of racial discrimination in the past" and those used to "exclude gays in the military now." "The parallel is inexact," they cautioned, because "a person's skin color is not the same as a person's sexual identity; race is self-evident to many whereas sexual orientation is not. Moreover, the history of African Americans is not equivalent to the history of lesbian, gay and bisexual people in this country." Yet, despite these qualifications, the CMS held firm to the analogy. "The bigotry expressed is the same; the discrimination is the same."[8]

The military responded with an attack on the race analogy as self-serving, racist, and offensive. They were aided by Senator Nunn, who skillfully managed the hearings in ways that exploited the whiteness of the CMS and their witnesses to advance the military's antigay agenda. Working in their favor was the fact that, unlike the CMS, the military had high-ranking officials who were African American. The chairman of the Joint Chiefs of Staff, Gen. Colin L. Powell, who opposed lifting the ban, responded to the CMS with the argument that the antigay policy was not analogous to racial segregation because "skin color" was a "benign characteristic" while homosexuality constituted conduct that was neither benign nor condoned by most Americans.[9] Another African American Army officer, Lt. Gen. Calvin Waller, Gen. Norman Schwarzkopf's deputy commander and the highest-ranking African American officer in Operation Desert Storm, attacked the race analogy with these words: "I had no choice regarding my race when I was delivered from my mother's womb. To compare my service in America's armed forces with the integration of avowed homosexuals is personally offensive to me."[10] Antigay white senators mimicked his outrage.

During the race analogy debates, the fact that only white witnesses made the analogy, drawing connections between antigay and racial discrimination without including people of color, reduced the power of their argument and the credibility it might have gained had it been made by advocates who had experienced the racial discrimination side of the analogy.[11] But without hearing these voices, everyone in the debate could imagine homosexuals as either people who do not experience racism (the military assumption) or as people who experience discrimination only as homosexuals (the pro-gay assumption)—two different routes that ultimately led to the same destination: the place where gay stays white, the place where the CMS chose to make its stand.

According to Mixner's memoir, the Senate Armed Services Committee "had asked CMS to suggest witnesses."[12] As gay gatekeepers to the hearings, the CMS utilized another whitening practice—*mirroring.* This is a political strategy that reflects back the whiteness of the men who run powerful institutions to persuade them to take "us" seriously, accept "us," and let "us" in because "we are just like you." From the witnesses they selected, it appears that the CMS tried to project an idealized image of the openly gay service member that mirrored the senators' racial makeup and their publicly espoused social values and sexual mores—the image of the highly competent, patriotic, sexually abstinent, young, male officer who had earned the right to serve with a proud record and therefore deserved equality. The CMS selected for the gay panel a group of articulate and courageous veterans—all white men, except for one white woman.[13] Cleverly, Senator Nunn's staff selected a panel of African American ministers opposed to lifting the ban to precede the gay white panel, so that both sides constructed and participated in a racialized dramatic conflict that reinforced the twin myths that gay is white and African Americans are antigay.

Missing was the testimony of service members whose lives bridged the hearings' false divide between black and gay—veterans who were both African American and lesbian, gay, or bisexual. In this context, a significant whitening practice at the hearings was the exclusion of Sgt. Perry Watkins as a witness. Watkins was an openly gay, African American veteran considered by many to be a military hero. Kicked out of the army as a homosexual shortly before his retirement, he successfully appealed his discharge to the Supreme Court, becoming what one attorney called "the first out gay soldier to retire from the Army with full honors."[14]

To my knowledge, there is no public record of how or why the CMS did not invite Watkins to testify.[15] (This is another privilege that comes with whiteness—the ability to make decisions that seriously affect people of color and then protect that decision-making process from public scrutiny or accountability.) Sabrina Sojourner, who recalls that she was the only African American at the CMS among the nonsupport staff, told me that she "got moved further and further from the decision-making process" because she "brought up race," including the problem of the racial dynamic set up by presenting only white witnesses to testify.[16]

There was a moment when I was personally involved with this process. As the author of *Coming Out Under Fire: The History of Gay Men and Women in World War Two,* I was asked by the CMS to prepare to fly from California to Washington to testify, but my appearance was not approved by the Senate staff, who allowed no open homosexuals to testify as expert witnesses.[17] During a phone conversation with a white CMS staff member, I remember getting up the courage to ask him why Watkins wasn't a witness and was told that "Perry is a difficult personality." I didn't push my question any further, getting the message that I shouldn't ask for complicated explanations during the heat of battle and deferring to their inside-the-beltway tactical decisions, thus forfeiting an important opportunity to seriously challenge Watkins's exclusion. More instances of this painful struggle over Watkins's participation in and around the hearings must have been going on behind the scenes.[18] Watkins believed he was shut out because he was a "queeny" African American.[19]

It seems that the CMS considered Watkins to be the opposite of their ideal witness. His military story was indeed more complicated than the generic coming-out story. During his 1968 induction physical exam in Tacoma, Washington, he had openly declared his homosexuality, checking "Yes" to the written question "Do you have homosexual tendencies?" and freely describing his sexual experiences to the induction psychiatrist. But the army drafted him nevertheless because it needed him to fight in Vietnam, along with other mostly working-class African American men, who accounted for 20 percent of US combat deaths in that war by 1966, when African Americans made up 11 percent of the US population and 12.6 percent of US troops in Vietnam. Journalist Randy Shilts, who later interviewed Watkins, reported that Watkins believed "the doctor probably figured Watkins would . . . go to Vietnam, get killed, and nobody would ever hear about it again."[20] So Watkins's story was not a white narrative. "If I had not been black," he told Mary Ann Humphrey in an oral history interview, "my situation would not have happened as it did. . . . Every *white* person I knew from Tacoma who was gay and had checked that box 'Yes' did not have to go into the service."[21] Watkins's story resonated more with how men of color experience antigay racism in the military than with the story so many white servicemen tell. That white narrative begins with how a gay serviceman never experienced discrimination until he discovered his homosexuality in the service and ends with his fighting an antigay discharge, without referring to how he lived this experience through his whiteness. But Watkins explicitly talked about how he lived his gay military experience through race. "People ask me," he explained, "'How have you managed to tolerate all that discrimination you have had to deal with in the military?' My immediate answer to them was, 'Hell, I grew up black. Give me a break.'"[22] Watkins had also, while in the military, danced and sung on US Army bases as the flamboyant "Simone," his drag persona; as a veteran he was HIV-positive; and in some gay venues he wore body piercings in public.[23]

Nevertheless, Watkins's testimony at the hearings could have struck familiar chords among many Americans, including working-class and African American communities, as the experience of someone who was *real* rather than an *ideal.* His story was so compelling, in fact, that after the hearings he was the subject of two films and a segment of the television news magazine *20/20.*[24] But the story of his military career—which he so openly lived through race (as an African American), sexuality (had a sex life), and gender (performed in drag)—seems to have been considered by the CMS as too contaminated for congressional testimony and too distracting for the personal media stories that were supposed to focus only on the gay right to serve.

Watkins's absence was a lost opportunity to see and hear in nationally televised Senate hearings a gay African American legal hero talk about his victory over antigay discrimination in the military and expose the racist hypocrisy of how the antigay ban was in practice suspended for African Americans during wartime. The lack of testimony from any other lesbian, gay, or bisexual veteran of color was a lost opportunity to build alliances with communities of color and to do something about the "(largely accurate) perception of the gay activist leadership in Washington as overwhelmingly white."[25] Their collective absence reinforced another powerful myth that, even in a military population that is disproportionately African American and Latino, the representative gay soldier is a white officer, and the most presentable gay face of military competence is a white face.

As the hearings progressed, some CMS activists, speaking in public forums outside the hearings, took the race analogy a step further by promoting the idea that the gay rights movement was *like* the civil rights movement. During the hearings, those who argued the race analogy had drawn parallels between racist and antigay bigotry and discrimination. But those who extended the race analogy to the civil rights movement analogy had to take several more steps. First, they had to reconceptualize the civil rights movement. They took a multiracial movement for human equality and human rights, which included many lesbian, gay, and bisexual activists, and changed it into a nongay, black movement for African American racial equality. Next, they had to imagine the gay movement as a white movement for homosexual rights rather than as a multiracial movement that grew out of and continued the work of the civil rights movement. Then they could make the analogy between these two now-separated movements—one just about race, the other just about homosexuality. The last step was to symbolically recast gay white men in the roles of African American civil rights leaders. These moves tried to correct a problem inherent in such whitening practices as excluding people of color and the wearing, mirroring, and selling of gay whiteness. Because such practices draw directly on the privileges of whiteness, they do not on their own carry much moral weight. The extended race analogy compensates for this weightlessness by first invoking the moral authority of the civil rights movement (while erasing its actual history), and then transferring that unearned moral authority to a white gay movement, without giving anything back. At its worst, the race analogy can become a form of historical erasure, political cheating, and, ultimately, a theft of cultural capital and symbolic value.

David Mixner's memoir reveals how the extended race analogy was used in and around the Campaign for Military Service. When President Clinton, at a press conference, revealed that he wouldn't rule out separating homosexuals from heterosexuals within the military, Mixner first interpreted Clinton's comments as condoning gay segregation, then began equating it with racial segregation. Mixner's account of what happened next does not include attempts to seek advice from or build alliances with people whose histories include long struggles against legal segregation. This despite solid support for lifting the ban from civil rights veterans including Coretta Scott King and Roger Wilkins, the Black Lesbian and Gay Leadership Forum, the Congressional Black Caucus (including Ron Dellums, chairman of the House Armed Services Committee and a former marine who eventually held House hearings to counter Nunn's Senate hearings), and, in public opinion polls, a majority of African Americans (in contrast to a minority of white Americans).[26] Mixner instead describes a series of decisions and actions in which he invokes scenes from the history of racial segregation and the civil rights movement and appears to be reenacting those scenes as if he were a gay (white) version of a black civil rights leader.

A telling moment was when Mixner asked his friend Troy Perry, a gay white minister who founded and heads the gay Metropolitan Community

Church, to let him use the Sunday pulpit at the MCC Cathedral in Dallas as a "platform from which to speak." Covered by network television, Mixner delivered a sermon to the nation about the gay "road to freedom." In his sermon he referred to the military's antigay policy as "ancient apartheid laws" and charged that "Sam Nunn is our George Wallace" and that "[b]igotry that wears a uniform is nothing more than a uniform with a hood." He angrily warned President Clinton, cast as antigay segregationist, that "with or without you we will be free . . . we will prevail!"[27] Shortly after the sermon, Tracy Thorne, a gay white Navy veteran who had courageously faced verbal abuse at the Senate hearings and who flew to Dallas to support Mixner, said out loud what had been implied by Mixner's words and actions. David Mixner "could be our Martin Luther King, no questions asked," Thorne told a reporter from a gay newspaper.[28]

Such dramatic race-analogy scenarios performed by white activists beg some serious questions. Are actual, rather than "virtual," people of color present as major actors in these scenarios, and if not, why not? What are they saying or how are they being silenced? How is their actual leadership being supported or not supported by the white people who are reenacting this racialized history? And who is the "we" in this rhetoric? Mixner's "we," for example, did not account for those Americans—including lesbian, gay, bisexual, and transgender activists from many racial backgrounds—who did not finally have or indeed need "our own George Wallace" or "our own Martin Luther King." "Martin Luther King is the Martin Luther King of the gay community," Dr. Marjorie Hill, board president of Unity Fellowship Church and former director of the New York City Mayor's Office for Lesbian and Gay Issues, has pointedly replied in response to those who were looking for King's gay equivalent. "His lesson of equality and truth and nonviolence was for everyone."[29] If the gay rights movement is already part of the ongoing struggle for the dignity of all people exemplified in the activism of Dr. Martin Luther King Jr., then there is no need for gay equivalents of Dr. King, racial segregation, or the civil rights movement. If the gay rights movement is not already part of the civil rights movement, then what is it? Answering this question from a white position with the race analogy—saying that white gay leaders and martyrs are "our" versions of African American civil rights leaders and martyrs—can't fix the problem and ultimately undermines the moral authority that is its aim. This use of the race analogy ends up reinforcing the whiteness of gay political campaigns rather than doing the work and holding onto the dream that would continue the legacy of Dr. King's leadership and activism.[30]

What would the gay movement look like if gay white men who use the race analogy took it more seriously? What work would we have to do to close the perceived moral authority gap between our gay activism and the race analogy, to directly establish the kind of moral authority we seek by analogy? What if we aspired to achieve the great vision, leadership qualities, grass-roots organizing skills, and union solidarity of Dr. Martin Luther King Jr., together with his opposition to war and his dedication to fighting with the poor and disenfranchised against the deepening race and class divisions in America and the world? How could we fight, in the words of US Supreme Court Justice Harry A. Blackmun, for the "fundamental interest all individuals have in controlling the nature of their intimate associations with others," in ways that build a broad civil rights movement rather than being "like" it, in ways that enable the gay movement to grow into one of many powerful and direct ways to achieve race, gender, and class justice?[31]

These, then, are only some of the many whitening practices that structure everyday life and politics in what is often called the "gay community" and the "gay movement"—making *race analogies; mirroring* the whiteness of men who run powerful institutions as a strategy for winning credibility, acceptance, and integration; *excluding* people of color from gay institutions; *selling* gay as white to raise money, make a profit, and gain economic power; and daily wearing the *pale protective coloring* that camouflages the unquestioned assumptions and unearned privileges of gay whiteness. These practices do serious damage to real people whenever they mobilize the power and privileges of whiteness to protect and strengthen gayness—including the privileges of gay whiteness—without using that power to fight racism—including gay white racism.

Most of the time, the hard work of identifying such practices, fighting racial discrimination and exclusion, critiquing the assumptions of whiteness, and racially integrating white gay worlds has been taken up by lesbian, gay, bisexual, and transgender people of color. Freed from this enforced daily recognition of race and confrontation with racism, some prominent white men in the gay movement have been able to advance a gay rights politics that, like the right to serve in the military, they imagine to be just gay, not about race. The gay rights movement can't afford to "dissipate our energies," Andrew Sullivan, former editor of the *New Republic,* warned on the

Charlie Rose television program, by getting involved in disagreements over nongay issues such as "how one deals with race . . . how we might help the underclass . . . how we might deal with sexism."[32]

But a gay rights politics that is supposedly color-blind (and sex-neutral and classless) is in fact a politics of race (and gender and class). It assumes, without ever having to say it, that gay must equal white (and male and economically secure); that is, it assumes white (and male and middle-class) as the default categories that remain once one discounts those who as gay people must continually and primarily deal with racism (and sexism and class oppression), especially within gay communities. It is the politics that remains once one makes the strategic decision, as a gay activist, to stand outside the social justice movements for race, gender, or class equality, or to not stand with disenfranchised communities, among whom are lesbian, bisexual, gay, or transgender people who depend on these movements for dignity and survival.

For those few who act like, look like, and identify with the white men who still run our nation's major institutions, for those few who can meet with them, talk to them, and be heard by them as peers, the ability to draw on the enormous power of a shared but unacknowledged whiteness, the ability never to have to bring up race, must feel like a potentially sturdy shield against antigay discrimination. I can see how bringing up explicit critiques of white privilege during high-level gay rights conversations (such as the Senate debates over gays in the military), or making it possible for people of color to set the agenda of the gay rights movement, might weaken that white shield (which relies on racial division to protect)—might even, for some white activists, threaten to "turn" the gay movement into something less gay, as gay bars "turn" when they're no longer predominantly white.

The threat of losing the white shield that protects my own gay rights raises even more difficult questions that I need to "clarify . . . for myself": What would *I* say and do about racism if someday my own whiteness helped me gain such direct access to men in the centers of power, as it almost did during the Senate hearings, when all I did was ask why Perry Watkins wasn't testifying and accept the answer I was given? What privileges would I risk losing if I persistently tried to take activists of color with me into that high-level conversation? How, and with whom, could I begin planning for that day?

Gay white men who are committed to doing antiracist activism *as* gay men have to work within and against these and other powerful whitening practices. What can we do, and how can we support each other, when we once again find ourselves involved in gay social and political worlds that are white and male?

Gay, White, Male, and HIV-Negative

A few years ago, in San Francisco, a friend invited me to be part of a new political discussion group of HIV-negative gay men. Arriving at a neighbor's apartment for the group's first meeting, I once again felt the relief and pleasure of being among men like me. All of us were involved in AIDS activism. We had supported lovers, friends, and strangers with HIV and were grieving the loss of too many lives. We didn't want to take time, attention, and scarce resources away from people with AIDS, including many people of color. But we did want to find a collective, progressive voice as HIV-negative men. We wanted to find public ways to say to gay men just coming out, "We are HIV-negative men, and we want you to stay negative, have hot sex, and live long lives. We don't want you to get sick or die." We were trying to work out a politics in which HIV-negative men, who are relatively privileged as not being the primary targets of crackdowns on people who are HIV-positive, could address other HIV-negative men without trying to establish our legitimacy by positioning ourselves as victims.

When I looked around the room, I saw only white men. I knew that many of them had for years been incorporating antiracist work into their gay and AIDS activism, so this seemed like a safe space to bring up the whiteness I saw. I really didn't want to hijack the purpose of the group by changing its focus from HIV to race, but this was important because I believed that not talking about our whiteness was going to hurt our work. Instead of speaking up, however, I hesitated.

Right there. That's the moment I want to look at—that moment of silence, when a flood of memories, doubts, and fears rushed into my head. What made me want to say something about our whiteness, and what was keeping me silent?

My memory took me back to 1990, when I spoke on a panel of gay historians at the first Out/Write conference of lesbian and gay writers, held in San Francisco. I was happy to be presenting with two other community-based historians working outside the academy. But I was also aware—and concerned—that we were all men. When the question period began, an African American writer in the audience, a man whose name I later learned was Fundi, stood up and asked us (as I recall) how it could happen, at this late date, that a gay history panel could have only white men on it. Awkward silence. I don't trust how I remember his question or what happened next—unreliable memory and bad thinking must be characteristics of inhabiting whiteness while it's being publicly challenged. As the other panelists responded, I remember wanting to distance myself from their whiteness while my own mind went blank, and I remember feeling terrified that Fundi would address me directly and ask me to respond personally. I kept thinking, "I don't know what to say, I can't think, I want to be invisible, I want this to be over, now!"

After the panel was over I spoke privately to Fundi. Later, I resolved never to be in that situation again—never to agree to be on an all-white panel without asking ahead of time why it was white, if its whiteness was crucial to what we were presenting, and, if not, how its composition might be changed. But in addition to wanting to protect myself from public embarrassment and to do the right thing, that writer's direct challenge made me understand something more clearly: that only by seeing and naming the whiteness I'm inhabiting, and taking responsibility for it, can I begin to change it and even do something constructive with it. At that panel, I learned how motivating, though terrifying, it can be as a white person to be placed in such a state of heightened racial discomfort—to be challenged to see the whiteness we've created, figure out how we created it, and then think critically about how it works.[33]

In the moment of silent hesitation I experienced in my HIV-negative group, I found myself imagining for the first time, years after it happened, what it must have been like for Fundi to stand up in a predominantly white audience and ask an all-white panel of gay men about our whiteness. My friend and colleague Lisa Kahaleole Hall, who is a brilliant thinker, writer, and teacher, says that privilege is "the ability not to have to take other people's existence seriously," the "ability not to have to pay attention."[34] Until that moment I had mistakenly thought that Fundi's anger (and I am not certain that he in fact expressed any anger toward us) was only about me, about us, as white men, rather than also about him—the history, desires, and support that enabled him to speak up, and the fears he faced and risks he took by doing it. Caught up in my own fear, I had not paid close attention to the specific question he had asked us. "The problem of conventional white men," Fundi later wrote in his own account of why he had decided to take the risk of speaking up, "somehow not being able, or not knowing how, to find and extend themselves to women and people of color had to be talked through. . . . My question to the panel was this: 'What direct skills might you share with particularly the whites in the audience to help them move on their fears and better extend themselves to cultural diversity?'"[35] I'm indebted to Fundi for writing that question down, and for starting a chain of events with his question that has led to my writing this essay.

I tried to remember who else I had seen bring up whiteness. The first images that came to mind were all white lesbians and people of color. White lesbian feminists have as a movement dealt with racism in a more collective way than have gay white men. In lesbian and gay activist spaces I and other gay white men have come to rely on white lesbians and people of color to raise the issue of whiteness and challenge racism, so that this difficult task has become both gendered as lesbian work and racialized as "colored" work. These images held me back from saying anything to my HIV-negative group. "Just who am I to bring this up?" I wondered. "It's not my place to do this." Or, more painfully, "Who will these men think I think I am? Will they think I'm trying to pretend I'm not a white man?"

Then another image flashed in my mind that also held me back. It was the caricature of the white moralist—another racialized phantom figure hovering in the room—who blames and condemns white people for our racism, guilt-trips us from either a position of deeper guilt or holier-than-thou innocence, claims to be more aware of racism than we are, and is prepared to catalog our offenses. I see on my mental screen this self-righteous caricature impersonating a person of color in an all-white group or, when people of color are present, casting them again in the role of spectators to a white performance, pushed to the sidelines from where they must angrily or patiently interrupt a white conversation to be heard at all. I understand that there is some truth to this caricature—that part of a destructive racial dynamic among white people is trying to determine who is more or less responsible for racism, more or less innocent and pure, more or less white. But I also see how the fear of becoming this caricature has been used by white people to keep each other from naming the whiteness of all-white groups we are in. During my moment of hesitation in the HIV-negative group, the fear of becoming this caricature was successfully silencing me.

I didn't want to pretend to be a white lesbian or a person of color, or to act like the self-righteous white caricature. "How do I ask that we examine our whiteness," I wondered, "without implying that I'm separating us into the good guys and bad guys and positioning myself as the really cool white guy who 'gets it' about racism?" I needed a way to speak intelligently from where I was standing without falling into any of these traps.

I decided to take a chance and say something.

"It appears to me," I began, my voice a little shaky, "that everyone here is white. If this is true, I'd like us to find some way to talk about how our whiteness may be connected to being HIV-negative, because I suspect there are some political similarities between being in each of these positions of relative privilege."

There was an awkward pause. "Are you saying," someone asked, "that we should close the group to men of color?"

"No," I said, "but if we're going to be a white group I'd like us to talk about our relationship to whiteness here."

"Should we do outreach to men of color?" someone else asked.

"No, I'm not saying that, either. It's a little late to do outreach, after the fact, inviting men of color to integrate our already white group."

The other men agreed and the discussion went on to other things. I, too, didn't really know where to take this conversation about our whiteness. By bringing it up, I was implicitly asking for their help in figuring this out. I hoped I wouldn't be the only one to bring up the subject again.

At the next month's meeting there were new members, and they all appeared to be white men. When someone reviewed for them what we had done at the last meeting, he reported that I'd suggested we not include men of color in the group. "That's not right," I corrected him. "I said that if we're going to be a white group, I'd like us to talk about our whiteness and its relation to our HIV-negative status."

I was beginning to feel a little disoriented, like I was doing something wrong. Why was I being so consistently misunderstood as divisive, as if I were saying that I didn't want men of color in the group? Had I reacted similarly when, caught up in my own fear of having to publicly justify our panel's whiteness, I had misunderstood Fundi's specific question—about how we could share our skills with other white people to help each other move beyond our fear of cultural diversity—as an accusation that we had deliberately excluded women and men of color? Was something structural going on here about how white groups respond to questions that point to our whiteness and ask what we can do with it?

Walking home from the meeting I asked a friend who'd been there if what I said had made sense. "Oh yes," he said, "it's just that it all goes without saying." Well, there it is. That *is* how it goes, how it stays white. "Without saying."

Like much of the rest of my gay life, this HIV-negative group turned out to be unintentionally white, although intentionally gay and intentionally male. It's important for me to understand exactly how that racial *unintentionality* gets *constructed,* how it's not just a coincidence. It seems that so long as white people never consciously decide to be a white group, a white organization, a white department, so long as we each individually believe that people of color are always welcome, *even though they are not there,* then we do not have to examine our whiteness because we can believe it is unintentional, it's not our *reason* for being there. That may be why I had been misunderstood to be asking for the exclusion of men of color. By naming our group as white, I had unknowingly raised the question of *racial intent—* implying that we had intended to create an all-white group by deliberately excluding men of color. If we could believe that our whiteness was purely accidental, then we could also believe that there was nothing to say about it because creating an all-white group, which is exactly what we had done, had never been anyone's intent, and therefore had no inherent meaning or purpose. By interrupting the process by which "it just goes without saying," by asking us to recognize and "talk through" our whiteness, I appeared to be saying that we already had and should continue to exclude men of color from our now very self-consciously white group.

The reality is that in our HIV-negative group, as in the panel of the Out/Write conference and in many other all-white groupings, we each did make a chain of choices, not usually conscious, to invite or accept an invitation from another white person. We made more decisions whether or not to name our whiteness when we once again found ourselves in a white group. What would it mean to make such decisions consciously and out loud, to understand why we made them, and to take responsibility for them? What if we intentionally held our identities as white men and gay men in creative tension, naming ourselves as gay *and* white, then publicly explored the possibilities for activism this tension might open up? Could investigating our whiteness offer us opportunities for reclaiming our humanity against the ways that racial hierarchies dehumanize us and disconnect us from ourselves, from each other, and from people of color? If we took on these difficult tasks, how might our gay political reality and purpose be different?[36]

When I told this story about our HIV-negative group to Barbara Smith, a colleague who is an African American lesbian writer and activist, she asked me a question that pointed to a different ending: "So why didn't you bring up the group's whiteness again?" The easy answer was that I left the group because I moved to New York City. But the more difficult answer was that I was afraid to lose the trust of these gay men whom I cared about and needed so much, afraid I would distance myself from them and be distanced by them, pushed outside the familiar circle, no longer welcomed as white and not belonging among people of color, not really gay and not anything else, either. The big fear is that if I pursue this need to examine whiteness too far, I risk losing my place among gay white men, forever—and then where would I be?

Pale, Male—and Antiracist

What would happen if we deliberately put together a white gay male group whose sole purpose was to examine our whiteness and use it to strengthen our antiracist gay activism?

In November 1995, gay historian John D'Emilio and I tried to do just that. We organized a workshop at the annual Creating Change conference of activists put on that year in Detroit by the National Gay and Lesbian Task Force. We called the workshop "Pale, Male—and Anti-Racist." At a conference of over 1,000 people (mostly white but with a large number of people of color), about thirty-five gay white men attended.[37]

We structured the workshop around three key questions: (1) How have you successfully used your whiteness to fight racism? (2) What difficulties have you faced in doing antiracist activism as a gay white man? And (3) what kind of support did you get or need or wish you had received from other gay white men?

Before we could start talking about our successes, warning lights began to flash. You could sense a high level of mistrust in the room, as if we were looking at each other and wondering, "Which kind of white guy are *you?*" One man wanted to make sure we weren't going to waste time congratulating ourselves for sharing our white privilege with people who don't have access to it or start whining about how hard it is to work with communities of color. Someone else wanted to make sure we weren't going to guilt-trip each other. Another said, "I'm so much more aware of my failures in this area, I can't even see the accomplishments."

But slowly, once all the cautions were out in the open, the success stories came out. About fighting an anti–affirmative action initiative. About starting a racism study group. About getting a university department to study why it had no teaching assistants who were students of color. About persuading a gay organization in Georgia to condemn the state's Confederate flag. "What keeps me from remembering," I wondered, "that gay white men publicly do this antiracist work? Why can't I keep their images in my mind?"

One possible answer to my question appeared in the next success story, which midway made a sharp turn away from our successes toward how gay white men can discipline each other for standing on the "wrong" side of the color line. A man from Texas, Dennis Poplin, told us about what happened to him as the only white man on the board of the San Antonio Lesbian and Gay Assembly (SALGA), a progressive, multiracial lesbian and gay alliance. When SALGA mobilized support that successfully canceled a so-called gay community conference whose planning committee was all-white—this in a city that was 65 percent Latina/Latino—a "community scandal" exploded, as he put it, "about political correctness, quotas, [and] reverse racism." A local newspaper, which was run by gay white men, started attacking SALGA. When a white reporter asked a man of color from SALGA why the group's board had no white men on it, and he replied that Dennis was on the board, the reporter said, "He's not white."[38]

Right away the men in the workshop started talking about the difficulties they'd had with other gay white men. "I find myself like not even knowing who it's safe to bring it up with," one man said. When he tries to talk about race, another said, "I'm just met with that smug, flippant, 'I'm tired of hearing about [all that].'" Others talked about fears of being attacked as too "PC."

At the "risk of opening a whole can of worms," as he put it, another man moved the discussion away from us to our relationships with white lesbians and people of color. Some men talked about how tired they were of being called "gay white men," feeling labeled then attacked for who they were and for what they tried to do or for not doing enough; about having to deal with their racism while they didn't see communities of color dealing with homophobia; and about how, after years of struggling, they felt like giving up. Yet here they all were at this workshop. I began to realize that all our frustrations were signs of a dilemma that comes with the privileges of whiteness: having the ability to decide whether to keep dealing with the accusations, resentments, racial categorizations, and other destructive effects of racism that divide people who are trying to take away its power; or, because the struggle is so hard, to walk away from it and do something else, using the slack our whiteness gives us to take a break from racism's direct consequences.

Bringing this dilemma into the open enabled us to confront our expectations about how the antiracist work we do should be appreciated, should be satisfying, and should bring results. One man admitted that he didn't make antiracist work a higher priority because "I [would have to face] a level of discomfort, irritation, boredom, frustration, [and] enter a lot of [areas where] I feel inept, and don't have confidence. It would require a lot of humility. All these are things that I steer away from."

Over and over the men at the workshop expressed similar feelings of frustration, using such phrases as "We tried, but . . . ," "No matter what you do, you can't seem to do anything right," and "You just can't win." These seemed to reflect a set of expectations that grew out of the advantages we have because we are American men and white and middle-class or even working-class—expectations that we *can* win, that we should know how to do it right, that if we try we will succeed.

What do we—what do I—expect to get out of doing antiracist work, anyway? If it's because we expect to be able to fix the problem, then we're not going to be very satisfied. When I talk with my friend Lisa Kahaleole Hall about these frustrations, she tells me, "Sweet pea, if racism were that easy to fix, we would have fixed it already." The challenge for me in relation to other gay white men—and in writing this essay—is to figure out how we can support each other in going exactly into those areas of whiteness where we feel we have no competence yet, no expertise, no ability to fix it, where we haven't even come up with the words we need to describe what we're trying to do. For me, it's an act of faith in the paradox that if we, together with our friends and allies, can figure out how our own whiteness works, we can use that knowledge to fight the racism that gives our whiteness such unearned power.

And whenever this struggle gets too difficult, many of us, as white men, have the option to give up in frustration and retreat into a more narrowly defined gay rights activism. That project's goal, according to gay author Bruce Bawer, one of its advocates, is "to achieve acceptance, equal rights, and full integration into the present social and political structure."[39] It's a goal that best serves the needs of men who can live our gayness through our whiteness and whose only or most important experience with discrimination is as homosexuals. James Baldwin, who wrote extensively about whiteness in America, noticed long ago the sense of entitlement embedded in a gay whiteness that experiences no other form of systematic discrimination. "[Y]ou are penalized, as it were, unjustly," he said in an interview.

"I think white gay people feel cheated because they were born, in principle, into a society in which they were supposed to be safe. The anomaly of their sexuality puts them in danger unexpectedly."[40]

The gay rights project that grows out of the shocking experience of being cheated unexpectedly by society because one is gay defines the gay political problem in its narrowest form. One solution is to get back the respect one has learned to expect as a white man. Some prominent, well-connected activists do this by educating the men who run our nation's powerful institutions, using reasoned arguments to combat their homophobia and expose discrimination as irrational—a strategy that sometimes does open doors but mostly to those who look and behave like the men in power. I have heard some of these activists express a belief that less privileged members of the "gay community" will eventually benefit from these high-level successes, but this would happen apparently without the more privileged having to do the work of fighting hierarchies that enforce race, class, and gender inequality. Their belief in a kind of "trickle-down" gay activism is based on the idea that powerful men, once enlightened, will generously allow equality to flow from the top to those near the top and then automatically trickle down to those down below. An alternative belief in "bottom-up activism" is based on the idea that, with great effort, democratic power must more slowly be built from the bottom up, and out, experimenting with more equal power relations along the way by creating links of solidarity across the divides of difference. Some gay white men explicitly reject, as nongay, this broader goal of joining activists who stand and work at the intersections of the many struggles to achieve social justice and to dismantle interlocking systems of domination. In the narrow world of exclusively gay "integrationist" activism, which its advocates privilege as the site of "practical" rather than "utopian" politics,[41] college-educated gay white men have a better chance of knowing what to say and how to be heard, what to do and how to succeed within existing institutions. Because when antigay barriers and attitudes are broken down but no other power relations are changed, we are the ones most likely to achieve "full integration into the present social and political structure." All it takes sometimes is being the white man at the white place at the white time.

When John and I asked the workshop participants our last question—"What would you need from each other to be able to continue doing antiracist work?"—the room went silent.

When push comes to shove, I wondered, holding back a sense of isolation inside my own silence, do gay white men as *white* men (including myself) have a lasting interest in fighting racism or will we sooner or later retreat to the safety of our gay white refuges? I know that gay white men as *gay* men, just to begin thinking about relying on each other's support in an on-going struggle against racism, have to confront how we've absorbed the anti-gay lies that we are all wealthy, irresponsible, and sexually obsessed individuals who can't make personal commitments, as well as the reality that we are profoundly exhausted fighting for our lives and for those we love through years of devastation from the AIDS epidemic. These challenges all make it hard enough for me to trust my own long-term commitment to antiracist work, let alone that of other gay white men.

Yet at this workshop we created the opportunity for us to see that we were not alone, to risk saying and hearing what we needed from each other in fighting racism, and to assess what support we could realistically hope to get. We wanted the opportunity to complain to another gay white man, to be held and loved when we get discouraged or feel attacked, whether justifiably or not. We wanted understanding for all the frustrations we feel fighting racism, the chance just to let them out with a gay white man who knows that it's not our racism he's supporting but the desire to see it and together figure out what to do next, so we won't give up or run away. We wanted other gay white men to take us seriously enough to call us on our racist shit in ways we could actually hear without feeling attacked. And we wanted to help each other lift at least some of the work and responsibility of supporting us from the shoulders of our friends and co-workers who are white women or people of color.

As time ran out at the workshop, I asked everyone to think about another difficult question: "Who is the gay white man who has had more experience than you in supporting other gay white men who are fighting racism, and who you can look to for advice on how to do it well?" "I think the more interesting question," one man answered, "is how many of us don't have anyone like that." We looked around at each other, wondering if any of us could name someone, until somebody said, "It's us."

Staying White

By trying to figure out what is happening with race in situations I'm in, I've embarked on a journey that I now realize is not headed toward innocence or winning or becoming not white or finally getting it right. I don't know where it leads, but I have some hopes and desires.

I want to find an antidote to the ways that whiteness numbs me, makes me not see what is right in front of me, takes away my intelligence, divides me from people I care about. I hope that, by occupying the seeming contradictions between the "antiracist" and the "gay white male" parts of myself, I can generate a creative tension that will motivate me to keep fighting. I hope to help end the exclusionary practices that make gay worlds stay so white. When I find myself in a situation that is going to stay white, I want to play a role in deciding what kind of white it's going to stay. And I want to become less invested in whiteness while staying white myself—always remembering that I can't just decide to stand outside of whiteness or exempt myself from its unearned privileges.[42] I want to be careful not to avoid its responsibilities by fleeing into narratives of how I have been oppressed as a gay man. The ways that I am gay will always be shaped by the ways that I am white.

Most of all, I want never to forget that the roots of my antiracist desires and my gay desires are intertwined. As James Baldwin's words remind me, acting on my gay desires is about not being afraid to love and therefore about having to confront this white society's terror of love—a terror that lashes out with racist and antigay violence. Following both my gay and antiracist desires is about being willing to "go the way your blood beats," as Baldwin put it, even into the heart of that terror, which, he warned, is "a tremendous danger, a tremendous responsibility."[43]

notes

This is an expanded version of a personal essay I presented at the Making and Unmaking of Whiteness conference at the University of California at Berkeley in April 1997. I want to acknowledge that my thinking has grown out of conversations with many friends and colleagues, including Nan Alamilla Boyd, Margaret Cerullo, John D'Emilio, Arthur Dong, Marla Erlein, Jeffrey Escoffier, Charlie Fernandez, Dana Frank, Wayne Hoffman, Amber Hollibaugh, Mitchell Karp, Jonathan Ned Katz, Judith Levine, William J. Mann, David Meacham, Dennis Poplin, Susan Raffo, Eric Rofes, Gayle Rubin, Sabrina Sojourner, Barbara Smith, Nancy Stoller, Carole Vance, and Carmen Vasquez; the editors of this collection, especially Matt Wray and Irene Nexica; the participants in the "Pale, Male—and Anti-Racist" workshop at the 1995 Creating Change conference in Detroit; Lisa Kahaleole Hall and the students I joined in her San Francisco City College class on Lesbian and Gay Communities of Color; and the students in the courses I taught at the University of California at Santa Cruz, Portland State University, Stanford University, and the New School for Social Research.

1. "Caught in the Storm: AIDS and the Meaning of Natural Disaster," *Out/Look: National Lesbian and Gay Quarterly* 1 (fall 1988), 8–19; "'Fitting In': Expanding Queer Studies beyond the *Closet* and *Coming Out*," paper presented at Contested Zone: Limitations and Possibilities of a Discourse on Lesbian and Gay Studies, Pitzer College, 6–7 April 1990, and at the Fourth

Annual Lesbian, Bisexual, and Gay Studies Conference, Harvard University, 26–28 October 1990; "Intellectual Desire," paper presented at La Ville en rose: Le premier colloque Québécois d'études lesbiennes et gaies (First Quebec Lesbian and Gay Studies Conference), Concordia University and the University of Quebec at Montreal, 12 November 1992, published in *GLQ: A Journal of Lesbian and Gay Studies* 3, no. 1 (February 1996): 139–57, reprinted in *Queerly Classed: Gay Men and Lesbians Write about Class,* ed. Susan Raffo (Boston: South End Press, 1997), 43–66; "Class Dismissed: Queer Storytelling Across the Economic Divide," keynote address at the Constructing Queer Cultures: Lesbian, Bisexual, Gay Studies Graduate Student Conference, Cornell University, 9 February 1995, and at the Seventeenth Gender Studies Symposium, Lewis and Clark College, 12 March 1998; "I Coulda Been a Whiny White Guy," *Gay Community News* 20 (spring 1995): 6–7, 28–30; and "Sunset Trailer Park," in *White Trash: Race and Class in America,* ed. Matt Wray and Annalee Newitz (New York: Routledge, 1997), 15–39.

2. *Dream Ships Sail Away* (forthcoming, Houghton Mifflin).

3. "'Go the Way Your Blood Beats': An Interview with James Baldwin (1984)," Richard Goldstein, in *James Baldwin: The Legacy,* ed. Quincy Troupe (New York: Simon and Schuster/Touchstone, 1989), 176.

4. Personal essays, often assembled in published collections, have become an important written form for investigating how whiteness works, especially in individual lives. Personal essays by lesbian, gay, and bisexual authors that have influenced my own thinking and writing about whiteness have been collected in James Baldwin, *The Price of the Ticket: Collected Nonfiction, 1948–1985* (New York: St. Martin's, 1985); Cherríe Moraga and Gloria Anzaldúa, eds., *This Bridge Called My Back: Writings by Radical Women of Color* (Watertown, Mass.: Persephone Press, 1981); Cherríe Moraga, *Loving in the War Years* (Boston: South End Press, 1983); Audre Lorde, *Sister Outsider* (Freedom, Calif.: Crossing Press, 1984); Elly Bulkin, Minnie Bruce Pratt, and Barbara Smith, *Yours in Struggle: Three Feminist Perspectives on Anti-Semitism and Racism* (Brooklyn: Long Haul Press, 1984); Essex Hemphill, ed., *Brother to Brother: New Writings by Black Gay Men* (Boston: Alyson, 1991); Mab Segrest, *Memoir of a Race Traitor* (Boston: South End Press, 1994); Dorothy Allison, *Skin: Talking about Sex, Class and Literature* (Ithaca, N.Y.: Firebrand, 1994); and Becky Thompson and Sangeeta Tyagi, eds., *Names We Call Home: Autobiography on Racial Identity* (New York: Routledge, 1996).

5. For discussion of how sexual identities are "lived through race and class," see Robin D. G. Kelley, *Yo' Mama's Dysfunktional!* (Boston: Beacon, 1997), 114.

6. Whiteness can grant economic advantages to gay as well as straight men, and gay male couples can sometimes earn more on two men's incomes than can straight couples or lesbian couples. But being gay can restrict a man to lower-paying jobs, and most gay white men are not wealthy; like the larger male population, they are lower-middle-class, working-class, or poor. For discussions of the difficulties of developing an accurate economic profile of the "gay community," and of how both the religious right and gay marketers promote the idea that gay men are wealthy, see Amy Gluckman and Betsy Reed, eds., *Homo Economics: Capitalism, Community, and Lesbian and Gay Life* (New York: Routledge, 1997).

7. David Mixner, *Stranger among Friends* (New York: Bantam, 1996), 291. For accounts of how the Campaign for Military Service was formed, see Mixner's memoir and Urvashi Vaid, *Virtual Equality: The Mainstreaming of Lesbian and Gay Equality* (New York: Anchor, 1995). Preceding the ad hoc formation of the Campaign for Military Service in January 1993 was the Military Freedom Project, formed in early 1989 by a group composed primarily of white feminist lesbians. Overshadowed during the Senate hearings by the predominantly

male Campaign for Military Service, these activists had raised issues relating the military's antigay policy to gender, race, and class; specifically, that lesbians are discharged at a higher rate than are gay men; that lesbian-baiting is a form of sexual harassment against women; and that African American and Latino citizens, including those who are gay, bisexual, or lesbian, are disproportionately represented in the military, which offers poor and working-class youth access to a job, education, and health care that are often unavailable to them elsewhere. Vaid, *Virtual Equality,* 153–59.

8. "The Race Analogy: Fact Sheet Comparing the Military's Policy of Racial Segregation in the 1940s to the Current Ban on Lesbians, Gay Men and Bisexuals," in *Briefing Book,* prepared by the Legal/Policy Department of the Campaign for Military Service, Washington, D.C. (1993).

9. Quoted from the *Legal Times,* 8 February 1993, in Mixner, *Stranger among Friends,* 286. Professor of history and civil rights veteran Roger Wilkins, responding to Powell's statement, argued that "lots of white people don't think that being black is benign even in 1993." Mixner, *Stranger among Friends,* 286.

10. Henry Louis Gates Jr., "Blacklash?" *New Yorker,* 17 May 1993.

11. For brief discussions of how the whiteness of those making the race analogy reduced the power of their arguments, see Gates, "Blacklash?" and David Rayside, *On the Fringe: Gays and Lesbians in Politics* (Ithaca, N.Y.: Cornell University Press, 1998), 243.

12. Mixner, *Stranger among Friends,* 319.

13. The gay service members on this panel were former Staff Sgt. Thomas Pannicia, Sgt. Justin Elzie, and Col. Margarethe Cammermeyer. Margarethe Cammermeyer, with Chris Fisher, *Serving in Silence* (New York: Penguin, 1994), 299. Other former gay service members who testified at the hearings were Sgt. Tracy Thorne and PO Keith Meinhold. Active-duty lesbian, gay, or bisexual service members could not testify without being discharged from the military as homosexuals, a situation that still exists under the current "don't ask, don't tell" military policy.

14. Mary Dunlap, "Reminiscences: Honoring Our Legal Hero, Gay Sgt. Perry Watkins 1949–1996," *Gay Community News* (winter 1996): 21.

15. In his memoir, *Stranger among Friends,* Mixner makes no mention of Watkins.

16. Author's personal conversation with Sabrina Sojourner, 19 October 1998.

17. An expert witness who was white, male, and not a gay historian was allowed to introduce a brief written synopsis of historical evidence from my book. I was one of the white men working with the CMS behind the scenes and from afar. Early in the hearings, Senator Edward Kennedy's staff asked me to compile a list of questions for him to ask during the hearings. In July, after the hearings were over and the "don't ask, don't tell" policy had been adopted, I submitted to the House Armed Services Committee written testimony, titled "Historical Overview of the Origins of the Military's Ban on Homosexuals," that critiqued the new policy and identified heterosexual masculinity, rather than the competence or behavior of homosexual service members, as the military problem requiring investigation. And I sent the CMS a copy of a paper I had given in April, "Stripping Down: Undressing the Military's Anti-Gay Policy," that used historical documents and feminist analysis to argue for investigating the military's crisis in heterosexual masculinity. In all these writings, I was trying, unsuccessfully, to get the CMS and the Senate to adopt a gender and sexuality analysis of the military policy; I used race and class analysis only to argue that the antigay policies disproportionately affected service members who were people of color and/or working-class.

18. After Watkins's death in 1996 from complications due to HIV, Mary Dunlap, a white civil rights attorney who for years had followed his appeal case, in a tribute addressed to him,

called him a "generous, tireless leader" who expressed "open and emphatic criticism and un-
abashed indictment of the racism of those among us who so blatantly and hurtfully excluded
your voice and face and words from the publicity surrounding the gaylesbitrans community's
challenge to 'Don't Ask, Don't Tell' in the early 90s." Dunlap, "Reminiscences," 21.

19. Shamara Riley, "Perry Watkins, 1948–1996: A Military Trailblazer," *Outlines*, 8 May
1996.

20. Randy Shilts, *Conduct Unbecoming: Gays and Lesbians in the U.S. Military* (New York:
St. Martin's, 1993), 60, 65; Mary Ann Humphrey, *My Country, My Right to Serve* (New York:
HarperCollins, 1990), 248–57. Statistics are from D. Michael Shafer, "The Vietnam-Era Draft:
Who Went, Who Didn't, and Why It Matters," in *The Legacy: The Vietnam War in the Amer-
ican Imagination*, ed. D. Michael Shafer (Boston: Beacon Press, 1990), 69.

21. Humphrey, *My Country*, 255–56.

22. Ibid.

23. Dunlap, "Reminiscences"; Shilts, *Conduct Unbecoming*, 155–56; Humphrey, *My Country*, 253–54.

24. A 1996 documentary film, *Sis: The Perry Watkins Story*, was coproduced by Chiqui
Cartagena and Suzanne Newman. On the *20/20* segment and a feature film on Watkins that
was in preproduction, see Jim Knippenberg, "Gay Soldier Story to Be Filmed," *Cincinnati
Enquirer*, 23 December 1997.

25. Rayside, *On the Fringe*, 243.

26. Keith Boykin, *One More River to Cross: Black and Gay In America* (New York: Anchor,
1996), 186–92.

27. Mixner, *Stranger among Friends*, 301–2, 308–10.

28. Garland Tillery, "Interview with Top Gun Pilot Tracy Thorne," *Our Own*, 18 May
1993.

29. Quoted from the documentary film *All God's Children*, produced by Dee Mosbacher,
Frances Reid, and Sylvia Rhue (Women Vision, 1996). I wish to thank Lisa Kahaleole Hall,
Stephanie Smith, and Linda Alban for directing me to this quotation.

30. One way to measure how much moral authority the race analogy tries to take from
the civil rights movement and transfuse it into a predominantly white gay movement is to
see what moral authority remains when the race analogy is removed. David Mixner would
be the David Mixner of the gay movement, the military's antigay policy would be a form of
antigay bigotry, and Sam Nunn would be "our" Sam Nunn. Or, to reverse the terms, other
movements for social change would try to gain moral authority by using a "gay analogy," de-
claring that their movement was "like" the gay movement. These moves do not seem to carry
the moral weight of the race analogy.

31. Quoted from Justice Blackmun's dissenting opinion in the US Supreme Court's 1986
Bowers v. Hardwick decision. "Blackmun's Opinions Reflect His Evolution of the 24 Court
Years," *New York Times*, 5 March 1999. I wish to thank Lisa Kahaleole Hall for the conversation we had on 24 October 1998, out of which emerged the ideas in this essay about how
the civil rights movement analogy works and is used as a strategy for gaining unearned moral
authority, although I am responsible for how they are presented here.

32. "Stonewall 25," *The Charlie Rose Show*, Public Broadcasting System, 24 June 1994. I
wish to thank Barbara Smith for lending me her videotape copy of this program.

33. For Fundi's reports on this panel and the entire conference, see "Out/Write '90 Report,
Part I: Writers Urged to Examine Their Roles, Save Their Lives," *San Diego GLN*, 16 March
1990, 7; "Out/Write Report, Part II: Ringing Voices," *San Diego GLN*, 23 March 1990, 7, 9;
and "Out/Write Report, Part III: Arenas of Interaction," *San Diego GLN*, 30 March 1990, 7, 9.

34. Lisa Kahaleole Chang Hall, "Bitches in Solitude: Identity Politics and Lesbian Community," in *Sisters, Sexperts, Queers: Beyond the Lesbian Nation,* ed. Arlene Stein (New York: Plume 1993), 223, and in personal conversation.

35. Fundi, "Out/Write Report, Part III," 7, 9.

36. I wish to thank Mitchell Karp for the long dinner conversation we had in 1996 in New York City during which we jointly forged the ideas and questions in this paragraph.

37. I have transcribed the quotations that follow from an audio tape of the workshop discussion.

38. I wish to thank Dennis Poplin for allowing me to use his name and tell his story.

39. Bruce Bawer, "Utopian Erotics," *Lambda Book Report* 7 (October 1998): 19–20.

40. Goldstein, "Go the Way," 180.

41. Bawer, "Utopian Erotics," 19–20.

42. I wish to thank Amber Hollibaugh for introducing me to this idea of "staying white" during a conversation about how a white person can be tempted to distance oneself from whiteness and escape the guilt of its privileges by identifying as a person of color. I was introduced to the idea that white privilege is unearned and difficult to escape at a workshop called White Privilege conducted by Jona Olssen at the 1995 Black Nations/Queer Nations Conference, sponsored by the Center for Lesbian and Gay Studies at the City University of New York. See also Peggy McIntosh, "White Privilege: Unpacking the Invisible Knapsack," *Peace and Freedom* (July/August 1989): 10–12.

43. Goldstein, "Go the Way," 177.

questioning privilege from within the special education process

Janet Sauer and Heather Powers Albanesi*

Introduction

The first author's son was presumed disabled shortly after birth based upon a blood test showing an extra twenty-first chromosome, while the second author's son was flagged for intervention at two years of age because he was not speaking. Both of these children were born into white American middle-class families to educated mothers and are currently provided with special education services based upon legislation focusing on their individually determined needs, but those services would likely look very different if these children had been born into different families. As another privileged parent acknowledged in an interview, the education system "is only fair for the people who are educated or who educate themselves and the other kids just suffer" (Ong-Dean, p. 41). This mother, a professional nurse who was married to a firefighter, voiced a common understanding among parents of children with disabilities that cultural and economic advantages are read-

---

*"Questioning Privilege from Within the Special Education Process," by Janet Sauer and Heather Albanesi. Forthcoming in *Understanding and Dismantling Privilege*. Reprinted with permission of the authors.

ily used in the education system to benefit certain individual children. In fact, the system was developed in response to calls from privileged parents for educational rights on behalf of their children. We do not blame these families, as we ourselves also advocate on behalf of our children, but we do have questions.

Janet: My questions about inequities within the educational structure emerged as a practicing elementary special education teacher who advocated for inclusive schooling for all students regardless of the impact of their impairment or category label of disability. Then I became a mother of a child born with an extra chromosome and the questions became personal. I was now directly impacted by the system in which I worked, in ways I had previously only imagined. I questioned the assumptions some of my colleagues, family, and friends made about my infant's future, when they presumed his diagnosis of Down syndrome predetermined restrictive educational placements and a life of dependence. Shortly thereafter I entered a doctoral program where I learned about disability studies and critical special education and began to revisit questions about the way children with disabilities were being labeled, sorted, and segregated systemically and the role I might have inadvertently played in the process. Reading and working with colleagues outside my educational discipline, such as Heather, provided me with the vocabulary and theoretical framework to analyze this structure from both a scholarly and personal perspective.

Heather: My research and teaching interests in both inequalities in education and the sociology of disability also predate the birth of my son. In particular, it was conversations with some of my undergraduate students with disabilities that initially sparked my interest in disability studies and my desire to address the glaring absence of any research on disability within the courses I taught. While there were indications of developmental issues prior to my son's second birthday (as he missed each pediatric speech milestone), it was after his second birthday that we were directed to early intervention services for a condition that was later diagnosed as ataxia (a neurological disorder of the cerebellum). It was in his transition into elementary school that I became increasingly aware and uncomfortable with the ways that schools structure the process for negotiating an Individualized Education Plan (IEP) in ways that I see as reproducing class and race privilege. In this ongoing process I find myself in conflict where, on one hand, I experience at a personal and emotional level the stigma and shame afforded individuals with disabilities in our society—compelling me to fight for my child's inclusion and acceptance, as hard as I can, using all of the re-sources that my privileged race and class status afford me—and on the other hand, unable to ignore questions raised as to the consequences of wielding this privilege.

The 2004 Individuals with Disabilities Education Act (P.L. 108–446), or IDEA, includes language requiring parental involvement in determining their children's *individual* education plan. Why is there such an emphasis on individuals, and what are the consequences? How has the law impacted the subsequent policies and practices of school personnel and the families with whom they work? Can privileged parents simultaneously advocate for their children and work toward systems-level change? These are some of the questions we explore in this chapter, as parents with privileges who un-derstand the inequitable educational system in which we play a part.

A Disability Studies Theoretical Framework

This paper examines the personal experiences of two children with disabil-ities from the perspective of their mothers using a disability studies (DS) theoretical framework. Disability studies offers a means by which to criti-cally analyze social and political structures. For the purposes of this piece we will refer to the following definition of DS:

> Disability Studies refers generally to the examination of disability as a social, cultural, and political phenomenon. In contrast to clinical, medical, or ther-apeutic perspectives on disability, Disability Studies focuses on how disability is defined and represented in society. From this perspective, disability is not a characteristic that exists in the person so defined, but a construct that finds its meaning in social and cultural context. (Taylor, 2003)

We are particularly interested in identifying the influences on the choices we are afforded and how we take advantage of our circumstances as self-identified parent advocates while recognizing the sociological and historical contexts in which decisions are made. In his sociological examination of disability and diversity, Mark Sherry argues "disability is always a sexed, gendered, racialized, ethnicized, and classed experience . . . [that] operates within a framework of multilayered and complex patterns of inequity and identities" (2008, p. 75). A disability studies theoretical framework offers an opportunity to examine the complexities involved in the daily (and sometimes moment-to-moment) decision-making processes we as parents are involved in. This critical self-examination is not something privileged parents are typically encouraged to participate in because it threatens to undermine the rights for educational access we seek for our children.

The authors acknowledge our privileged positions within the special education process and through this chapter grapple with the moral dilemma involved with advocating for our children while recognizing how we might implicitly contribute to systemic inequities based on our various forms of capital (economic, cultural, social, symbolic, etc.). We explore Ong-Dean's (2009) claim that "our current expectations for parent advocacy may make it difficult for parents and others to see the role privilege plays" (p. 7). As such, we uncover some of the privileges we have enjoyed, by offering some specific examples of our experiences, and analyze them with regard to the current related literature across various disciplines and through a disability studies lens.

Intersections in Special Education

Important questions about the negative influence of special education legislation were first raised in the late 1960s. Lloyd Dunn (1968), for instance, asked the now oft-cited question, "Special education for the mildly retarded—is much of it justifiable?" He questioned why minority students were labeled mentally retarded because they were considered by teachers as "disruptive" or "slow learners." The unnatural overrepresentation of poor and minority students in special education is well documented (Donovan and Cross, 2002; Ferri and Connor, 2005; Harry and Klingner, 2006; Skrtic and McCall, 2010; Sleeter, 1987). We know, for instance, that only about 1 percent of whites are labeled as having mental retardation, while 2.6 percent of black students carry this label (Donovan and Cross, 2002). Interestingly, this overrepresentation is not evident in the disability categories based in physical or biological etiologies, such as visual or hearing impairments. Furthermore, those students of color identified for special education are often served in more restrictive settings than their white counterparts. In this chapter we consider the various ways that parental involvement in the IEP process helps to reproduce these inequities.

Utilizing critical race theory, disability studies scholars have argued that rather than IDEA serving as civil rights legislation, it is used "to maintain the effects of the unacceptable and illegal segregation by race" (Beratan,

2008, p. 337). Sleeter (2010) points out that "differential opportunities afforded to students in schools are not determined by the variety of children and youth who attend, but rather by how that variety is understood and responded to." Sleeter's comment points to the importance of the power of our social interactions and the underlying assumptions and biases in which we base those interactions, something she found when asking the question more than twenty years earlier: "Why are there learning disabilities?" Her answer: "Rather than being a product of progress, the category was essentially conservative in that it helped schools continue to serve best those whom schools have always served best: the White middle and upper-middle class" (Sleeter, 1987, p. 212). As Sleeter suggests, in addition to race, class is a social dynamic involved in the intersectionality of the special education process.

In her research about the role of class in schools, Brantlinger (2003) describes the way "affluent mothers narrate their own and other people's children" (p. 35). She explains how advantages are secured through educational structures and policies, noting that even those in positions of power, such as principals and superintendents, "succumb to the demands of the powerful constituencies," such as the interests of affluent families. She describes teachers she interviewed who, despite expressing frustration about the situations they observed, passively complied with inequitable practices. Instead of focusing on the problem of class-based educational stratification, Brantlinger's study examines the people in power. She refers to Ball (1994), who "insists that to transform social hierarchies, it is necessary to understand groups that have the power to control them" (p. 189). This argument suggests the value of self-examination as we try to figure out the rationale we make for our decisions.

Parental Involvement and the Individualized Strategy

The first process we consider is how parents with privilege are encouraged and expected to pursue the individualized strategy (e.g., "save my son") over collective strategies (e.g., "how do we equitably address the needs of all children with disabilities?"). Considerable research contemplates the "home/school relation" as a primary locus for how the education system reproduces class inequality (Domina, 2005; Lareau, 2000). The individualized parent advocacy strategy can be located within broader trends in the educational system. One set of research in both the US and the UK looks at the level of discourse, pointing to the dominance within the K–12 educational system of the intertwined discourses of parental involvement and parent choice. The former discourse has strongly influenced school reform policy toward the goal of increasing parental involvement in the perhaps misguided hopes that this will redress class and race inequity (Domina, 2005). Instead, researchers have generally found the parental involvement to privilege middle-class families in producing educational outcomes (Brantlinger, 2003; Kainz and Aikens, 2007). Studies looking at the ascendance of parent choice agendas (which David, 1993, connects to the ideology of "parentocracy") have examined the consequences of this popular trend. In particular, researchers have suggested that despite the potential attraction of parents to this discourse, it creates a trade-off between freedom and equity (Reinoso, 2008). Kainz and Aikens (2007) similarly consider the bias of this discourse of involvement, in that it articulates with a particular set of privileged parental resources:

> Instead, we argue that selective access to the dominant discourse—selectivity due to strictly bounded cultural, gender, and family structure expectations— works to privilege certain groups of children and families at the expense of others, particularly because a dominant discourse on parent involvement obscures diversity in viewpoints, family structure, and resources for expected home/school relations. (pp. 301–302)

This move toward a parent choice model is also connected to the creation of "quasi-markets" within the educational system that researchers argue reproduce and intensify existing inequalities (Cookson, 1994; Whitty, 1997).

Mirroring the literature on discourse is research that looks at actual practices, in particular patterns of parental involvement/intervention. For example, a significant body of work within the sociology of education considers the effect of parental privilege on educational outcomes, including economic, cultural, social, symbolic, and emotional capital (Lareau, 2000; Reay, 1998).

Economic Capital

One of the most obvious ways privileged parents affect their children's education is through the choice of where they live and the resulting quality and resources of the area's local schools. While the quality of local schools affects all children, research finds higher SES (socioeconomic status) schools are more likely to offer inclusive (versus segregated) special education services, and children with learning disabilities who attend these schools are more likely to attend college (LeRoy and Kulik, 2003). Local economic resources also affect the quality of teachers working with children with disabilities. Low SES children with disabilities are more likely to have uncertified or provisionally licensed teachers and to graduate with a certificate of attendance or completion rather than a high school diploma (Chamberlain, 2005).

Personal examples of economic capital. Take, for instance, the privilege Janet's son has enjoyed because she and her husband have the funds to find a house in the neighborhood where she wants her son to be educated. She describes the time and resources her family used in their search for an inclusive school when they moved across the country (Sauer, in press). Similarly, Kluth and her colleagues (2007) interviewed twelve families who sought out schools that they felt would offer their individual children the services they thought were best suited to support their children's education. In a case study, Ryndak and colleagues (2011) describe a series of advocacy efforts by an advantaged mother named Sarah that secured support services including horseback-riding lessons, private speech therapy, respite care, and behavior interventions in the home, and she herself at times provided homeschooling and a supplemental reading program for her son. Some research also suggests that there is a "digital divide," where privileged families have increased access to assistive technologies (or just generic technologies, such as an iPad) (Clark and Gorski, 2001). Again, Janet and her husband used their economic advantage to purchase an iPad for their son to use in both the home and school environments prior to the schoolwide adoption of the technology. The effect of the boy's role as a "trend-setter" in his school is unclear, but ready access to the technology was shown to directly affect his academic achievement, as evidenced in his IEP.

Heather's family also was in the financial position (and had flexible work schedules) to pursue every type of medical testing and private speech therapy recommended by the pediatric neurologist. While some of this was covered by insurance, much of it was not. But the documented results of all of these tests went into her son's IEP file and clearly bolstered his case, serving as evidence and justification for particular IEP accommodations. Heather's perception was that the school's special education teachers were quite receptive to this type of data—that it was "speaking their language" (versus parents expressing a vague sense that "something is just not right" with their kid). How many poor families have the time or financial resources to provide these opportunities for their children? As we have seen here and will again describe later in greater detail, race and class play important roles in parent advocacy, whether for certain diagnostic labels, for services, and/or for placements where those services are provided.

Cultural Capital

Much of the work on transmitting class privilege via the home/school relation focuses on how cultural capital shapes parenting practices. Lareau (2003) characterizes middle-class parenting as following the logic of "concerted cultivation." She theorizes that concerted cultivation has three aspects: intensive language use, "over"-scheduling of children's free time, and intervening with institutions such as schools on behalf of the child. In this chapter we focus on the last one: how parents negotiate with various institutions to maximize benefit and accommodation for the individual child. Lareau (2003) suggests these practices have twofold results: the direct accommodation afforded middle-class children (the squeaky wheel) and the modeling of middle-class behavior to the next generation, that is, teaching the child to advocate for him/herself and the child feeling entitled to do so. In his book *Distinguishing Disability: Parents, Privilege, and Special Education,* Ong-Dean (2009) writes about the "burden of advocacy" the IDEA legislation has imposed upon families of disabled children. He argues for the "need to acknowledge that parents differ in how far they can shoulder this burden" (p. 2) based upon their cultural and economic resources.

Personal examples of cultural capital. Both authors are keenly aware of the many opportunities within the IEP process to exercise cultural capital. While interacting/negotiating with special education teachers in a parental role, we are both armed with the specialized language, acronyms, and historical knowledge of, research on, and meaning of decisions such as those to determine the least restrictive environment (LRE) and how services might be provided ("pull out" or "push in" the child); scientific/medical language; and the ability to take on (or at least confidently convey) the role of "expert" with regard to the child's "condition." Janet's master's and doctoral degrees in special education certainly add credibility to her particular interpretations of assessment reports. Take, for example, the request from a school psychologist for an intelligence test to determine a numeric quotient for Janet's son upon arriving at a new school. She questioned the validity of the proposed assessment tool, arguing that she had used the tool herself and taught a college-level course on assessment illustrating the issues concerning so-called intelligence testing, so it was with ease that she quickly referenced related scholarly work (Borthwick, 1996; Kliewer and Biklen, 1996; Linneman, 2001). Janet also provided curriculum-based assessments she had secured from her son's previous teachers as an alternative illustration of her son's abilities. Few parents would have had this kind of skill set and the confidence needed to challenge the supposed power of the psychologist. Similarly, Janet's specific training in special education sensitized her to the "hidden curriculum" of the IEP process so she might expend time and resources to prepare for IEP meetings. On occasion Janet found errors in the IEP document itself that she brought to the attention of the teachers or case managers, directly leading to changes in placement and services.

Race and Cultural Capital

While drawing important attention to the ways in which parenting styles help reproduce class privilege, Lareau's work has been criticized for underestimating the effects of race (Bodovski, 2010; see also Lareau and Horvat, 1999). Bodovski (2010), using a large-scale representative survey, found that while socioeconomic status is related to cultural capital, race has an independent effect. Thus Bodovski (2010) found that black middle-class parents were less engaged in concerted cultivation than white middle-class parents. In addition, research suggests that factors such as race can affect institutional responses to similar displays of cultural capital. So when black and white (both middle-class) parents actively negotiate for accommodations that are in their child's interest, educators perceive those interactions differently due to race. For example, Lareau and Horvat (1999) found that

> many black parents, given the historical legacy of racial discrimination in schools, cannot presume or trust that their children will be treated fairly in school. Yet, they encounter rules of the game in which educators define desirable family-school relationships as based on trust, partnership, coopera-

tion, and deference. These rules are more difficult for black than white parents to comply with. (p. 42) . . .

The teachers repeatedly praised parents who had praised them. They liked parents who were deferential, expressed empathy with the difficulty of teachers' work, and had detailed information about their children's school experiences. In addition, the teachers often stressed the importance of parents "understanding" their children's educational situations, by which they meant that the parents should accept the teacher's definitions of their children's educational and social performance. (p. 43)

McGrath and Kuriloff (1999) similarly find that African-American parents who express criticism of existing school policies and procedures were negatively evaluated by white elite mothers (seen as "always complaining"). This negative evaluation was used by white elite mothers to exclude black mothers from PTA (parent-teacher association) involvement.

Personal examples of racial privilege. Racial privilege is perhaps more difficult than class to identify when one is white. But as whites in (vast) majority-white school systems, Janet and Heather are both aware that their ability to assertively negotiate for their sons is aided by their race. While the research discussed above finds that African-American parents display similar assertive behavior, it is often perceived by white educators (and other white parents) as aggressive and racially motivated.

Cultural Capital: "Individuality" and Middle-Class Parenting

Another element of cultural capital that researchers have identified is middle-class parents' tendency to emphasize their child's unique academic talents, preferred learning styles, competencies, and so on (Lareau, 2003). This tendency can be seen as within the larger picture of classed differences in interacting with the educational institution. Gillies (2005) found "parents' accounts demonstrated the extent to which the middle-class interviewees were invested in constructing their children as 'unique' and distinct from others" (p. 843). Similarly, Ong-Dean (2009) states:

While the creation of educational rights for disabled children follows in the footsteps of social reforms of the 1960s and 1970s, through which previously

marginalized social groups gained access to new opportunities, this latest reform, unlike many of its predecessors, did not emphasize collective action or
the goal of social justice. Instead individual families were to advocate for individual children's rights toward the goal of meeting their "individualized"
needs. (p. 2)

Sleeter's (1987) analysis of the development of the category of learning
disabilities similarly highlights how "the ideology of individual difference"
masks the political purpose of "protecting" white middle-class children
from lower-class minority children. The idea is that parents can maintain
their child's inclusion among those considered of "normal intelligence"
while arguing for variance in their child's individualized learning support
needs. This approach sees both the problem and solution as located within
the individual child rather than examining broader societal systems.

Personal examples of individualizing processes. This one is tricky because
the "logic" of a child's uniqueness is so central to the IEP process (starting
with the title—"individualized" educational plan). There is also the obvious
appeal to parents of a process that seems to acknowledge and appreciate
their child's uniqueness (although the various learning-disability, or LD, labels also constrain our understanding of the child as fitting into precon-
ceived boxes). Unfortunately, another downside of this approach is that it
creates a binary division (children with and without IEPs) where those without IEPs are seen as not unique (normative or slow learners, but not unique)
and the kids with IEPs are separated for special accommodation.

In this chapter, we have examined how interactions with schools are
structured to encourage an individual ("save my son") approach over more
collective approaches that might result in institutional change. While we
are critical of the individual approach, we are aware that our perspective
may not represent those of other similarly privileged parents. Research on
upper-middle-class parents suggests that this individual-advocate approach
is actually consistent with and reflective of parental desire, not in opposition
to it, particularly in the context of fighting for scarce resources. For example,
McGrath and Kuriloff (1999) find "that elite parents' advocacy for tracking
is often driven by their desires to separate their children from those of lesser
social status and to gain for their children access to the highest proportion
of educational resources possible—often at the expense of other parents'
children (though we make no claim that upper-middle-class parents con-

sciously recognize these distributive consequences)" (p. 606). Here, educators are seen as holding the more progressive and egalitarian position (i.e., detracking) while parents are the conservative force (McGrath and Kuriloff, 1999; Wells and Serna, 1996). McGrath and Kuriloff (1999) find this extends to special education, where elite parents also angle for a competitive advantage for their children:

> Wealthier parents with children in the special education program often approached the school with similar intentions. For instance, some upper-middle-class parents sought to separate their special education children from other special education children, especially African American children. Often, they demanded that the district pay for private school placements. (p. 619)

The authors continue, "Similarly, these (White elite) parents sought the most resources that they could get for their own children" (p. 621). In their study, Ong-Dean, Daly, and Park (2011) found evidence that parents with higher economic and cultural capital were more successful in securing public school resources, such as reimbursement claims for private educational costs, than other parents. Brantlinger, Majd-Jabbari, and Guskin (1996) found that even middle-class, educated mothers who claim a liberal identity and commitment to integrated and inclusive education "often support segregated and stratified school structures that mainly benefit students of the middle class" (p. 590).

Cultural Capital, Preferential Labeling, and Placement

As discussed above, researchers have analyzed the crucial role of middle-class parents in creating the "learning disability" category (Blanchett, 2006; Ong-Dean, 2009; Sleeter, 1987), reflecting the desire for middle-class parents for preferential labels within the special education context, and rejection of negatively stigmatized labels (e.g., behavior, "mentally retarded," etc.) (Blair and Scott, 2002). Even Dunn, back in 1968, warned that the special education categories risked labels and that related placements were being used to re-sort children based on disability, race, culture, language, and social class. The overrepresentation of minorities in certain less preferential categories continues today, which is why in Colorado we have Indicator 9, requiring schools to put into place protections against such problems

(Smith, 2004). In fact, IDEA 2004 requires all states to collect demographic data regarding disability determination, but recent reports indicate only twenty-six states focused their monitoring and improvement efforts on the disproportionate representation of racial/ethnic groups in special education (US Commission on Civil Rights, USCCR, 2009). Those states reporting results from 2003 indicate "African American students are three times as likely to receive services for mental retardation under IDEA Part B as are their age peers from the other racial/ethnic groups combined" (USCCR, p. 36). It is abundantly clear that cultural capital plays a role in preferential labeling of students who need educational supports.

Privilege has also been found to lead to different LRE (least restrictive environment) placements (cf. Conway, 2005). In her discussion of the role race, class, and culture play in perpetuating segregation resulting from white middle-class families seeking privileged eligibility categories (such as learning disabilities rather than mental retardation), Blanchett (2010) outlines the inequitable treatment families of color receive in the special education process. Using large-scale national data sets from 2005 through 2009, she points out that despite four decades of research into addressing the over-representation of minorities in special education who end up in even more segregated settings than their white counterparts with the same labels, the problem persists. Interestingly, state-and district-level differences also suggest similar trends, but the intricacies of how labels and placements are determined is largely undocumented. What we do know is that there are large variances in the way the federal laws are interpreted and implemented at local levels. Blanchett (2010) explains,

> When the privilege conferred by the LD label is compounded by the privilege of whiteness and social class privilege, it greatly advantages those students. However, when LD intersects with lower socio-economic status or class and with being African American or of color, the privileges . . . that are often associated with LD are denied these students. ("Learning Disabilities: A Category of Privilege" section, para. 6)

The 27th Annual Report to Congress (2005) illustrates the daily impact these differences have in educating students. It noted the concern of the finding that black students with disabilities were more likely than students with disabilities from other racial/ethnic groups to be educated outside the regular classroom more than 60 percent of the day. This is important because a relationship has been found between more restrictive placements and increased dropout rates, resulting in inequitable postschool opportunities. In an effort to explain why these discrepancies persist, Blanchett (2010) calls racism, white privilege, and white dominance and supremacy "the primary culprits."

Some disability-studies scholars discuss how a "special" education, particularly when students are "pulled out" of the regular classroom, can be seen as segregation, where students with disabilities are socially isolated and stigmatized (Barnes, Mercer, & Shakespeare, 1999; Irvin, 2004; Linton, 1998). Even when individualized "special" services are "pushed in" to the classroom, (e.g., a paraprofessional assigned to work with a single student), stigmatization from other students is an issue. As Conway (2005) points out, "Because special education often separates children with disabilities from their nondisabled peers, whether physically or nominally, it can also promote the very stereotypes of freakishness, pity, and lack of ability from which people with disabilities struggle to be free. Special education can be a subtle, or not-so-subtle, form of discrimination that tracks children according to their 'ability' or other 'distinctive' characteristics" (Conway, 2005, p. 6). By contrast, many educators, who tend not to come from a disability studies perspective, view special education as the solution that represents every child's right to an education (Council for Exceptional Children, 2012). Given the uneven adoption of inclusive (versus traditional "special education") approaches, considerable variation exists in the United States among educators as to which approach is in the best interest of a child with disabilities. It would likely follow that those parents with the least cultural capital would be most likely to capitulate to the strategies embraced by educators (Lareau, 2003).

Preferential Labeling and "Twice Exceptional"

Perhaps the gold ring for parents of children with disabilities, the additive label (and corresponding resource pool) of "gifted and talented" (making the child "twice exceptional"), has obvious appeal. On the one hand, it fits well with a diversity model open to the possibility of unique talents, learning differences, and strengths. But, as seen with the competition for preferential labeling within special education, it is subject to the same inequities in application. For example, in her discursive analysis of the justification of "highly gifted and talented" programs, Young (2010) argues these programs serve to reproduce class and racial stratification.

Personal examples of prereferential labeling. As previously mentioned, upon moving to Colorado, Janet refused IQ testing and the suggestion by some educational personnel to ascribe the state-based presumed label of SLIC, or significantly limited intellectual capacity for students with Down syndrome (see Sauer, in press). The family spent hours in discussion, e-mail exchanges, and phone calls with the schools, negotiating the label to be ascribed to Janet's son. Some professionals threatened a loss of future services if the parents were to refuse the recommended label. In the end it was agreed to adopt "physical disability" as the primary disabling condition and speech/language/communication as the secondary label. The family in this case was acutely aware of the social stigma related to labels such as SLIC or mental retardation, as well as its effect on teachers' expectations. At the same time, they were conscious of their right to refuse testing and knew if necessary they could recruit "experts" on their own behalf through parent advocacy groups and professional colleagues. In fact, each time an educator offered the family the parents' rights booklet that outlined these legal guidelines, Janet would give the teacher a knowing smile that seemed to communicate the shared understanding that these parents were very aware of their rights.

In the process of testing Heather's son, the neuropsychologist verbally expressed the opinion that (in addition to various other diagnoses) he had attention-deficit/hyperactivity disorder (ADHD). While accepting the other "more palatable" labels, Heather rejected the ADHD label and asked that it not be included (at least as a definitive diagnosis) in the report that would be shared with the school. The external (to the school) neuropsychological testing Heather's son received allowed for preferential labels (medical/neurological diagnosis of ataxia, "twice exceptional"). The parents rejected non-preferred labels (ADHD) that the testing had also generated.

Social Capital

Whereas cultural capital is understood as an individual's stock of high-status etiquette, tastes, preferences, and behaviors, social capital is composed of the interpersonal networks or connections that individuals can draw on for support, information, and other favors (Coleman, 1988). A number of studies have indicated that middle-class parents are able to more successfully leverage their social capital in school interactions than less privileged parents (Pong, Hao, and Gardner, 2005; Horvat, Weininger, and Lareau, 2003).

McGrath and Kuriloff (1999) summarize their finding: "The social networks that upper-middle-class parents form through schools help them to gain crucial knowledge about the workings of schools and to make influential social contact" (p. 606).

Personal examples of social capital. Heather has had many conversations with other parents of children with IEPs. These conversations can be viewed as an example of social capital, including shared experiences of problematic negotiations and what kinds of accommodations other children are getting. In one conversation where parents were sharing their frustration with the consistent lack of follow-through on the written IEP, one parent mentioned that it was "obvious" and "expected" that parents would need to get a lawyer to force the school into compliance. While Heather has never felt compelled to hire a lawyer, just knowing that such recourse was out there (and having the financial resources to employ it) potentially shifts the balance of power in the IEP meeting. Throughout her son's fifteen years, Janet has employed her social capital in her advocacy efforts. She regularly provides her son's teachers and therapists with current literature and at times she has served as a volunteer parent and professional consultant, and educational researcher to schools. Through her work in preservice education she has collaborated with teachers who have come to the university as guest speakers and copresented at conferences and workshops. As Janet occasionally chooses to point out, she was a teacher before becoming a mother and those identities do not have clearly delineated boundaries. Perhaps a less obvious but equally significant example of social (and economic) capital is that Janet typically brings food to the school meetings, recognizing that when she was a teacher she enjoyed meetings where food was shared.

Symbolic Capital

In addition to the actual knowledge accumulation (or human capital) assumed to be reflected in a professional degree, a doctoral degree confers symbolic capital based on prestige. Our case is interesting because whereas most parents enter school decision-making meetings (such as IEP meetings) with educators at a comparative disadvantage in terms of information and power (Fine, 1993), in our case that balance of power is questionable. While it is hard to demonstrate specific advantages gained because we have professional degrees, it would seem naive to assume they had no effect. As

Ong-Dean et al. (2011) argue, "Whether they request a hearing or not, their words and actions are backed up by a material and symbolic power, which may be effective in the moment or may stand as a reminder of what could happen if they chose to fully exercise their rights" (p. 396). Another form of symbolic privilege worth noting is that of our married, heterosexual statuses. While mothers do the vast majority of interaction with their children's schooling (Reay, 1998), research does suggest that, perhaps due in part to its relative scarcity, father involvement has a positive and mediating effect on educational outcomes (McBride, Schoppe-Sullivan, and Ho, 2005).

Personal examples of symbolic privilege. In both Janet's and Heather's cases, their husbands typically attend every IEP meeting, if only to try to compensate for the large numbers of school professionals in an IEP meeting (usually five to eight). While it is difficult to point to a specific payoff for this effort, it would at a minimum seem to impress upon the IEP team the seriousness with which these parents take their children's education (all taking off work) and willingness to fight for the desired accommodations. In Heather's case, her husband has been the only man present at any of the IEP meetings (and any interaction with the elementary school). Janet has noticed subtle differences in the communication style in meetings when her husband is present.

Rehabilitative Approach Versus Disability Studies Approach

The second process we consider is how parents are pushed to accept the rehabilitative approach over an approach that questions the construction of "disability" and the range of possible institutional responses to it. Current orientations toward disability are based in a history of "otherness" that necessitates a rehabilitative approach to educating students who might experience impairments (Kliewer and Biklen, 2007). The systems that emerged from the deinstitutionalization movement of the 1960s and 1970s (Larsen, 1976) were framed as issues of access for people considered to experience significant disabilities (Jackson, 2005).

However, public discourse continues to rely upon a historical consciousness whereby impairment is pitied and viewed through a medical/deficit model. In the lives of American youth with disabilities, the rehabilitative approach has meant segregated education. The thinking is, "You are broken, you cannot 'fit' among your nondisabled peers, and thus you need to go elsewhere to get some specialized education or related services and then you can return/reenter the general education learning environment." Despite the unevenness in which different states and school districts determine placement of services, students considered to have more moderate or severe disabilities are typically removed (IDEA data). Even students with the most "mild" of disabilities are often removed from their general education classrooms for therapy sessions.

Jackson (2005) explains how arguments regarding segregation in disability parallel those used to justify slavery:

> As an analogy, it has been said that slave traders justified their vocation by arguing that while slavery may be bad, the natives were better off because they were now in the new world and not in Africa. Likewise, many special educators acknowledge that restrictive placements can be problematic because of their enforced isolation from peers and typical experiences of life, but some then argue that the educational benefits of such placements outweigh the negative effects of segregation. In severe disabilities, neither the research data nor the day to day experiences of persons who know the field support the educational benefits argument for segregation. Only when such reasoning is set aside can significant access concerns be resolved, and only at this point can equity and quality concerns assume their rightful place as important determinants of the critical issues in the discourse of our profession. (p. 7)

Restrictive placement justifications are regularly made as part of the IEP process, but few families describe this intellectual negotiation as open, flexible, or clearly explained. Despite legislation guaranteeing active parent involvement and a process whereby the placement of services is to be determined only after assessment and goal-setting discussion, some families report that placement decisions were made before meetings. The link between labels and placement in practices across the United States is important because this has been a factor in families' ability to advocate for particular labels based upon cultural capital.

Finally, from a disability studies theoretical framework, we question how our participation in these two processes helps reproduce the existing structures of inequality. Goodley and colleagues (2010) write, "Disability must be analyzed as a social and cultural phenomenon, which says as much about normalizing/non-disabled society as it does about the constitution of disability. Indeed, in the current economic climate, the need for analyses of disablism in everyday cultural life is arguably more necessary than ever" (p. 3). We write from a place of privilege, torn between two roads. The first follows our inclination to avail ourselves of the various form of capital (cultural, social, symbolic, economic) we can access with relative ease to benefit our own children in the immediate future (potentially at the expense of less privileged children). The second involves working toward systemic change that can influence the lives of children less privileged that will take more time. While this problem and the possible solutions are not necessarily mutually exclusive, it seems worthwhile to reexamine the underlying reason for the tension. Who benefits from these structures and practices? Are we being duped into thinking it is okay to work toward our own children's "appropriate education" at the expense of other children and their teachers and families?

Personal examples of the rehabilitative approach. The following quote from Heather's son's neuropsychology report illustrates the rehabilitative or medical model:

> Robbie is fortunate to have parents who are highly invested in promoting his development and well-being. They have provided excellent advocacy for his needs and should be commended for their dedication to seeing that Robbie's potential is maximized. It was a pleasure working with Robbie and his family.

Heather found this statement somewhat bizarre and questioned its purpose and meaning. She interpreted it as a reward for pursuing the individual advocacy strategy and encouragement to continue to work within the current structure. This was one of a number of times that she felt embraced by the educational institution, reflecting a good "fit" between the "type" of parents we are and the institutional practices at play (see Doucet, 2011, and Van Galen, 1987, for a discussion of how schools structure and constrain parental involvement).

On the other hand, rather than using a parent support group for parents of students with disabilities to bring disability into equity discussions, Janet joined the PTA and its discussions of racism. Being keenly aware of her white race, Janet listened to a fellow parent chaperone at their children's middle-school dance talk about the recent use of racial epitaphs against her "mixed-race" daughter. This mother was one of a growing number of parents at their small, predominantly white school who felt the need to meet with the district leaders and discuss what seemed like a spike in prejudice against students of color. Janet and her husband joined what became known as the "angry parent meetings" and they tried to explain how the racial tension was part of a larger issue regarding a lack of respect for student diversity. It's unclear how these discussions might have changed other families' or the school personnel's attitudes toward the idea expressed by Martin Luther King (1963):

> I am cognizant of the interrelatedness of all communities and states. I cannot sit idly by in Atlanta and not be concerned about what happens in Birmingham. Injustice anywhere is a threat to justice everywhere.

Janet used this quote in a complaint letter she wrote to the school upon learning that her son with disabilities was socially excluded from an activity celebrating King's birthday.

Discussion

This chapter provides personal experiences illustrating how privilege is implicated in the way certain parents interact with schools regarding their children served through special education. Skrtic and McCall (2011) consider how legislation enacted to support children with disabilities differentially benefited children of white, middle-class (professional) families through access to decision-making and due process. They argue that antidemocratic practices resulted from IDEA because the practices are case-based, individualized, and "closed," thus "muting" the broad systemic issues. They contend a reinterpretation of "needs politics" is needed from one based on a decontextualized rights-based struggle to one where the "medium of struggle [is] in an institutional context," which provides a space of opposition that is more empowering and democratic. Their work highlights experiences of the "least privileged" where schools used delay tactics and questioned families' credibility and thus their rights for access to due process. In this chapter, we reverse the focus to questioning ourselves as (unintentional) reproducers of inequity. As Sleeter (1987) turned her gaze to critical self-reflection in her early critique of special education, we, too, hope that our experiences and perspectives offer a "standpoint from which to view schools and society" (Sleeter, 2010). We believe that by sharing our personal experiences analyzed through a disability studies lens, we have contributed to a greater understanding of the effect our individual responses to disability seem to perpetuate problems in the field, particularly for families of children with disabilities who are already marginalized due to their class or race.

Ball (1994) "insists that to transform social hierarchies, it is necessary to understand groups that have the power to control them" (as cited in Brantlinger, 2003, p. 189). Indeed, we have implicated ourselves by bringing these personal stories forward. The process has been at times demoralizing and somewhat embarrassing, but it can also be viewed as a first step in moving forward in the process of change by seeking the critical feedback from our colleagues, both personal and professional, in our attempt to unpack and make public the ways we ourselves have become oppressors. The sharing of our stories is not intended to be used by other parents as strategies for individual advocacy on behalf of children. Rather, we hope families might see themselves in these stories and share in recognizing how our role in navigating the educational system works to perpetuate historical inequalities. Once these are realized, we think we can more readily assent to (or take leadership in creating) changes on the systemic level.

Educational leaders, too, can take into account these personal examples and the related literature to more critically inform their practices. They might become more aware of the ways in which they ignore or even contribute to perpetuating practices that privilege certain families. At a time when public education is increasingly scrutinized and resources are limited, educational leaders could exercise their own agency to become change agents. Critical dispositions are necessary for inclusive school leaders to, in the words of Frattura, "choose to be emancipators" (Theoharis and Causton-Theoharis, 2008, p. 243). Initiatives that honor democratic principles for social justice in inclusive, culturally responsive classrooms have been developed (for example, see the *International Journal of Whole Schooling*), but they need leaders to enact them. Through critical self-examination, families and educators could find opportunities to collaborate on developing a broad shared vision for inclusive schooling that would focus energies on redirecting practices and creating policies away from reliance on individualism and move toward collective work that recognizes the value of our interconnectedness. It is important to include families whose children are not directly involved in the special education process to become informed about these inequities so they might become allies. Just as Janet has pushed for inclusive education as a right and benefit for all children, she has found it important to infuse disability into PTA conversations about diversity.

As society has come to realize the need to address economic disparity, we need to address the ways in which social and cultural capital are used in the special education process. We suggest that expanding access to a disability studies theoretical framework in educational preservice programs and parent advocacy will help facilitate a broader, interdisciplinary audience where we can build alliances toward changing educational inequities.

references

Ball, S. J. (1994) *Education Reform: A Critical and Post-Structural Approach.* Buckingham: Open University Press.

Barnes, C., Mercer, G., & Shakespeare, T. (1999) *Exploring disability: A sociological introduction.* Cambridge, UK: Blackwell.

Beratan, G. D. (2008) The song remains the same: Transposition and the disproportionate representation of minority students in special education. *Race, Ethnicity, and Education, 11*(4), 337–354. doi: 10.1080/13613320802478820

Blair, C., & Scott, J.C. (2002) Proportion of LD placements associated with low SES status: Evidence of a gradient, *Journal of Special Education, 36*(1), 14–22. doi: 10.1177/00224669020360010201

Blanchett, W. (2006). Disproportionate representation of African American students in special education: Acknowledging the role of white privilege and racism, *Educational Researcher, 35*(6), 24–28. doi: 10.3102/0013189X035006024

_____. (2010) Telling it like it is: The role of race, class, & culture in the perpetuation of LD as a privileged category for the white middle class. *Disability Studies Quarterly, 30* (2). Retrieved from http://dsq-sds.org/issue/view/46.

Bodovski, K. (2010) Parental practices and educational achievement: Social class, race, and habitus. *British Journal of Sociology of Education, 31*(2), 139–156. doi: 10.1080/01425690903539024

Borthwick, C. (1996) Racism, IQ, and Down's syndrome. *Disability & Society, 11*(3), 403–410.

Brantlinger, E. (2003) *Dividing classes: How the middle class negotiates and rationalizes school advantage.* New York: RoutledgeFalmer.

Brantlinger, E., Majd-Jabbari, M., & Guskin, S. L. (1996) Self-interest and liberal educational discourse: How ideology works for middle-class mothers. *American Educational Research Journal, 33*(3), 571–597.

Chamberlain, S. (2005) Recognizing and responding to cultural differences in the education of culturally and linguistically diverse learners. *Intervention in School & Clinic, 40*(4), 195–211. doi: 10.1177/10534512050400040101

Clark, C., & Gorski, P. (2001) Multicultural education and the digital divide: Focus on race, language, socioeconomic class, sex, and disability. *Multicultural Perspectives, 3*(3), 39–44.

Coleman, J. (1988) Social capital in the creation of human capital. *American Journal of Sociology, 94*, 95–120.

Conway, M. (2005) Introduction: Disability studies meets special education. *Review of Disability Studies: An International Journal, 3*(1), 3–9.

Cookson, P. (1994) *School choice: The struggle for the soul of American education.* New Haven, CT: Yale University Press.

Council for Exceptional Children (CEC). (2012) *Open letter to U.S. Congress and U.S. Secretary of Education Arne Duncan from the Council for Exceptional Children and the special education research community.* Author. Retrieved from www.cec .sped.org/~/media/Files/Policy/Research/special_education_research_open_ letter.pdf.

David, M. (1993) Parents, gender, and education. *Educational Policy, 7*(2), 184–205. doi: 10.1177/0895904893007002004

Domina, T. (2005) Leveling the home advantage: Assessing the effectiveness of parental involvement in elementary school. *Sociology of Education, 78*(3), 233–249. doi: 10.1177/003804070507800303

Donovan, M. S., & Cross, C. T. (2002) The committee on minority representation in special education. *Minority Students in Special and Gifted Education.* National Academy Press.

Doucet, F. (2011) Parent involvement as ritualized practice. *Anthropology & Education Quarterly, 42*(4), 404–421. doi: 10.1111/j.1548-1492.2011.01148.x

Dunn, L. (1968) Special education for the mildly retarded—Is much of it justifiable? *Exceptional Children, 35*(1), 5–22.

Ferri, B., & Connor, D. (2005) Tools of exclusion: Race, disability, and (re)segregated education. *Teachers College Record, 107*(3), 453–474.

Gillies, V. (2005) Raising the "meritocracy": Parenting and the individualization of social class. *Sociology, 39*(5), 835–853.

Goodley, D., Mallet, R., Lawthom, R., Burke, L., & Bolt, D. (2010) Theorizing culture and disability: Interdisciplinary dialogues. *Review of Disability Studies: An International Journal, 6*(3). Retrieved from www.rds.hawaii.edu.

Harry, B., & Klingner, J. K. (2006) *Why are so many minority students in special education? Understanding race and disability in schools.* New York: Teachers College Press.

Horvat, E., Weininger, E., & Lareau, A. (2003) From social ties to social capital: Class differences in the relations between school and parent networks. *American Educational Research Journal, 40*(2), 319–351.

Irvin, C. (2004) *Homebound: Growing up with a disability in America.* Philadelphia: Temple University Press.

Jackson, L. (2005) *Issues in severe disabilities.* National Center on Severe and Sensory Disabilities. Retrieved from www.unco.edu/ncssd.

Kainz, K., & Aikens, N. L. (2007) Governing the family through education: A genealogy on the home/school relation. *Equity & Excellence in Education, 40*(4), 301–310.

King, M. L., Jr. (1963) The Negro is your brother. *The Atlantic, 212*(2), 78–88. Retrieved from www.theatlantic.com/ideastour/civil-rights/king-excerpt.html.

Kliewer, C., & Biklen, D. (1996) Labeling: Who wants to be called retarded? In W. Stainbeck & S. Stainbeck (Eds.), *Controversial issues confronting special education: Divergent perspectives* (pp. 83–95).

———. (2007) Enacting literacy: Local understanding, significant disability, and a new frame for educational opportunity. *Teachers College Record, 109*(12), 2579–2600.

Kluth, P., Biklen, D., English-Sand, P., & Smukler, D. (2007) Going away to school: Stories of families who move to seek inclusive educational experiences for their children with disabilities. *Journal of Disability Policy Studies, 18*(1), 43–56.

Lareau, A. (2000) *Home advantage: Social class and parental intervention in elementary education*. Lanham, MD: Rowman & Littlefield.

———. (2003) *Unequal Childhoods: Class, race and family life*. Berkeley: University of California Press.

Lareau, A., & Horvat, E. (1999, January) Moments of social inclusion and exclusion: Race, class and cultural capital in family-school relationships. *Sociology of Education, 72*, 37–53.

Larsen, L. A. (1976) Deinstitutionalization. In M. A. Thomas (Ed.), *HEY, don't forget about me!* (pp. 124–145). Reston, VA: Council for Exceptional Children.

LeRoy, B., & Kulik, N. (2003) The demography of inclusive education in Michigan: State and local district findings. Detroit, MI: Developmental Disabilities Institute. Retrieved from http://ddi.wayne.edu/publications.php.

Linneman, R. D. (2001) *Idiots: Stories about mindedness and mental retardation*. New York: Peter Lang.

Linton, S. (1998) *Claiming disability: Knowledge and identity*. New York: New York University Press.

McBride, B. A., Schoppe-Sullivan, S. J., & Ho, M. (2005) The mediating role of fathers' school involvement on student achievement. *Journal of Applied Developmental Psychology, 26*(2), 201–216. doi.org/10.1016/j.bbr.2011.03.031

McGrath, D. J., & Kuriloff, P. J. (1999) "They're going to tear the doors off this place": Upper-middle-class parent school involvement and the educational opportunities of other people's children. *Educational Policy, 13*(5), 603–629.

Ong-Dean, C. (2009) *Distinguishing disability: Parents, privilege, and special education*. Chicago: University of Chicago Press.

Ong-Dean, C., Daly, A. J., & Park, V. (2011) Privileged advocates: Disability and education policy in the USA. *Policy Futures in Education, 9*(3), 392–405. doi.org/10.2304/pfie.2011.9.3.392

Pong, S., Hao, L. & Gardner, E. (2005) The roles of parenting styles and social capital in the school performance of immigrant Asian and Hispanic adolescents. *Social Science Quarterly. 86*(4), 928–950. doi: 10.1111/j.0038–4941.2005.00364.x

Reay, D. (1998) *Class work: Mothers' involvement in their children's primary schooling*. London: UCL Press.

Reinoso, A. (2008) Middle-class families and school choice: Freedom versus equity in the context of a "local education market." *European Educational Research Journal, 7*(2), 176–194.

Ryndak, D., Orlando, A., Storch, J. F., Denney, M. K., and Huffman, J. (2011) A mother's perceptions of her ongoing advocacy efforts for her son with significant disabilities: Her twelve-year journey. *International Journal of Whole Schooling, 7*(2). Retrieved from www.wholeschooling.net/Journal_of_Whole_Schooling/articles/7–2b%20Ryndak.pdf.

Sauer, J. (in press) What's behind the curtain?: A family's search for an inclusive Oz. *Review of Disability Studies, an International Journal.*

Sherry, M. (2008) *Disability and diversity: A sociological perspective.* New York: Nova Science Publishers.

Skrtic, T., & McCall, Z. (2010) Ideology, institutions, and equity: Comments on Christine Sleeter's "Why is there learning disabilities?" *Disability Studies Quarterly, 30,* 2. Retrieved from http://dsq-sds.org/issue/view/46.

_____. (2011) The irony of access: Intersectional needs politics and the stratifying practices of special education. Presentation at the Second City Conference Disability Studies in Education, Chicago, IL.

Sleeter, C. E. (1987) Why is there learning disabilities? A critical analysis of the birth of the field in its social context. In T. S. Popkewicz (Ed.), *The formation of school subjects: The struggle for creating an American institution* (pp. 210–238). London: Falmer Press.

_____. (2010) Building counter-theory about disability. *Disability Studies Quarterly, 30*(2). Retrieved from http://dsq-sds.org/issue/view/46.

Smith, P. (2004) Whiteness, normal theory, and disability studies. *Disability Studies Quarterly, 24*(2). Retrieved from http://dsq-sds.org/article/view/491/668.

Taylor, S. (2003) *Introduction.* Disability studies: Information and resources. Retrieved from http://thechp.syr.edu/Disability_Studies_2003_current.html.

Theoharis, G., & Causton-Theoharis, J. (2008) Oppressors or emancipators: Critical dispositions for preparing inclusive school leaders. *Equity & Excellent, 41*(2), 230–246. doi: 10.1080/10665680801973714

US Commission on Civil Rights (USCCR). (2009) Retrieved from www.usccr.gov.

US Department of Education. (2008) Office of Special Education and Rehabilitation Services, Office of Special Education Programs, *27th Annual Report to Congress on the Implementation of the Individuals with Disabilities Education Act, 2005, vol. 1,* Washington, DC.

Van Galen, J. (1987) Maintaining control: The structuring of parent involvement. In G. W. Noblit and W. T. Pink (Eds.), *Schooling in social context* (pp. 78–90). Norwood, NJ: Ablex.

Wells, A., & Serna, I. (1996) The politics of culture: Understanding local political resistance to detracking in racially mixed schools. *Harvard Educational Review, 66*(1), 93–118.

Whitty, G. (1997) Creating quasi-markets in education: A review of recent research on parental choice and school autonomy in three countries. *Review of Research in Education, 22,* 3–47.

Winzer, M. A. (1993) *The history of special education: From isolation to integration.* Washington, DC: Gallaudet University Press.

Young, K. (2010) LD and the rise of highly gifted and talented programs: Examining similar rationales across decades and designations. *Disability Studies Quarterly, 30,* 2. Retrieved from http://dsq-sds.org/issue/view/46.

discussion questions & activities

Discussion Questions

1. Each chapter in this section examines the intersections of multiple social identities. For each chapter, identify some of the ways in which our knowledge of one specific social identity would be limited by examining it in isolation:

   a. Kimmel and Coston: How would our understanding of masculinity be limited by ignoring ability and sexual identity? What would the consequences be?

   b. hooks: How would our understanding of race be limited by ignoring class privilege? What would the consequences be?

   c. Bérubé: How would our understanding of heterosexual privilege be limited by ignoring race? What would the consequences be?

   d. Sauer and Albanesi: How would our understanding of disability be limited by ignoring race and class privilege? What would the consequences be?

Personal Connections

The following questions and activities are designed to be completed either on your own or in class and then discussed as a group with others. As you share your insights with others, think about the patterns and similarities that emerge, as well as the differences among your answers.

A. Dissecting Privilege and Intersectionality in Your Own Life

Moving beyond the cases in this text, consider the many other ways in which our avoidance of intersectional complexities limits our understanding and knowledge of specific social identities and the dynamics of privilege.

- Identify the most significant social identity in your life. How has ignoring some of the privileged identities you benefit from limited your understanding of that specific identity? When you begin to examine that prominent identity in the context of these other privileged identities, does it change anything? Reveal anything? Make you think about yourself or others differently in any way? For example, if you have always seen being a woman as the most significant identity in your life, does considering your race, class, sexual identity, or ability lead to a different understanding of your experience as a woman?

B. Bringing Privilege and Intersectionality into Your Studies

- Select one book or article you have read for another class or research project, that focuses specifically on one social identity. Identify and discuss the ways that knowledge of the issue would be advanced by bringing an intersectional perspective into the research.
- Select one subject you are interested in researching. Approaching the subject from an intersectional perspective, which social identities do you think would be most important for you to examine, and why?

part four

making new connections

17

whiter shades of pale

On the Plurality of Whitenesses

Clifford Leek*

Introduction

I have spent the past several years of my life attempting to keep one foot in the field of critical studies of whiteness and one foot in the field of studies on men and masculinity while focusing on where the fields intersect. In the process, I have noticed the fields experiencing parallel debates and struggling through similar sites of contention. I believe that these sites of contention, namely the defining of core terms, turmoil over the relationship between those key terms and biology, and diversity within their categories of analysis, are places where the studies of whiteness and masculinity have the opportunity to learn from one another. Before I dive headfirst into the sites of contention in these fields, it is important to understand their parallel political orientations and trajectories.

In the fields of gender and race, the positions of men and white people had been neglected as sites of critical study before men's studies and whiteness studies emerged. Brod compared the omission of men from the critical gaze to the

---

neglect of women from the vast majority of scholarly work: "While women have been obscured from our vision by being too much in the background, men have been obscured by being too much in the foreground" (1987a, p. 40). The need is not for more research on men and white people, but rather for more "studies that critically address men in the context of gendered power relations" (Hearn, 2004) and, likewise, more studies that critically address white people in the context of race relations. According to Pease (2004),

> the task then identified by many anti-racist activists and scholars is to make whiteness more visible. Just as feminism has challenged men to critically reflect upon their masculinity, so anti-racism challenges white people to reflect upon what it means to be white. Just as men have been challenged to not take "male" for granted, so white people have been challenged to not take "white" for granted. (p. 120)

So, these fields of study on whiteness and masculinity, originating from studies of positions of marginalization, subordination, and oppression, strive to analyze positions and relations of dominance without reifying or "re-centering" them (Cuomo and Hall, 1999; Shome, 2000). The aim is not for men's studies to become the new center of gender studies or for whiteness studies to become the new center of ethnic studies, but rather to "(re)turn the gaze of critical race studies to how whites are socially produced, maintained, and constructed as 'white'" (Shome, 2000, p. 366) and to utilize critical feminist thinking to comprehend how men too are produced, maintained, and constructed as "men."

Even with similar political and academic orientations, men's studies and whiteness studies have taken markedly separate paths. Before the heyday of whiteness studies, Brod predicted that "certain aspects of men's studies may indeed share principles in common with studies of other ruling groups" (1987a, p. 62), and I argue that he is very right. However, what he may not have foreseen is the way the two fields operate mostly in isolation from each other when they could gain from continuous dialogue. A few scholars have shown just how valuable increased dialogue between the two fields can be. For example, in his book *Affirmative Reaction*, Hamilton Carroll (2011) illustrates several cases in which formulations of white masculinity have shifted to maintain dominance. Abby Ferber (2007) makes the case in "Whiteness Studies and the Erasure of Gender" that whiteness studies in particular can benefit from increased dialogue with masculinity studies.

In his reflection on these two fields, Pease argues that "increasing aware-ness of debates within profeminism may heighten awareness of some of the tensions and dangers in critical white studies" (2004, p. 126), and I argue here that the learning can go both ways.

Definitions

Challenges to men's studies and whiteness studies have addressed the issue of how key terms are defined (Arnesen, 2001; Clatterbaugh, 1998; Hearn, 1996; Kolchin, 2002; Pascoe, 2007).

Masculinity

According to Clatterbaugh, "It may be the best kept secret of the literature on masculinities that we have an extremely ill-defined idea of what we are talking about" (1998, p. 27). Every responsible critique of men's studies lit-erature comments on the difficulty of defining, and thus operationalizing, the term "masculinity." In the literature, a number of definitions have emerged that frame masculinity as a stereotype or norm (Bem, 1993; Wieg-man, 2002), as a set of attributes (Petersen, 2003), or as a set of behaviors or practices (Connell and Messerschmidt, 2005; Donovan, 1998). In the canon-ical work *Masculinities*, Connell (1995) outlines four definitional tendencies in the field: "essentialist," "positivist," "normative," and "semiotic," which, re-spectively, result in analyses of a single feature thought to encompass mas-culinity, discussions of what men actually are, notions of what men ought to be, and oversimplified conceptualizations of masculinity as "not-femininity."

The most commonly utilized definition of masculinity, though, seems to be as a set of practices (Burke, 2011; Connell, 1995; Connell, 2002; Con-nell and Messerschmidt, 2005; Donovan, 1998; Paechter, 2003; Pascoe, 2007), and the most coherent articulation of this framework comes from Connell and Messerschmidt (2005):

> Masculinity is not a fixed entity embedded in the body of personality traits of individuals. Masculinities are configurations of practice that are accom-plished in social action and, therefore, can differ according to the gender re-lations in a particular social setting. (p. 836)

The unanswered question that arises from this definition is how we de-cide which behaviors or practices to attribute to masculinity and which to attribute to other factors (Clatterbaugh, 1998; Hearn, 1996). A similar question must be asked of definitions that address masculinity as norms or attributes.

As a result of these mostly unanswered questions about definitions of masculinity, some men's studies scholars have called for a moratorium on using the term (Hearn, 1996; MacInnes, 1998; McMahon, 1993). Hearn (1996) argues that

> it would probably be helpful to conceptualize the material discursive practices of and about men in terms of the extent to which and the ways in which they are "masculinized" rather than to speak of some independent substance of masculinity itself. (p. 214)

According to Hearn, the prominent usage of masculinity as an analytical tool in men's studies scholarship often leads us to assume that masculinity is relevant and meaningful in any given situation rather than asking whether it is.

Whiteness

Similar to the debates surrounding masculinity, whiteness studies continue to negotiate definitions of whiteness as pillars of the field. Kincheloe rightly claims that "in the emerging sub-discipline of whiteness studies scholars seem better equipped to explain white privilege than to define whiteness itself" (1999, p. 162). The literature on whiteness reveals two conflicting trends in definitions of whiteness. Some define whiteness as a set of practices that function to protect and maintain privilege, while others define whiteness simply as the experience of privilege.

The definition of whiteness as a set of practices (Frankenberg, 1997a; Hughey, 2010; Shome, 2000) is the one most parallel to definitions of masculinity. This framework is sometimes expressed through language of strategies (Leonardo, 2002; Nakayama and Krizek, 1995), but the implication of practice remains. Hughey frames whites as a "configuration of meanings and practices that simultaneously produce and maintain racial cohesion and difference" (2010, p. 1290), while Leonardo understands it as a "collection of everyday strategies ... characterized by the unwillingness to name the contours of racism, the avoidance of identifying with a racial experience group, the minimization of racist legacy, and other similar evasions" (2002, p. 32).

The framework of whiteness as practice experiences the same dilemmas as the articulation of masculinity as practice. The question must be asked: Which behaviors or practices can we attribute to whiteness and which should be attributed to other factors? Frankenberg argues that "whiteness turns out on closer inspection to be more about the power to include and exclude groups and individuals than about the actual practices of those who are to be let in or kept out" (1997, p. 13). This definition invites work such as that by Waters (1990), Ignatiev (1995), and Roediger (1999), all of which analyze the ways a category of whiteness has been constructed over time through inclusion and exclusion. While these historical and macro-social approaches to the practices of whiteness are important, what is missing in the field is a more in-depth discussion of the micro-social practices of whiteness. What practices by individual white people can be attributed to whiteness? How does whiteness function interpersonally?

A growing number of scholars have taken on the micro-social practices of whiteness (Alegria, 2012; Bonilla-Silva, 2006; Burke, 2012; Kendall, 2006; Rains, 1998), but such studies are still rare. One of the scholars who has taken on these micro-social practices of whiteness makes the case that often seemingly "benign" practices of whiteness reinforce white supremacy in meaningful ways (Rains, 1998). Rains argues that one reason scholars of whiteness with the political agenda of dismantling white supremacy avoid focusing on micro-social practices is that "when racism is constructed as individualistic, it is much easier to think that it has no relationship to the vast majority of Whites" (1998, p. 81). But in avoiding discussion of the micro-social practices of whiteness, we fail to address the full range of practices reinforcing white supremacy.

Bodies

A perpetual problem in defining both whiteness and masculinity has been the role of bodies in relationship to the practices, hierarchies, or attitudes to be analyzed. The question here is whether "whiteness" and "masculinity," as concepts, can be applied to "not-white" and "not-male." Cheng summarizes the debate within masculinities by stating that "one should not assume that 'masculine' behavior is performed only by men, and by all men, while 'feminine' behavior is performed only by women and by all women" (1999, p. 295). Indeed, many scholars have shown that masculine behavior can be associated with bodies that would not be biologically categorized as male

(Halberstam, 1998, 2002b; Messerschmidt, 2004; Pascoe, 2007). The point here is that masculinity in men's studies scholarship is not biological fact and behaviors we identify as "masculine" are not restricted to being performed by male bodies.

Similarly, studies that have shown historical flexibility of the boundaries of whiteness challenge any conceptualization of whiteness that relies upon white bodies (Hale, 2010; Ignatiev, 1995; Roediger, 1999, 2005; Tehranian, 2008). Other studies have shown how black and Latino people often understand whiteness in terms of practices and that those practices can be enacted by people who are not labeled as white (Ramos-Zayas, 2001; Twine, 1996; Warren and Twine, 1997). This particular understanding of whiteness detaches whiteness from the bodies of white people and therefore broadens the scope of future studies of whiteness. In light of findings of this nature, Wiegman advocates for a location of whiteness in "complex economic and political processes and practices" rather than in the "epidermal 'reality' of white skin" (1999, p. 135). Here, again, the scholarship is clearly marking whiteness as something other than biological fact and "whiteness" is not restricted to being performed by people with white skin.

The separation of masculinity and whiteness from biology has important political implications. Some men's studies and whiteness studies scholars have at times called for the abolition of these dominant identities. Wiegman argues that "if whiteness is historically produced, and if its production requires something more than the physical characteristic of skin color, then whiteness as a form of political identification, if not racial identity, can be abolished" (1999, p. 136) and the same must also be true of masculinity. Whether these identities and practices *should* be abolished is a political debate that whiteness studies, but not men's studies, has engaged in (Moon and Flores, 2000; Roediger, 1994; Wiegman, 1999).

In addition to the political ramifications, there are analytical ramifications of separating whiteness and masculinity from bodies. According to Nayak, "The potential of a social constructionist approach to engage with whiteness as fluid, mutable and ever changing is curtailed when it is tethered to the weighty anchor, and seemingly fixed idea of the white body" (2007, p. 742). When bodily practices are central to the construction of conceptualizations of whiteness and masculinity, the ability to discuss "others" utilizing the behaviors, attitudes, and strategies typically associated with these terms is hindered.

The movement toward separating whiteness and masculinity from white and male bodies is also a movement toward greater inclusivity. Recognizing performances of masculinity by non-male bodies is crucial to queer studies (Halberstam, 1998, 2002a), and recognizing performances of whiteness by bodies we might not typically identify as white opens new lines of questioning in relationship to performances by multiracial people and racial "passing."

It is important to note, however, that the whiteness–white bodies and the masculinity–male bodies links should not be completely discarded. Important scholarship in both fields points out important spaces and moments where those links are crucial. The links between bodies and these social categories continue to be important in regards to intimate relationships (Davidson, 2001; Dines, 2006; Stokes, 2001) and sports (Hokowhitu, 2011; Light, 2008; Messner, 1995; Young, McTeer, and White, 1994), to name only two prominent examples. It is important to temper the inclination to discuss whiteness and masculinity as disembodied practices with an understanding that we cannot sever the relationship to bodies entirely. Finding this balance has proven to be a difficulty, if not *the* difficulty, in establishing functional definitions of whiteness and masculinity.

Intersectionalities

Both men's studies and whiteness studies have made moves toward recognizing that their central concepts vary along other intersecting axes of identity and power. That is, masculinity and whiteness, whether they are understood as configurations of behaviors or attitudes, are not formed, enacted, or reinforced in the same way for everyone. The notion of intersectionality is operationalized in men's studies under the terminology of "masculinities," and I propose that it be operationalized in whiteness studies as "whitenesses." Masculinities as a concept was popularized, among other reasons, because it pushed men's studies to move beyond the field's ethnocentric and heteronormative roots (Brod, 1987b). The theoretical construction of masculinities has been a huge success in men's studies but it has also led the field into a spiral of increasingly meaningless typologies. On the other hand, whitenesses as a concept has not yet had the same level of popularity and its absence may be seen as an indicator that whiteness studies has not yet seriously considered intersectionality.

Masculinities

Masculinities, as Connell (1995) imagined in the process of his theorization of hegemonic masculinity, come in four forms: hegemonic masculinity, subordinated masculinities, complicit masculinities, and marginalized masculinities. The relationships between hegemonic masculinity, subordinated masculinities, and complicit masculinities are considered internal to the gender order, while the relationship between hegemonic masculinity and marginalized masculinity supposedly extends beyond the gender order.

Hegemonic masculinity is theorized as "the configuration of gender practice which embodies the currently accepted answer to the problem of the legitimacy of patriarchy [and] guarantees (or is taken to guarantee) the dominant position of men and the subordination of women" (Connell, 1995, p. 77). Subordinated masculinities are those with positions beneath hegemonic masculinity in a hierarchy of masculinities. Connell offers a monolithic "gay masculinity" as an example of a subordinated masculinity (1995, p. 79). Complicit masculinities are those that do not explicitly support the maintenance of men's dominance, but also do not challenge it. Finally, marginalized masculinities are generated by "the interplay of gender with other structures such as class and race" (Connell 1995, p. 80). Marginalized masculinities are those that are denied authority by the dominant group.

In addition to these four categories of masculinities, Spector-Mersel (2006) also maps two different contexts in which we can discuss masculinities: "across persons and within persons" (p. 68). The plurality across persons allows us to analyze the variety of masculinities that exist in society at-large, while plurality within a person facilitates exploration of the ways in which individuals can perform a range of masculinities in relationship to the contexts of their lives. Burke (2011) and Pascoe (2003, 2007) touch on both of these aspects of plurality in their analyses of masculinities in the context of secondary education. Pascoe's findings complicate theories of masculinities because her interviews indicate that rather than "each boy enacting a different type of masculinity . . . they are attempting to infuse their own identity with recognizably masculine characteristics" (2003, p. 1435). Pascoe argues that "slotting boys into masculinity types, as is commonly done in the multiple masculinities model" (2003, p. 1435) does not tell the full story of the role of masculinity in their lives. In this statement, Pascoe is clearly critiquing the growing tendency in studies of men and masculinities to create masculine categories containing sets of practices that we expect subjects to fit neatly into. This downward spiral of typologies has dominated studies of men and masculinities as of late and is precisely why any pluralization of whiteness must be carefully theorized.

Moving Toward Whitenesses

Shortly before studies of men and masculinity turned to a notion of masculinities, some scholars in the field began to discuss a notion of hegemonic masculinity (Carrigan, Connell, and Lee, 1985; Pleck, 1983). Hegemonic masculinity was theorized to allow scholars of men and masculinity to make sense of how some men, and some masculine practices, had power and dominance over others. The same process that brought about the concept of hegemonic masculinity also led to a theorization of masculinities (Connell, 1987).

I open this section with this very brief history of masculinities because the pattern so closely matches the current work in critical studies on whiteness. In 2004 Lewis theorized hegemonic whiteness as "a shifting configuration of practices and meanings that occupy the dominant position in a particular racial formation and that successfully manage to occupy the empty space of 'normality' in our culture" and claimed that "hegemonic whiteness is not a quality inherent to individual whites but is a collective social force that shapes their lives just as it shapes the lives of racial minorities" (2004, p. 634). In 2010 Matthew Hughey proposed a notion of hegemonic whiteness because "white racial identities cannot be distilled into static political formations that are distinct and separable; rather they share a common allegiance to dominant racial (and often racist) ideologies that transcend differing belief systems" (2010, p. 1306). Hegemonic whiteness, as Lewis and Hughey present it, allows us to talk about the heterogeneity of white racial identity without critical white studies' focus on power and privilege.

This theorization of hegemonic whiteness also addresses one of the most prominent critiques of current conceptualizations of whiteness. Hartigan argues that one of the weak points in theorizations of whiteness is its "rendering white people as a homogenous cultural identity or order" (1997, p. 502), and Pease criticizes the "tendency in much of the critical whiteness literature to overlook the differences and social divisions that exist within whiteness" (2004, p. 127). According to Rasmussen, many conceptualizations of whiteness do not answer "the question of how whites themselves are internally differentiated, how the same white skin that has facilitated the integration, assimilation, and enrichment of some does not guarantee that others—such as poor whites and queer whites—might not also experience deprivation, stigmatization, and subjugation" (2001, p. 8). These concerns are similar to the concerns that led men's studies from masculinity to masculinities, and just as studies of men and masculinity turned to masculinities, I propose a turn in critical studies of whiteness to a concept of whitenesses.

Many whiteness studies scholars have chosen to begin from a place of recognition of multiple whitenesses without implementing the terminology or fully theorizing the implications (Frankenberg, 1997b; Giroux, 1997; Hyde, 1995; Lewis, 2004; Shome, 2000; Winant, 1997). Hyde holds that "whiteness has multiple meanings and interpretations, which are further complicated with the inclusion of class, sexual orientation or other forms of identity" (1995, p. 94), while Shome maintains that "whiteness is not a monolithic formation—it is constantly made and remade through its participation in other unequal social relations" (2000, p. 368).

But even as an understanding that whiteness is plural is present in whiteness studies, whitenesses as a conceptual framework seems to have been avoided. This avoidance may be a result of lessons learned from the conceptualization of masculinities, but may also be a result of the political position of whiteness studies. As I began writing this chapter, some white anti-racist activists expressed concern to me that a conceptualization of whitenesses risks breaking down into a discussion of good versus bad, healthy versus unhealthy, or racist versus nonracist whiteness when the social construction of whiteness itself needs to be problematized. Melanie Bush puts it well when she states, "I do not subscribe to the notion that our primary task is to forge a positive white identity, because if race was constructed as a tool to dominate and subordinate, how can we render it positive?" (2004, p. 7). That is to say, the goal of utilizing whitenesses should not be to construct a hierarchy of good and bad whites, but rather to enable an examination of variance in practices in relationship to the persistence of racial inequality.

There may be a fear among scholars of whiteness that pluralizing whiteness disaggregates the role that white people play in the maintenance of racial inequality. Lewis counters this position by arguing that "recognizing that there are multiple forms of whiteness, some of which provide more rewards than others, does not mean that some whites are unaffected by race" (2004, p. 635). The goal here is to disaggregate the practices of whiteness for closer examination, which is not the same as diluting white responsibility or accountability for racial inequality. A conceptualization of whitenesses enables us to redirect our analytical lens from macro-social and historical analyses of white identity construction and boundary-making to the various and wide-ranging micro-social and interpersonal practices that maintain racial inequality in our daily lives.

Even as the field of critical studies of whiteness has avoided taking up a conceptualization of whitenesses, a few prominent authors have fleetingly mentioned a need for pluralization of whiteness or have illustrated the existence of multiple whitenesses through their empirical work (Bérubé, 2001; Carroll, 2011; Frankenberg, 1997b; Hughey, 2010). Hughey (2010), in his work "The (Dis)Similarities of White Racial Identities," illustrates how two seemingly different white communities, one politically affiliated as antiracist and one as white supremacist, enact some shared racial discursive practices. Meanwhile, Bérubé (2001) hints in his discussion of gay male whiteness that one can be different kinds of white. In *Affirmative Reaction*, Carroll (2011) analyzes media discourse surrounding ethnic whiteness, and gay whiteness, to name only two. A theory of whitenesses allows us to bring this work together under one framework. It allows us to begin understanding the power relationships within the category of whiteness, the individual practices that support the larger structure of racial inequality, and how practices operating in defense of white privilege vary from person to person or from community to community.

As there has been no consistent conceptualization of whitenesses in the context of whiteness studies, there has also been no consistent conceptualization of hegemonic, subordinated, complicit, and marginalized whitenesses. The field could very well benefit from a further development of the previously mentioned theorizations of hegemonic whiteness by Hughey (2010) and Lewis (2004). It is also easy to imagine theorizations of subordinated, complicit, and marginalized whitenesses as well. Just as in the case of masculinity, a subordinated whiteness could be understood as the whiteness of Jews (Brodkin, 1998) or Slavs (Jacobson, 1998). Many whiteness studies scholars would label "color-blind" whites as complicit (Bonilla-Silva, 2006; Frankenberg, 1993), while others would label color-conscious antiracists as complicit (Hughey, 2007). Marginalized whitenesses would be those of poor whites, gay or transgender whites, and whites with disabilities, to name only a few.

Whiteness studies has already rejected the idea that whiteness is monolithic, but I propose that whiteness studies begins to take that rejection seriously. In not developing a notion of whitenesses, the field of whiteness studies has failed to fully address the interaction of other axes of power and identity, such as class, gender, and sexuality. We must strive to disaggregate the historically aggregated category of whiteness to foster research into the neglected power relations within the category of whiteness and the various contemporary practices of whiteness that reinforce racial inequality.

references

Alegria, S. 2012. "Constructing racial difference through group talk: An analysis of white focus groups' discussion of racial profiling." *Ethnic and Racial Studies.*

Arnesen, E. 2001. "Whiteness and the historians' imagination." *International Labor and Working Class History* 60 (Fall 2001):3–32.

Bem, S. L. 1993. *The lenses of gender: Transforming the debate on sexual inequality.* New Haven, CT: Yale University Press.

Bérubé, A. 2001. "How gay stays white and what kind of white it stays." *The making and unmaking of whiteness.* B. B. Rasmussen et al. (eds.). Durham, NC: Duke University Press, 234–265.

Bonilla-Silva, E. 2006. *Racism without racists: Color-blind racism and the persistence of racial inequality in the United States.* Lanham, MD: Rowman & Littlefield.

Brod, H. 1987a. "A case for men's studies." *Changing Men: New Directions in Research on Men and Masculinity.* Michael Kimmel (ed.). Newbury Park, CA: Sage.

———. 1987b. "Introduction: Themes and theses of men's studies." *The Making of Masculinities,* volume 10. Boston: Allen & Unwin.

Brodkin, K. 1998. *How Jews became white folks and what that says about race in America.* New Brunswick, NJ: Rutgers University Press.

Burke, Kevin. 2011. *Masculinities and other hopeless causes at an all-boys Catholic school.* New York: Peter Lang.

Burke, M. A. 2012. "Discursive fault lines: Reproducing white habitus in a racially diverse community." *Critical Sociology* 38:645–668.

Bush, M. E. L. 2004. *Breaking the code of good intentions: Everyday forms of whiteness.* Lanham, MD: Rowman & Littlefield.

Carrigan, T., B. Connell, and J. Lee. 1985. "Toward a new sociology of masculinity." *Theory and Society* 14:551–604.

Carroll, Hamilton. 2011. *Affirmative reaction: New formations of white masculinity.* Durham, NC: Duke University Press.

Cheng, Cliff. 1999. "Marginalized masculinities and hegemonic masculinity: An introduction." *Journal of Men's Studies* 7:295.

Clatterbaugh, K. 1998. "What is problematic about masculinities?" *Men and Masculinities* 1:24.

Connell, R. W. 1987. *Gender and power: Society, the person and sexual politics.* Stanford, CA: Stanford University Press.

———. 1995. *Masculinities.* Berkeley: University of California Press.

———. 2002. *Gender.* Cambridge: Polity Press.

Connell, R. W., and J. W. Messerschmidt. 2005. "Hegemonic masculinity." *Gender and Society* 19:829–859.

Cuomo, C. J., and K. Q. Hall. 1999. *Whiteness: Feminist philosophical reflections.* Lanham, MD: Rowman & Littlefield.

Davidson, J. O. C. 2001. "The sex tourist, the expatriate, his ex-wife and her other: The politics of loss, difference and desire." *Sexualities* 4:5–24.

Dines, G. 2006. "The white man's burden: Gonzo pornography and the construction of black masculinity." *Yale JL & Feminism* 18:283.

Donovan, B. 1998. "Political consequences of private authority: Promise Keepers and the transformation of hegemonic masculinity." *Theory and Society* 27:817–843.

Ferber, A. L. 2007. "Whiteness studies and the erasure of gender." *Sociology Compass* 1:265–282.

Frankenberg, R. 1993. *White women, race matters: The social construction of whiteness.* Minneapolis: University of Minnesota Press.

————. 1997a. *Displacing whiteness: Essays in social and cultural criticism.* Durham, NC: Duke University Press.

————. 1997b. "Introduction: Local whitenesses, localizing whiteness." *Displacing whiteness: Essays in social and cultural criticism,* pp. 1–33.

Giroux, H. A. 1997. "Rewriting the discourse of racial identity: Towards a pedagogy and politics of whiteness." *Harvard Educational Review* 67:285–321.

Halberstam, J. 1998. *Female masculinity.* Durham, NC: Duke University Press.

————. 2002a. "An introduction to female masculinity: Masculinity without men." *The masculinity studies reader.* Malden, MA: Blackwell.

————. 2002b. "An introduction to female masculinity: masculinity without men." *The masculinity studies reader,* pp. 355–374.

Hale, G. E. 2010. *Making whiteness: The culture of segregation in the South, 1890–1940.* New York: Knopf Group E-Books.

Hartigan, J., Jr. 1997. "Establishing the fact of whiteness." *American Anthropologist* 99:495–505.

Hearn, J. 1996. "A critique of the concept of masculinity." In M. Mac An Ghaill, ed., *Understanding masculinities.* Buckinghamshire: Open University Press.

————. 2004. "From hegemonic masculinity to the hegemony of men." *Feminist Theory* 5:49.

Hokowhitu, B. 2011. "Race tactics: The racialised athletic body." *Junctures: The Journal for Thematic Dialogue.*

Hughey, M. W. 2007. "Racism with antiracists: Color-conscious racism and the unintentional persistence of inequality." *Social Thought and Research* 28:67–108.

————. 2010. "The (dis)similarities of white racial identities: The conceptual framework of 'hegemonic whiteness.'" *Ethnic and Racial Studies* 33:1289–1309.

Hyde, C. 1995. "The meanings of whiteness." *Qualitative Sociology* 18:87–95.

Ignatiev, N. 1995. *How the Irish became white.* New York: Routledge.

Jacobson, M. F. 1998. *Whiteness of a different color.* Cambridge, MA: Harvard University Press.

Kendall, F. E. 2006. *Understanding white privilege: Creating pathways to authentic relationships across race.* New York: Routledge.

Kincheloe, J. L. 1999. "The struggle to define and reinvent whiteness: A pedagogical analysis." *College Literature* 26:162–194.

Kolchin, P. 2002. "Whiteness studies: The new history of race in America." *Journal of American History* 89:154–173.

Leonardo, Z. 2002. "The souls of white folk: critical pedagogy, whiteness studies, and globalization discourse." *Race, Ethnicity and Education* 5:29–50.

Lewis, A. E. 2004. "'What group?' Studying whites and whiteness in the era of 'color-blindness.'" *Sociological Theory* 22:623–646.

Light, R. 2008. "Boys, the body, sport and schooling." *Sport, Education and Society* 13:127–130.

MacInnes, J. 1998. *The end of masculinity: The confusion of sexual genesis and sexual difference in modern society.* Buckingham, UK: Open University Press.

McMahon, A. 1993. "Male readings of feminist theory: The psychologization of sexual politics in the masculinity literature." *Theory and Society* 22:675–695.

Messerschmidt, J. W. 2004. *Flesh and blood: Adolescent gender diversity and violence.* Lanham, MD: Rowman & Littlefield.

Messner, M. A. 1995. *Power at play: Sports and the problem of masculinity.* Boston, MA: Beacon Press.

Moon, D., and L. A. Flores. 2000. "Antiracism and the abolition of whiteness: Rhetorical strategies of domination among 'race traitors.'" *Communication Studies* 51:97–115.

Nakayama, T. K., and R. L. Krizek. 1995. "Whiteness: A strategic rhetoric." *Quarterly Journal of Speech* 81:291–309.

Paechter, C. 2003. "Masculinities and femininities as communities of practice." *Women's Studies International Forum* 26, no. 1:69–77.

Pascoe, C. J. 2003. "Multiple masculinities?" *American Behavioral Scientist* 46:1423–1438.

———. 2007. *Dude, you're a fag: Masculinity and sexuality in high school.* Berkeley: University of California Press.

Pease, B. 2004. "Decentring white men: Critical reflections on masculinity and white studies." *Whitening race: Essays in social and cultural criticism.* Moreton-Robinson, Aileen (eds). Canberra, A.C.T.: Aboriginal Studies Press, 119.

Petersen, A. 2003. "Research on men and masculinities." *Men and Masculinities* 6:54.

Pleck, J. H. 1983. *The myth of masculinity.* Cambridge, MA: The MIT Press.

Rains, F. V. 1998. "Is the benign really harmless? Deconstructing some 'benign' manifestations of operationalized white privilege." *White reign: Deploying whiteness in America.* 77–102. J. L. Kincheloe, S. R. Steinberg, N. M. Rodriguez, & R. E. Chennault (eds.). New York: St. Martin's Press.

Ramos-Zayas, A. Y. 2001. "All this is turning white now: Latino constructions of 'white culture' and whiteness in Chicago." *Centro Journal* 13:73–95.

Rasmussen, B. B. 2001. "Introduction." *The making and unmaking of whiteness.* Durham, NC: Duke University Press.

Roediger, D. R. 1994. *Towards the abolition of whiteness: Essays on race, politics, and working class history.* London: Verso Books.

———. 1999. *The wages of whiteness: Race and the making of the American working class.* London: Verso Books.

———. 2005. *Working toward whiteness: How America's immigrants became white: The strange journey from Ellis Island to the suburbs.* New York: Basic Books.

Shome, R. 2000. "Outing whiteness." *Critical Studies in Media Communication* 17, no. 3.

Stokes, M. 2001. *The color of sex: Whiteness, heterosexuality, and the fictions of white supremacy.* Durham, NC: Duke University Press.

Tehranian, J. 2008. *Whitewashed: America's invisible Middle Eastern minority*. New York: New York University Press.

Twine, F. W. 1996. "Brown-skinned white girls: Class, culture and the construction of white identity in suburban communities." *Gender, Place and Culture: A Journal of Feminist Geography* 3:205–224.

Warren, J. W., and F. W. Twine. 1997. "White Americans, the new minority? Non-blacks and the ever-expanding boundaries of whiteness." *Journal of Black Studies* 28:200–218.

Waters, M. 1990. *Ethnic options: Choosing identities in America*. Berkeley: University of California Press.

Wiegman, R. 1999. "Whiteness studies and the paradox of particularity." *Boundary* 2(26):115–150.

_____. 2002. "Unmaking: Men and masculinity in feminist theory." *Masculinity Studies and Feminist Theory: New Directions*. Judith Kagan Gardiner (ed.). New York: Columbia University Press, 31–59.

Winant, H. 1997. "Behind blue eyes: Whiteness and contemporary US racial politics." *New Left Review* 225:73–88.

Young, K., W. McTeer, and P. White. 1994. "Body talk: Male athletes reflect on sport, injury, and pain." *Sociology of Sport Journal* 11:175–194.

18

we aren't just color-blind,
we are oppression-blind!

Abby L. Ferber*

The ideology of color-blind racism, the contemporary framework for under-standing and defending white privilege, is part of a broader, overarching ide-ology I refer to as "oppression-blindness." It is not only race-based privilege that we actively render invisible today, but many other systems of oppression and privilege as well, including class, gender, sexuality, nationality, ability, age, and religion. We have already examined most of these systems throughout this book, and read about many examples where these systems interact and intersect in shaping our lives. We have read important arguments by leading scholars compelling us to consider these social identities not as discrete, stand-alone properties, but as specific axes of power that imbue the social structures we shape and are shaped by day in and day out. In this chapter I will take these arguments further by examining the multifaceted ways in which the ideological justifications for each of these various systems of in-equality work to reinforce one another. Each one is made stronger by its place-ment in the broader context of a hierarchically organized society with ever-evolving narratives that work to rationalize and justify inequality as nat-

*This chapter is a slightly revised version of the article that appeared as "The Culture of Priv-ilege: Color-blindness, Post-feminism, and Christonormativity," *Journal of Social Issues* 68, no. 1 (2012): 63–77.

ural and inevitable. Situating these specific systems of oppression and privilege within this broader narrative framework can help us to understand why each one remains so elusive and difficult to abolish despite the work of active social justice movements over the past three hundred years.

Intersectionality

Kimberle Crenshaw coined the term "intersectionality" to direct attention to the interaction of multiple social identities in shaping the reality of oppression and privilege (African American Policy Forum, 2009). She argues that we must embrace an intersectional approach to analyze social problems and develop more effective social movement responses. An intersectional framework can be employed at every level of analysis. Traditionally, analysts of racial inequality and racism have identified three levels for analysis: the individual level, the cultural level, and the structural level (Blumenfeld, 2006; Hardiman and Jackson, 1997).

Intersectional analyses focus most often on those who are multiply disadvantaged by numerous systems of inequality. There is less research, however, examining systems of privilege intersectionally (Coston and Kimmel, 2012). In this chapter, I examine privilege from an intersectional perspective and focus specifically on the level of culture. Culture gives meaning to our experiences and shapes the ways we make sense of the world. Race itself is a cultural construct, and it is through culture that we learn to "see" and "read" race (Ferber, 1998; Hartigan, 2010). Culture is key in socializing people into a system of racial inequality, and cultural constructions of race shape our own individual identities, as well as our participation in institutions and systems that reproduce inequality (Blumenfeld, 2006; Hardiman and Jackson, 1997).

Researchers from many disciplines identify racial ideology as one of the most important factors in ongoing racial inequality (Blumenfeld, 2006; Bonilla-Silva, 2010; Feagin, 2001; Ferber, 1998; Hartigan, 2010). Ideology is a central feature of culture that "consists of broad mental and moral frameworks, or 'grids,' that social groups use to make sense of the world, to decide what is right and wrong, true or false, important or unimportant" (Bonilla-Silva, 2010, p. 62). Racial ideology mediates individuals and institutions, providing rationalization for the nature of current race relations. It provides a system of assumptions and rules that inform individuals' decisions, behaviors, and interactions. Racial ideology is an interpretive repertoire that provides story lines, narratives, and common frames for making sense of race relations.

The Defense of White Privilege: Color-Blind Ideology

Sociologists, psychologists, social workers, and economists continue to research the ways in which racial oppression remains entrenched in the United States (Feagin, 2001; Plaut, 2010). Centuries of what Feagin (2001) calls "undeserved impoverishment and undeserved enrichment" (p. 21) provide some people a huge head start and plenty of help along the way.

Yet many white people believe that discrimination against people of color is a thing of the past (Plaut, 2010). For example, despite all evidence to the contrary, white people generally believe that whites are actually more likely to face job discrimination than people of color (Pincus, 2003). As Collins (2004) argues,

> Recognizing that racism even exists remains a challenge for most White Americans, and increasingly for African-Americans as well. They believe that the passage of civil rights legislation eliminated racially discriminatory practices and that any problems that Blacks may experience now are of their own doing. (p. 5)

To understand this gap between reality and the stories we tell, we need to examine the cultural framework informing our stories. Plaut (2010) argues that we must

> [examine] the cultural ideas and beliefs that are prevalent in people's social worlds. These socially, culturally, and historically constituted ideas and beliefs, or cultural models, get inscribed in institutions and practices (e.g., language, law, organizational policies), and daily experiences (e.g., reading the newspaper, watching television, taking a test) such that they organize and coordinate individual understandings and psychological processes (e.g., categorization, attitudes, anxiety, motivation) and behavior. (p. 82)

Over time our hegemonic stories and narratives about race change, connected to the changing social and economic organization of race relations. Just when the blatantly discriminatory policies and practices of Jim Crow racism were finally crumbling under attack, the early foundations of a "new racism" were taking form (Irons, 2010.) This new racism is much less overt, its predominant operating narrative characterized as an ideology of color-blind racism that avoids the use of blatantly racist terminology (Bonilla-Silva, 2010; Irons, 2010; Plaut, 2010).

A color-blind perspective assumes that discrimination is a thing of the past and denies the reality of race and racial inequality today. This approach argues that we should treat people as simply human beings, rather than as racialized beings (Plaut, 2010).

According to Bonilla-Silva (2010), color-blind ideology consists of four key frames that organize our understandings of racial inequality:

1. *Abstract liberalism*: relies upon the language of political liberalism, referring to abstract concepts of equal opportunity, rationality, free choice, individualism, etc. (i.e., discrimination is no longer a problem, and any individual who works hard can succeed).
2. *Naturalization*: reframes ongoing inequality as the result of natural processes, rather than social relations (i.e., segregation today is the result of the natural inclination of people to live near others of the same race).
3. *Cultural racism*: reframes ongoing inequality as the result of inherent cultural differences between racialized groups.
4. *Minimization of racism*: assumes that we now have a fairly level playing field, everyone has equal opportunities to succeed, and racism is no longer a real problem.

Color-blind racism assumes racial discrimination has ended, people are being treated in a color-blind fashion, and any differences we see in the success of racial groups is therefore due to inherent differences in the groups themselves. Color-blind ideology leads to the conclusion that we've done all we can. For many whites, the election of Barack Obama as president has been evoked to confirm their assumptions of a color-blind nation (Bonilla-Silva, 2010; Cunnigen and Bruce, 2010). While many people naively embrace this view as nonracist, it reinforces and reproduces contemporary systemic racial inequality by denying its reality.

These scripts are so ubiquitous that they are drawn upon to explain other forms of inequality as well. Color-blind racism needs to be examined from an intersectional perspective, making visible the ways it is connected and mutually constitutive of other ideologies of privilege. In the remainder of this chapter, I will examine discourses of oppression and privilege that rationalize male and Christian privilege, and argue that we must examine how these ideologies mirror color-blind racism and reinforce one another. Post-feminism has emerged to justify and rationalize gender inequality, just as Christonormativity works to naturalize and protect Christian privilege. As Plaut argues, these cultural ideologies work together; therefore, each one must be dismantled to advance the cause of social justice.

From New Racism to Postfeminism

Intersectional analyses of both the civil rights and women's movements of the 1960s have revealed how their failures to address the concerns, needs, and demands of women of color limited their success. Exclusion of women from leadership in the civil rights movement, and the women's movement's failure to fully engage issues of race and sexuality (both the first and second waves), led to divisions in both movements.

There are also striking similarities among the predominant narratives of backlash to both of these movements, yet efforts to respond and attack these narratives still proceed from separate silos, with little collaboration. I argue that the same four frames of color-blindness identified by Bonilla-Silva operate to defend and normalize gender inequality (Ferber, 2007). It is common today for journalists and conservative commentators to argue that we have moved beyond the need for feminism, and have entered a *postfeminist* phase. Like the civil rights movement, the women's movement did much to advance formal, legal equality for women. Nevertheless, gender inequality remains widespread, and feminist scholars have observed the rise of a new discourse around gender, remarkably similar to new racism's color-blind framework.

The ideology of postfeminism assumes that the law and society are now "gender-blind" in their treatment of men and women, reflecting the use of a "minimization of racism/discrimination" frame. Mainstream media promotes the assumption that the women's movement has accomplished its goals and barriers facing women have been removed. According to the advocates of postfeminism, men and women now have equal opportunities: women now have the right to vote, legal protection from discrimination, and the same legal rights as men (Douglas, 2010; McRobbie, 2004).

Some commentators argue that the push for equality has gone too far, saying that men are now victims of feminist frenzy. Just as the advocates of color-blind racism believe that racial inequality is a thing of the past and that further attempts to remedy inequality lead to "reverse discrimination" against whites, we see similar arguments about gender. This rearticulation of the minimization of discrimination frame leads to reifying the values of *abstract liberalism*, where feminism is attacked for violating the values of individualism and equal opportunity. After all, if everyone is already equal, then interventions aimed at women violate the principle of equal opportunity and hurt men. Faludi (1991) examines the "steady stream of indictments" of feminism that began in the 1980s in the mainstream media. Problems women face are often framed as the result of feminism, and women's push for equality, rather than the product of inequality itself. In this way, feminism is discredited and claims of ongoing inequality dismissed. McRobbie (2004) writes that postfeminist culture is undermining the gains of the women's movement and feminism, arguing that "equality is achieved, in order to install a whole repertoire of new meanings which emphasize that it is no longer needed" (p. 255).

Consistent with the abstract liberalism frame, women's status today is depicted as a product of their own individual choices. According to the logic of the postfeminist story line, women legally have the same opportunities and rights as men; therefore, if women are more likely to be found in low-paying, part-time jobs, it must be because of their own choosing, since "women are now free to choose for themselves" (McRobbie, 2004, p. 259). Job segregation and the persistent wage gap are often dismissed with the "prevailing ideological constructions of women as carers," which is also used to explain why women are more likely to be found in the home, responsible for child care, elder care, and housework. Further, as an extension of women's caregiving "natures," they are assumed to be more likely than men to choose careers in nursing, teaching, day care, or social work, knowing that these jobs pay significantly less compared to male careers requiring similar skills and education levels (Glenn, 2010). Here we have moved into the frames of *naturalization* and *cultural racism/sexism*. Both natural, biological differences between men and women, as well as gender-based cultural differences, are invoked to rationalize gender inequality (Cole, Avery, Dodson, and Goodman, 2012). In *Forced to Care*, Glenn (2010) examines the ways this gender ideology of caring, in conjunction with ideologies of race, relegate women of color to the lowest-paying, least valued caregiving jobs, such as working in nursing homes. She strikingly reveals the coercion at the heart of this enterprise, examining the state's role in enforcing women's obligation to provide "care," including the training of Native American women in boarding schools and the formal "Americanization" programs for immigrant women. A tremendous amount of effort and force has been extended to make women acquiesce with the ideology of women as natural caregivers.

Yet postfeminism makes this history and enforcement invisible; "there is little trace . . . of the enduring inequities which still mark out the relations between men and women" (McRobbie, 2004, p. 260). Any inequality between men and women, therefore, is seen as a result of men's and women's different natures, and the choices men and women make. Both color-blind racism and postfeminism ignore the vast body of literature that examines the ways the social institutions of education, work, health care, criminal justice, and the family shape and constrain all of our choices and opportunities (Crittenden, 2001; Faludi, 1991; Feagin, 2001; Glenn, 2010; Lewis, 2003; Van Ausdale and Feagin, 2001).

Given the ideological similarities of color-blind racism and postfeminism, we need to examine both discourses within a broader framework of political backlash against the social movements of the '60s and '70s. According to Coppock, Haydon, and Richter (1995), "the proclamation of 'post-feminism' has occurred at precisely the same moment as acclaimed feminist studies demonstrate that not only have women's real advancements been limited, but also that there has been a backlash against feminism of international significance" (p. 3). The concept of postfeminism itself is part of this backlash, an "attempt to retract the handful of small and hard-won victories that the feminist movement did manage to win for women" (Faludi, 1991, p. 12).

Similarly, Bonilla-Silva (2003) argues that color-blind racism "has become a formidable political tool for the maintenance of the racial order [serving] as the ideological armor for a covert and institutionalized system [of racial oppression] in the post–Civil Rights era" (p. 3). Both postfeminism and color-blind racism are part of an ideology of "oppression-blindness" that operates to defend the culture of privilege against perceived attacks (Ferber, 2003, 2007; Ferber and Samuels, 2010; Pratto and Stewart, 2012).

This discourse results in blaming the victim for his or her own oppression. William Ryan first described the contours of blaming the victim in 1971. Ryan emphasizes that blaming the victim is essentially a defense of privilege: "those who buy this solution with a sigh of relief are inevitably blinding themselves to the basic causes of the problems being addressed. They are, most crucially, rejecting the possibility of blaming, not the victims, but themselves" (p. 583). In this way, blaming the victim allows privilege to remain intact and unexamined, not simply rationalizing, but reproducing, privilege.

Christonormativity

I now turn to a third category, Christian privilege. Christonormativity refers to the normalization and privileging of Christianity as the dominant religious and spiritual culture in the United States (Steinberg and Kincheloe, 2009). Todd (2010) argues that Christianity "not only dominates other religious and atheistic traditions in this country, but is implicated in virtually every other category of oppression: racism, sexism, heterosexism, ableism, classism . . . every one of these categories has been undergirded by Christian theological justifications" (p. 142). Indeed, Christianity played a central role historically in constructing racial categories, and continues to affect decisions over who counts as "white." Tehranian's (2009) recent work on Middle-Eastern Americans demonstrates that when the majority of Arab immigrants to the United States were Christian, they were more likely to be defined legally as white, yet as the percentage of Arab immigrants who are Muslim has grown, that is changing. "As it has grown less Christian, the Middle Eastern population in the United States is thought of as less assimilable and, consequently, less white" (p. 70).

A few years back, I published a blog examining the pervasive atmosphere of Christian privilege I was observing (Ferber, 2009). In the blog, I argue that Christonormativity is a system of privilege that marginalizes and excludes those who are not Christian, especially during the winter holiday season. In the blog, I described a typical December day:

> I woke up and turned on my favorite morning show. I learned new recipes for the favorite holiday drink—egg nog; tips on how to decorate for the holidays on a budget by trimming the mantel and staircase with wreaths, green swags, and small lights; followed by the best toys to buy for kids this holiday season. I then read my local newspaper, which featured a big story about how the Colorado governor's mansion has been decorated for the holidays, accompanied by a large photo of the Christmas tree. . . . I entered my office building, where a large Christmas tree sat in the lobby. Due to concerns raised a few years back about the heavy focus on Christmas, the tree has now been renamed "The Giving Tree." It is decorated by ornaments made by children

at the campus day care center, with requests for donations as a part of our annual Holiday Service Project. I wonder how Jewish, Muslim, and other non-Christian students feel each time they enter the building.

On my way home, I stop off on a few errands. In the grocery store, I am greeted by another large Christmas tree. As I wander the aisles I hum along to "Jingle Bells," "All I Want for Christmas," "Blue Christmas," "Feliz Navidad," and "Here Comes Santa Claus." . . . So you see, while it may not seem like a big deal that someone wishes me a "Merry Christmas," and I genuinely appreciate the good will and cheer being offered, for non-Christians like myself, this time of year can be anything but merry (24% of the U.S. population of about 304 million do not define themselves as Christian). . . . Not only is it all-pervasive, all day long, when I do the math, I discover that it adds up to about ten years of my life that I live in this exclusionary Christian culture. (If I live to be eighty, one and a half months per year of that time adds up to ten years over a lifetime!). . . . The question is *not* how do we stop the celebrations, but instead, how do we create a more inclusive culture, a climate where everybody feels included? (full text of blog can be found at www.huffingtonpost.com/abby-ferber/please-dont-wish-me-a-mer_b_389824.html)

My arguments here are threefold. First, I introduce the concept of Christonormativity, documenting the manner in which Christian culture has become the normative, dominant culture in the United States at this time of year. Like other forms of privilege, it is often invisible and unexamined. Second, I highlight the way attempts to make Christian privilege visible are rearticulated as an attack on Christianity. This is another example of blaming the victim. Finally, I ask that we think about what it means to be inclusive.

Defending Christian Privilege

I received a flood of negative responses to this blog. The blog appeared on the *Huffington Post*, a news/blog site generally characterized as liberal. I have a regular blog there, and in previous blogs I have received a maximum of twenty-one comments, while this post received seventy-nine comments. I often focus on issues of race and gender. I wrote an entry titled "I Am Racist" and have often written about white privilege, yet received very few negative responses. I was therefore shocked by the number of negative responses to this post. Of the seventy-nine, forty were explicitly negative or sarcastic and contained elements of an oppression-blind ideology. The remaining responses consisted of short replies to other posts, were neutral, or were positive. In examining the responses, there is a clear pattern that can be discerned. Like the discourses of color-blind racism and postfeminism, these oppression-blind ideologies minimize Christian privilege and reframe the issue in the abstract liberal terms of free choice and individualism.

One of the most common themes I found was the *minimization of discrimination* and the concomitant attempt to preserve the culture of privilege:

- "The only thing Christian about Christmas is the name 'Christ'mas . . . about 95% of all Christmas traditions are non-Christian . . . growing up I never really noticed the Christ in Christmas. . . . To me it's like Thanksgiving."
- "Christ was born in September, the holiday that you are so offended by is a secular holiday, there are no real Christian holidays. . . . The American Christmas is a family celebration of giving and love . . . everyone can join in, it's really not Christian in any real sense."
- "May I suggest you go to 'Blintzes and Bling' and get a Star of David necklace the size of a hub cap so that I know you are Jewish. Then I promise to wish you a Happy Hanukkah. . . . People of all faiths are dying across the globe for their religious beliefs. December is a month of hope and light and joy for most faiths—and also for those of no particular faith—who can enjoy the secular spirit of giving and cheer."

These quotes and many others argue that there is no evidence of privilege or exclusion. Christmas is reframed in universal terms, depicted as good fun that everyone can be a part of. These responses also provide evidence of the *naturalization* of Christianity. Christian values are naturalized as simply human values inherent in all people. As one respondent put it, "These are universal beliefs, that for this time of year, just happen to be wrapped in green and red bows."

Not only do the respondents minimize and trivialize Christian discrimination and privilege, they draw upon the abstract liberalism frame by emphasizing the abstract principles of individualism, rationality and free choice:

- "What an awful whiner. . . . The vast majority of this country is Christian, and even many secular people celebrate Christmas; is it any wonder that the average person is assumed to celebrate it? Anybody who is 'offended' or 'uncomfortable' really needs to find something new to complain about."

- "You have two choices. You can either be terribly offended and act pissy when someone smiles and wishes you a Merry Christmas or you can embrace the friendly, positive sentiment as it was intended and smile back. How you react says much about who you are."

- "We can choose to continue to live in a world where we seek out an offense where none is intended and continue down this dangerous path of perpetuating the 'us vs. them' mentality that serves to divide us more than we are already. Or we can decide to be participants in a world where we look beyond our differences."

- "As an atheist, I am constantly bombarded with God from the government, from friends and strangers alike. However, I am not offended by anyone wishing me Merry Christmas, Happy Hanukkah, Happy Kwanzaa etc. . . . I would be in a constant state of irritation if I let these things bother me."

- "I am not a Christian. I could choose to feel excluded and marginalized because a lot of people are celebrating a holiday important to their religion, or I can choose my own interpretation of a winter holiday with rituals and traditions that I select and enjoy the lights and colors and giving and general goodwill. It's of no relevance to me what the holiday means to anyone else, and mine is of no matter to them. If I choose to forgo Christmas completely (and I've done that in previous years), I certainly don't resent others continuing to celebrate nor do I take offense that they assume that I share in their celebration."

These arguments are the very same arguments used to justify color-blind racism and postfeminism. They erase from view Christian privilege, reinscribing Christianity as normative. They blame the victim for choosing to focus on differences. Like advocates of affirmative action or those "frenzied feminists," anyone who argues that race, gender, and religious differences still matter in shaping people's daily lives is attacked. The reality of institutional inequality is ignored, and the issue is reduced to simply one of individual choice.

Our failure to examine the interconnections among these three narratives carries consequences and undermines our efforts to advance social justice. When we only interrogate this cultural story line of privilege and oppression in terms of its implications for racial inequality, we leave the broader story line in place. While the goals of most research on white privilege are to contribute to antiracist activism, approaches that focus only on race have limited potential. For example, the belief that legal obstacles to equality have been removed and everyone has equal opportunities to succeed is used to justify not only race, but gender and religious inequality, which is rearticulated as the product of the poor choices of individuals, rather than a systemic issue. When we hear the very same arguments offered to explain each of these systems of inequality, it gives them more legitimacy. The more familiar the arguments, the more they feel intuitively right to people. The frames are more likely to resonate and to feel like "common sense." Wherever we are situated, we will have greater potential for success if we attack the entire ideology of oppression-blindness and victim blaming in all of its forms, rather than only one of its manifestations.

Focusing on only one social classification, such as race, is like trying to pull one strand out of a tapestry. Even if we are successful, the tapestry itself remains intact, and thus that strand can always be picked up and woven back in; perhaps in new ways, so that the overall pattern and design shift over time. Nevertheless, the ever-present tapestry remains in place and ready to reincorporate new threads.

It is the entire tapestry we must unravel. We need to analyze all of our "-isms" as strands in a broader, comprehensive ideological tapestry explaining away inequality and trying to naturalize and justify oppression and privilege.

references

African American Policy Forum. 2009. A primer on intersectionality. http://aapf.org/wp-content/uploads/2009/03/aapf_intersectionality_primer.pdf.

Blumenfeld, W. 2006. "Christian Privilege and the Promotion of 'Secular' and not-so 'Secular' Mainline Christianity in Public Schooling and in the Larger Society." *Equity and Excellence in Education* 39: 195–210. doi: 10:1080/10665680600788024.

Blumenfeld, W. J., and K. Jaekel. "Exploring Levels of Christian Privilege Awareness Among Preservice Teachers." *Journal of Social Issues* 68: xx–xx.

Blumenfeld, W. J., K. Y. Joshi, and E. E. Fairchild. 2009. *Investigating Christian Privilege and Religious Oppression in the United States.* Rotterdam, Denmark: Sense Publishers.

Bonilla-Silva, E. 2010. *Racism Without Racists: Color-blind Racism and the Persistence of Racial Inequality in the United States,* 3rd ed. Lanham, MD: Rowman & Littlefield.

_____. 2003. "'New Racism,' Color-blind Racism, and the Future of Whiteness in America." In A. W. Doane and E. Bonilla-Silva, eds., *White Out: The Continuing Significance of Race.* New York: Routledge.

Brown, C., and T. Augusta-Scott. 2007. *Narrative Therapy: Making Meaning, Making Lives*. Thousand Oaks, CA: Sage.

Case, K. 2012. "Discovering the Privilege of Whiteness: White Women's Reflections on Antiracist Identity and Ally Behavior." *Journal of Social Issues* 68, no. 1: 78–96.

Cole, E. R., L. R. Avery, C. Dodson, and K. D. Goodman. 2012. "Against Nature: How Arguments About the Naturalness of Marriage Privilege Heterosexuality." *Journal of Social Issues* 68, no. 1: 42–62.

Collins, P. H. 2000. *Black Feminist Thought: Knowledge, Consciousness, and the Politics of Empowerment*, 2nd ed. New York: Routledge.

_____. 2004. *Black Sexual Politics: African Americans, Gender, and the New Racism*. New York: Routledge.

Coppock, V., Haydon, D., and Richter, I. 1995. *The Illusions of "Post-feminism."* London: Taylor and Francis.

Coston, B. M., and Kimmel, M. S. 2012. "Seeing Privilege Where It Isn't: Marginalized Masculinities and the Intersectionality of Privilege." *Journal of Social Issues* 68: xx–xx.

Crittenden, A. 2001. *The Price of Motherhood: Why the Most Important Job in the World Is Still the Least Valued*. New York: Henry Holt.

Cunnigen, D., and M. Bruce. 2010. *Race in the Age of Obama*. Bingley, UK: Emerald Group Publishing.

Doane, A. W. 2003. Rethinking Whiteness Studies. In A. W. Doane and E. Bonilla-Silva, eds., *White Out: The Continuing Significance of Race* (pp. 3–18). New York: Routledge.

Doane, A. W., and E. Bonilla-Silva, eds. 2003. *White Out: The Continuing Significance of Race*. New York: Routledge.

Douglas, S. 2010. *Enlightened Sexism: The Seductive Message that Feminism's Work Is Done*. New York: Times Books.

Fairchild, E. E. 2009. "'I Believe' in Education." In W. J. Blumenfeld, K. Y. Joshi, and E. E. Fairchild, eds., *Investigating Christian Privilege and Religious Oppression in the United States* (pp. 151–157). Rotterdam, Denmark: Sense Publishers.

Faludi, S. 1991. *Backlash: The Undeclared War Against American Women*. New York: Doubleday.

Feagin, J. R. 2001. *Racist America: Roots, Current Realities, and Future Reparations*. New York: Routledge.

Ferber, A. L. 1998. *White Man Falling: Race, Gender, and White Supremacy*. Lanham, MD: Rowman & Littlefield.

_____. 2003. "Defending the Culture of Privilege." In M. S. Kimmel and A. L. Ferber, eds., *Privilege: A Reader* (pp. 319–329). Boulder, CO: Westview Press.

_____. 2007. "Whiteness Studies and the Erasure of Gender." *Sociology Compass* 1: 265–282, doi 10.1111/j.1751–9020.2007.00014.x

_____. 2009. "Please Don't Wish Me a Merry Christmas." *Huffington Post*, www.huffingtonpost.com/abby-ferber/please-dont-wish-me-a-mer_b_389824.html.

Ferber, A. L., C. Jimenez, A. H. O'Reilly, and D. Samuels, eds. 2008. *The Matrix Reader: Examining the Dynamics of Privilege and Oppression*. New York: McGraw-Hill.

Ferber, A. L., and D. Samuels. 2010. Oppression Without Bigots." Factsheet. *Network News*. Sociologists for Women in Society, Winter.

Glenn, E. N. 2010. *Forced to Care: Coercion and Caregiving in America*. Cambridge, MA: Harvard University Press.

Hardiman, R., and B. Jackson. 1997. "Conceptual Foundations for Social Justice Courses." In M. Adams, L. A. Bell, and P. Griffin, eds., *Teaching for Diversity and Social Justice Courses* (pp. 16–29). New York: Routledge.

Hartigan, J. Jr. 2010. *Race in the 21st Century: Ethnographic Approaches.* New York: Oxford University Press.

Irons, J. 2010. "Reconstituting Whiteness: The Mississippi State Sovereignty Commission." Nashville, TN: Vanderbilt University Press.

Kendall, F. E. 2006. *Understanding White Privilege: Creating Pathways to Authentic Relationships Across Race.* New York: Routledge.

Kimmel, M. S., and A. L. Ferber, eds. 2009. *Privilege: A Reader,* 2nd ed. Boulder, CO: Westview Press.

Kincheloe, J. L. 2009. Selling a New and Improved Jesus: Christotainment and the Power of Political Fundamentalism. In S. Steinberg and J. L. Kincheloe, eds., *Christotainment: Selling Jesus Through Popular Culture* (pp. 1–22). Boulder, CO: Westview.

Lewis, A. 2003. *Race in the Schoolyard: Negotiating the Color Line in Classrooms and Communities.* New Brunswick, NJ: Rutgers University Press.

McRobbie, A. 2004. "Post-feminism and Popular Culture." *Feminist Media Studies* 4: 255–264. doi 10.1080/1468077042000309937

Nelson, J. 2009. "Christian Teachers and Christian Privilege." In W. J. Blumenfeld, K. Y. Joshi, and E. E. Fairchild, eds., *Investigating Christian Privilege and Religious Oppression in the United States* (pp. 135–149). Rotterdam, Denmark: Sense Publishers.

Pincus, F. L. 2003. *Reverse Discrimination: Dismantling the Myth.* Boulder, CO: Lynne Rienner.

Plaut, V. C. 2010. "Diversity Science: Why and How Difference Makes a Difference." *Psychological Inquiry* 21: 77–99. doi: 10.1080/10478401003676501

Pratto, F., and A. L. Stewart. 2012. "Group Dominance and the Half-blindness of Privilege." *Journal of Social Issues* 68, no. 1: 28–45.

Ryan, W. 1971. *Blaming the Victim.* New York: Pantheon Books.

Steinberg, S. 1995. *Turning Back: The Retreat from Racial Justice in American Thought and Policy.* Boston: Beacon Press.

Steinberg, S. R., and J. L. Kincheloe. 2009. *Christotainment: Selling Jesus Through Popular Culture.* Boulder, CO: Westview.

Stewart, T. L., I. M. Latu, and H. T. Denney. 2012. "White Privilege Awareness and Efficacy to Reduce Racial Inequality Improve White Americans' Attitudes Toward African Americans." *Journal of Social Issues* 68, no. 1: 11–27.

Sutton, B. 2010. *Bodies in Crisis: Culture, Violence, and Women's Resistance in Neoliberal Argentina.* New Brunswick, NJ: Rutgers University Press.

Tehranian, J. 2009. *Whitewashed: America's Invisible Middle Eastern Minority.* New York: New York University Press.

Todd, J. 2010. "Confessions of a Christian Supremacist." *Reflections: Narratives of Professional Helping* 16: 140–146.

Van Ausdale, D., and J. R. Feagin. 2001. *The First R: How Children Learn Race and Racism.* Lanham, MD: Rowman & Littlefield.

19

toward a new vision

Race, Class, and Gender as Categories of Analysis and Connection

Patricia Hill Collins*

> The true focus of revolutionary change is never merely the oppressive situations which we seek to escape, but that piece of the oppressor which is planted deep within each of us.
>
> —AUDRE LORDE, *SISTER OUTSIDER*

Audre Lorde's statement raises a troublesome issue for scholars and activists working for social change. While many of us have little difficulty assessing our own victimization within some major system of oppression, whether it be by race, social class, religion, sexual orientation, ethnicity, age, or gender, we typically fail to see how our thoughts and actions uphold someone else's subordination. Thus, White feminists routinely point with confidence to their oppression as women but resist seeing how much their white skin privileges them. African-Americans who possess eloquent analyses of racism

---

*"Toward a New Vision: Race, Class, and Gender as Categories of Analysis and Connection," by Patricia Hill Collins. Adapted from an article originally published in *Race, Sex, and Class* 1, no. 1, Fall 1993. Reprinted by permission of Jean Ait Belkhir, Founder and Editor of the *Race, Gender & Class* journal.

often persist in viewing poor White women as symbols of white power. The radical left fares little better. "If only people of color and women could see their true class interests," they argue, "class solidarity would eliminate racism and sexism." In essence, each group identifies the type of oppression with which it feels most comfortable as being fundamental and classifies all other types as being of lesser importance.

Oppression is full of such contradictions. Errors in political judgment that we make concerning how we teach our courses, what we tell our children, and which organizations are worthy of our time, talents, and financial support flow smoothly from errors in theoretical analysis about the nature of oppression and activism. Once we realize that there are few pure victims or oppressors, and that each one of us derives varying amounts of penalty and privilege from the multiple systems of oppression that frame our lives, then we will be in a position to see the need for new ways of thought and action.

To get at that "piece of the oppressor which is planted deep within each of us," we need at least two things. First, we need new visions of what oppression is, new categories of analysis that are inclusive of race, class, and gender as distinctive yet interlocking structures of oppression. Adhering to a stance of comparing and ranking oppressions—the proverbial "I'm more oppressed than you"—locks us all into a dangerous dance of competing for attention, resources, and theoretical supremacy. Instead, I suggest that we examine our different experiences within the more fundamental relationship of domination and subordination. To focus on the particular arrangements that race, class, and gender take in our time and place without seeing these structures as sometimes parallel and sometimes interlocking dimensions of the more fundamental relationship of domination and subordination may temporarily ease our consciences. But while such thinking may lead to short-term social reforms, it is simply inadequate for the task of bringing about long-term social transformation.

While race, class, and gender as categories of analysis are essential in helping us understand the structural bases of domination and subordination, new ways of thinking that are not accompanied by new ways of acting offer incomplete prospects for change. To get at that "piece of the oppressor which is planted deep within each of us," we also need to change our daily behavior. Currently, we are all enmeshed in a complex web of problematic relationships that grant our mirror images full human subjectivity while stereotyping and objectifying those most different from us. We often assume that the people we work with, teach, send our children to school with, and sit next to . . . will act and feel in prescribed ways because they belong to given race, social class, or gender categories. These judgments by category must be replaced with fully human relationships that transcend the legitimate differences created by race, class, and gender as categories of analysis. We require new categories of connection, new visions of what our relationships with one another can be. . . .

[This discussion] addresses this need for new patterns of thought and action. I focus on two basic questions. First, how can we reconceptualize race, class, and gender as categories of analysis? Second, how can we transcend the barriers created by our experiences with race, class, and gender oppression in order to build the types of coalitions essential for social exchange? To address these questions I contend that we must acquire both new theories of how race, class, and gender have shaped the experiences not just of women of color, but of all groups. Moreover, we must see the connections between the categories of analysis and the personal issues in our everyday lives, particularly our scholarship, our teaching, and our relationships with our colleagues and students. As Audre Lorde points out, change starts with self, and relationships that we have with those around us must always be the primary site for social change.

How Can We Reconceptualize Race, Class, and Gender as Categories of Analysis?

To me, we must shift our discourse away from additive analyses of oppression (Spelman, 1982; Collins, 1989). Such approaches are typically based on two key premises. First, they depend on either/or, dichotomous thinking. Persons, things, and ideas are conceptualized in terms of their opposites. For example, Black/White, man/woman, thought/feeling, and fact/opinion are defined in oppositional terms. Thought and feeling are not seen as two different and interconnected ways of approaching truth that can coexist in scholarship and teaching. Instead, feeling is defined as antithetical to reason, as its opposite. In spite of the fact that we all have "both/and" identities (I am both a college professor and a mother—I don't stop being a mother when I drop my child off at school, or forget everything I learned while scrubbing the toilet), we persist in trying to classify each other in either/or categories. I live each day as an African-American woman—a race/gender–specific experience. And I am not alone. Everyone has a race/gender/class–

specific identity. Either/or, dichotomous thinking is especially troublesome when applied to theories of oppression because every individual must be classified as being either oppressed or not oppressed. The both/and position of simultaneously being oppressed and oppressor becomes conceptually impossible.

A second premise of additive analyses of oppression is that these dichotomous differences must be ranked. One side of the dichotomy is typically labeled dominant and the other subordinate. Thus, Whites rule Blacks, men are deemed superior to women, and reason is seen as being preferable to emotion. Applying this premise to discussions of oppression leads to the assumption that oppression can be quantified, and that some groups are oppressed more than others. I am frequently asked, "Which has been most oppressive to you, your status as a Black person or your status as a woman?" What I am really being asked to do is divide myself into little boxes and rank my various statuses. If I experience oppression as a both/and phenomenon, why should I analyze it any differently?

Additive analyses of oppression rest squarely on the twin pillars of either/or thinking and the necessity to quantify and rank all relationships in order to know where one stands. Such approaches typically see African-American women as being more oppressed than everyone else because the majority of Black women experience the negative effects of race, class, and gender oppression simultaneously. In essence, if you add together separate oppressions, you are left with a grand oppression greater than the sum of its parts.

I am not denying that specific groups experience oppression more harshly than others—lynching is certainly objectively worse than being held up as a sex object. But we must be careful not to confuse this issue of the saliency of one type of oppression in people's lives with a theoretical stance positing the interlocking nature of oppression. Race, class, and gender may all structure a situation but may not be equally visible and/or important in people's self-definitions. In certain contexts, such as the antebellum American South and contemporary South America, racial oppression is more visibly salient, while in other contexts, such as Haiti, El Salvador, and Nicaragua, social class oppression may be more apparent. For middle-class White women, gender may assume experiential primacy unavailable to poor Hispanic women struggling with the ongoing issues of low-paying jobs and the frustrations of the welfare bureaucracy. This recognition that one category may have salience over another for a given time and place does not minimize the theoretical importance of assuming that race, class, and gender as categories of analysis structure all relationships.

In order to move toward new visions of what oppression is, I think that we need to ask new questions. How are relationships of domination and subordination structured and maintained in the American political economy? How do race, class, and gender function as parallel and interlocking systems that shape this basic relationship of domination and subordination? Questions such as these promise to move us away from futile theoretical struggles concerned with ranking oppressions and toward analyses that assume race, class, and gender are all present in any given setting, even if one appears more visible and salient than the others. Our task becomes redefined as one of reconceptualizing oppression by uncovering the connections among race, class, and gender as categories of analysis.

1. Institutional Dimension of Oppression

Sandra Harding's contention that gender oppression is structured along three main dimensions—the institutional, the symbolic, and the individual—offers a useful model for a more comprehensive analysis encompassing race, class, and gender oppression (Harding, 1989). Systemic relationships of domination and subordination structured through social institutions such as schools, businesses, hospitals, the workplace, and government agencies represent the institutional dimension of oppression. Racism, sexism, and elitism all have concrete institutional locations. Even though the workings of the institutional dimension of oppression are often obscured with ideologies claiming equality of opportunity, in actuality, race, class, and gender place Asian-American women, Native American men, White men, African-American women, and other groups in distinct institutional niches with varying degrees of penalty and privilege.

Even though I realize that many . . . would not share this assumption, let us assume that the institutions of American society discriminate, whether by design or by accident. While many of us are familiar with how race, gender, and class operate separately to structure inequality, I want to focus on how these three systems interlock in structuring the institutional dimension of oppression. To get at the interlocking nature of race, class, and gender, I want you to think about the antebellum plantation as a guiding metaphor for a variety of American social institutions. Even though slavery is typically analyzed as a racist institution, and occasionally as a class institution, I suggest that slavery was a race-, class-, and gender-specific institution. Removing any one piece from our analysis diminishes our understanding of the true nature of relations of domination and subordination under slavery.

Slavery was a profoundly patriarchal institution. It rested on the dual tenets of White male authority and White male property, a joining of the political and the economic within the institution of family. Heterosexism was assumed and all Whites were expected to marry. Control over affluent White women's sexuality remained key to slavery's survival because property was to be passed on to the legitimate heirs of the slave owner. Ensuring affluent White women's virginity and chastity was deeply intertwined with maintenance of property relations.

Under slavery, we see varying levels of institutional protection given to affluent White women, working-class and poor White women, and enslaved African women. Poor White women enjoyed few of the protections held out to their upper-class sisters. Moreover, the devalued status of Black women was key in keeping all White women in their assigned places. Controlling Black women's fertility was also key to the continuation of slavery, for children born to slave mothers themselves were slaves.

African-American women shared the devalued status of chattel with their husbands, fathers, and sons. Racism stripped Blacks as a group of legal rights, education, and control over their own persons. African-Americans could be whipped, branded, sold, or killed, not because they were poor, or because they were women, but because they were Black. Racism ensured that Blacks would continue to serve Whites and suffer economic exploitation at the hands of all Whites.

So we have a very interesting chain of command on the plantation—the affluent White master as the reigning patriarch; his White wife helpmate to serve him, help him manage his property, and bring up his heirs; his faithful servants, whose production and reproduction were tied to the requirements of the capitalist political economy; and largely propertyless, working-class White men and women watching from afar. In essence, the foundations for the contemporary roles of elite White women, poor Black women, working-class White men, and a series of other groups can be seen in stark relief in this fundamental American social institution. While Blacks experienced the most harsh treatment under slavery, and thus made slavery clearly visible as a racist institution, race, class, and gender interlocked in structuring slavery's systemic organization of domination and subordination.

Even today, the plantation remains a compelling metaphor for institutional oppression. Certainly the actual conditions of oppression are not as severe now as they were then. To argue, as some do, that things have not changed all that much denigrates the achievements of those who struggled for social change before us. But the basic relationships among Black men, Black women, elite White women, elite White men, working-class White men, and working-class White women as groups remain essentially intact.

A brief analysis of key American social institutions most controlled by elite White men should convince us of the interlocking nature of race, class, and gender in structuring the institutional dimension of oppression. For example, if you are from an American college or university, is your campus a modern plantation? Who controls your university's political economy? Are elite White men overrepresented among the upper administrators and trustees controlling your university's finances and policies? Are elite White men being joined by growing numbers of elite White women helpmates? What kinds of people are in your classrooms grooming the next generation who will occupy these and other decision-making positions? Who are the support staff that produce the mass mailings, order the supplies, fix the leaky pipes? Do African-Americans, Hispanics, or other people of color form the majority of the invisible workers who feed you, wash your dishes, and clean up your offices and libraries after everyone else has gone home?

If your college is anything like mine, you know the answers to these questions. You may be affiliated with an institution that has Hispanic women as vice presidents for finance, or substantial numbers of Black men among the faculty. If so, you are fortunate. Much more typical are colleges where a modified version of the plantation as a metaphor for the institutional dimension of oppression survives.

2. The Symbolic Dimension of Oppression

Widespread, societally sanctioned ideologies used to justify relations of domination and subordination comprise the symbolic dimension of oppression. Central to this process is the use of stereotypical or controlling images of diverse race, class, and gender groups. In order to assess the power of this dimension of oppression, I want you to make a list, either on paper or in your head, of "masculine" and "feminine" characteristics. If your list is anything like that compiled by most people, it reflects some variation of the following:

Masculine	Feminine
aggressive	passive
leader	follower
rational	emotional
strong	weak
intellectual	physical

Not only does this list reflect either/or dichotomous thinking and the need to rank both sides of the dichotomy, but ask yourself exactly which men and women you had in mind when compiling these characteristics. This list applies almost exclusively to middle-class White men and women. The allegedly "masculine" qualities that you probably listed are only acceptable when exhibited by elite White men, or when used by Black and Hispanic men against each other or against women of color. Aggressive Black and Hispanic men are seen as dangerous, not powerful, and are often penalized when they exhibit any of the allegedly "masculine" characteristics. Working-class and poor White men fare slightly better and are also denied the allegedly "masculine" symbols of leadership, intellectual competence, and human rationality. Women of color and working-class and poor White women are also not represented on this list, for they have never had the luxury of being "ladies." What appear to be universal categories representing all men and women instead are unmasked as being applicable to only a small group.

It is important to see how the symbolic images applied to different race, class, and gender groups interact in maintaining systems of domination and subordination. If I were to ask you to repeat the same assignment, only this time, by making separate lists for Black men, Black women, Hispanic women, and Hispanic men, I suspect that your gender symbolism would be quite different. In comparing all of the lists, you might begin to see the interdependence of symbols applied to all groups. For example, the elevated images of White womanhood need devalued images of Black womanhood in order to maintain credibility.

While the above exercise reveals the interlocking nature of race, class, and gender in structuring the symbolic dimension of oppression, part of its importance lies in demonstrating how race, class, and gender pervade a wide range of what appears to be universal language. Attending to diversity in our scholarship, in our teaching, and in our daily lives provides a new angle of vision on interpretations of reality thought to be natural, normal, and "true." Moreover, viewing images of masculinity and femininity as universal gender symbolism, rather than as symbolic images that are race, class, and gender specific, renders the experiences of people of color and of non-privileged White women and men invisible. One way to dehumanize an individual or a group is to deny the reality of their experiences. So when we refuse to deal with race or class because they do not appear to be directly relevant to gender, we are actually becoming part of someone else's problem.

Assuming that everyone is affected differently by the same interlocking set of symbolic images allows us to move forward toward new analyses. Women of color and White women have different relationships to White male authority, and this difference explains the distinct gender symbolism applied to both groups. Black women encounter controlling images such as the mammy, the matriarch, the mule, and the whore, that encourage others to reject us as fully human people. Ironically, the negative nature of these images simultaneously encourages us to reject them. In contrast, White women are offered seductive images, those that promise to reward them for supporting the status quo. And yet seductive images can be equally controlling. Consider, for example, the views of Nancy White, a 73-year-old Black woman, concerning images of rejection and seduction:

> My mother used to say that the black woman is the white man's mule and the white woman is his dog. Now, she said that to say this: we do the heavy work and get beat whether we do it well or not. But the white woman is closer to the master and he pats them on the head and lets them sleep in the house, but he ain't gon' treat neither one like he was dealing with a person. (Gwaltney, 1980, p. 148)

Both sets of images stimulate particular political stances. By broadening the analysis beyond the confines of race, we can see the varying levels of rejection and seduction available to each of us due to our race, class, and gender identity. Each of us lives with an allotted portion of institutional privilege and penalty, and with varying levels of rejection and seduction inherent in the symbolic images applied to us. This is the context in which we make our choices. Taken together, the institutional and symbolic dimensions of oppression create a structural backdrop against which all of us live our lives.

3. The Individual Dimension of Oppression

Whether we benefit or not, we all live within institutions that reproduce race, class, and gender oppression. Even if we never have any contact with members of other race, class, and gender groups, we all encounter images of these groups and are exposed to the symbolic meanings attached to those images. On this dimension of oppression, our individual biographies vary tremendously. As a result of our institutional and symbolic statuses, all of our choices become political acts.

Each of us must come to terms with the multiple ways in which race, class, and gender as categories of analysis frame our individual biographies. I have lived my entire life as an African-American woman from a working-class family, and this basic fact has had a profound impact on my personal biography. Imagine how different your life might be if you had been born Black, or White, or poor, or of a different race/class/gender group than the one with which you are most familiar. The institutional treatment you would have received and the symbolic meanings attached to your very existence might differ dramatically from what you now consider to be natural, normal, and part of everyday life. You might be the same, but your personal biography might have been quite different.

I believe that each of us carries around the cumulative effect of our lives within multiple structures of oppression. If you want to see how much you have been affected by this whole thing, I ask you one simple question—who are your close friends? Who are the people with whom you can share your hopes, dreams, vulnerabilities, fears, and victories? Do they look like you? If they are all the same, circumstance may be the cause. For the first seven years of my life I saw only low-income Black people. My friends from those years reflected the composition of my community. But now that I am an adult, can the defense of circumstance explain the patterns of people that I trust as my friends and colleagues? When given other alternatives, if my friends and colleagues reflect the homogeneity of one race, class, and gender group, then these categories of analysis have indeed become barriers to connection.

I am not suggesting that people are doomed to follow the paths laid out for them by race, class, and gender as categories of analysis. While these three structures certainly frame my opportunity structure, I as an individual always have the choice of accepting things as they are, or trying to change them. As Nikki Giovanni points out, "we've got to live in the real world. If we don't like the world we're living in, change it. And if we can't change it, we change ourselves. We can do something" (Tate 1983, p. 68). While a piece of the oppressor may be planted deep within each of us, we each have the choice of accepting that piece or challenging it as part of the "true focus of revolutionary change."

How Can We Transcend the Barriers Created by Our Experiences with Race, Class, and Gender Oppression in Order to Build the Types of Coalitions Essential for Social Change?

Reconceptualizing oppression and seeing the barriers created by race, class, and gender as interlocking categories of analysis is a vital first step. But we must transcend these barriers by moving toward race, class, and gender as categories of connection, by building relationships and coalitions that will bring about social change. What are some of the issues involved in doing this?

1. Differences in Power and Privilege

First, we must recognize that our differing experiences with oppression create problems in the relationships among us. Each of us lives within a system that vests us with varying levels of power and privilege. These differences in power, whether structured along axes of race, class, gender, age, or sexual orientation, frame our relationships. African-American writer June Jordan describes her discomfort on a Caribbean vacation with Olive, the Black woman who cleaned her room:

> Even though both "Olive" and "I" live inside a conflict neither one of us created, and even though both of us therefore hurt inside that conflict, I may be one of the monsters she needs to eliminate from her universe and, in a sense, she may be one of the monsters in mine. (1985, p. 47)

Differences in power constrain our ability to connect with one another even when we think we are engaged in dialogue across differences. Let me give you an example. One year, the students in my course "Sociology of the Black Community" got into a heated discussion about the reasons for the upsurge of racial incidents on college campuses. Black students complained vehemently about the apathy and resistance they felt most White students expressed about examining their own racism. Mark, a White male student, found their comments particularly unsettling. After claiming that all the Black people he had ever known had expressed no such beliefs to him, he questioned how representative the viewpoints of his fellow students actually were. When pushed further, Mark revealed that he had participated in conversations over the years with the Black domestic worker employed by his family. Since she had never expressed such strong feelings about White racism, Mark was genuinely shocked by class discussions. Ask yourselves whether that domestic worker was in a position to speak freely. Would it have been wise for her to do so in a situation where the power between the two parties was so unequal?

In extreme cases, members of privileged groups can erase the very presence of the less privileged. When I first moved to Cincinnati, my family and I went on a picnic at a local park. Picnicking next to us was a family of White Appalachians. When I went to push my daughter on the swings, several of the children came over. They had missing, yellowed, and broken teeth, they wore old clothing, and their poverty was evident. I was shocked. Growing up in a large eastern city, I had never seen such awful poverty among Whites. The segregated neighborhoods in which I grew up made White poverty all but invisible. More importantly, the privileges attached to my newly acquired social class position allowed me to ignore and minimize the poverty among Whites that I did encounter. My reactions to those children made me realize how confining phrases such as "well, at least they're not Black" had become for me. In learning to grant human subjectivity to the Black victims of poverty, I had simultaneously learned to demand White victims of poverty. By applying categories of race to the objective conditions confronting me, I was quantifying and ranking oppressions and missing the very real suffering which, in fact, is the real issue.

One common pattern of relationships across differences in power is one that I label "voyeurism." From the perspective of the privileged, the lives of people of color, of the poor, and of women are interesting for their entertainment value. The privileged become voyeurs, passive onlookers who do not relate to the less powerful, but who are interested in seeing how the "different" live. Over the years, I have heard numerous African-American students complain about professors who never call on them except when a so-called Black issue is being discussed. The students' interest in discussing race or qualifications for doing so appear unimportant to the professor's efforts to use Black students' experiences as stories to make the material come alive for the White student audience. Asking Black students to perform on cue and provide a Black experience for their White classmates can be seen as voyeurism at its worst.

Members of subordinate groups do not willingly participate in such exchanges but often do so because members of dominant groups control the institutional and symbolic apparatuses of oppression. Racial/ethnic groups, women, and the poor have never had the luxury of being voyeurs of the lives of the privileged. Our ability to survive in hostile settings has hinged on our ability to learn intricate details about the behavior and world view of the powerful and adjust our behavior accordingly. I need only point to the difference in perception of those men and women in abusive relationships. Where men can view their girlfriends and wives as sex objects, helpmates, and a collection of stereotyped categories of voyeurism—women must be attuned to every nuance of their partners' behavior. Are women "naturally" better in relating to people with more power than themselves, or have circumstances mandated that men and women develop different skills? . . .

Coming from a tradition where most relationships across difference are squarely rooted in relations of domination and subordination, we have much less experience relating to people as different but equal. The classroom is potentially one powerful and safe space where dialogues among individuals of unequal power relationships can occur. The relationship between Mark, the student in my class, and the domestic worker is typical of a whole series of relationships that people have when they relate across differences in power and privilege. The relationship among Mark and his classmates represents the power of the classroom to minimize those differences so that people of different levels of power can use race, class, and gender as categories of analysis in order to generate meaningful dialogues. In this case, the classroom equalized racial difference so that Black students who normally felt silenced spoke out. White students like Mark, generally unaware of how they had been privileged by their whiteness, lost that privilege in the classroom and thus became open to genuine dialogue. . . .

2. Coalitions Around Common Causes

A second issue in building relationships and coalitions essential for social change concerns knowing the real reasons for coalition. Just what brings people together? One powerful catalyst fostering group solidarity is the presence of a common enemy. African-American, Hispanic, Asian-American, and women's studies all share the common intellectual heritage of challenging what passes for certified knowledge in the academy. But politically expedient relationships and coalitions like these are fragile because, as June Jordan points out:

> It occurs to me that much organizational grief could be avoided if people understood that partnership in misery does not necessarily provide for partnership for change. When we get the monsters off our backs all of us may want to run in very different directions. (1985, p. 47)

Sharing a common cause assists individuals and groups in maintaining relationships that transcend their differences. Building effective coalitions involves struggling to hear one another and developing empathy for each other's points of view. The coalitions that I have been involved in that lasted and that worked have been those where commitment to a specific issue mandated collaboration as the best strategy for addressing the issue at hand.

Several years ago, master's degree in hand, I chose to teach in an inner-city parochial school in danger of closing. The money was awful, the conditions were poor, but the need was great. In my job, I had to work with a range of individuals who, on the surface, had very little in common. We had White nuns, Black middle-class graduate students, Blacks from the "community," some of whom had been incarcerated and/or were affiliated with a range of federal anti-poverty programs. Parents formed another part of this community, Harvard faculty another, and a few well-meaning White liberals from Colorado were sprinkled in for good measure.

As you might imagine, tension was high. Initially, our differences seemed insurmountable. But as time passed, we found a common bond that we each brought to the school. In spite of profound differences in our personal biographies, differences that in other settings would have hampered our ability to relate to one another, we found that we were all deeply committed to the education of Black children. By learning to value each other's commitment and by recognizing that we each had different skills that were essential to actualizing that commitment, we built an effective coalition around a common cause. Our school was successful, and the children we taught benefited from the diversity we offered them. . . .

None of us alone has a comprehensive vision of how race, class, and gender operate as categories of analysis or how they might be used as categories of connection. Our personal biographies offer us partial views. Few of us can manage to study race, class, and gender simultaneously. Instead, we each know more about some dimensions of this larger story and less about others. . . . Just as the members of the school had special skills to offer to the task of building the school, we have areas of specialization and expertise, whether scholarly, theoretical, pedagogical, or within areas of race, class, or gender. We do not all have to do the same thing in the same way. Instead, we must support each other's efforts, realizing that they are all part of the larger enterprise of bringing about social change.

3. Building Empathy

A third issue involved in building the types of relationships and coalitions essential for social change concerns the issue of individual accountability. Race, class, and gender oppression form the structural backdrop against which we frame our relationship—these are the forces that encourage us to substitute voyeurism . . . for fully human relationships. But while we may not have created this situation, we are each responsible for making individual, personal choices concerning which elements of race, class, and gender oppression we will accept and which we will work to change.

One essential component of this accountability involves developing empathy for the experiences of individuals and groups different from us. Empathy begins with taking an interest in the facts of other people's lives, both as individuals and as groups. If you care about me, you should want to know not only the details of my personal biography but a sense of how race, class, and gender as categories of analysis created the institutional and symbolic backdrop for my personal biography. How can you hope to assess my character without knowing the details of the circumstances I face?

Moreover, by taking a theoretical stance that we have all been affected by race, class, and gender as categories of analysis that have structured our treatment, we open up possibilities for using those same constructs as categories of connection in building empathy. For example, I have a good White woman friend with whom I share common interests and beliefs. But we know that our racial differences have provided us with different experiences. So we talk about them. We do not assume that because I am Black, race has only affected me and not her or that because I am a Black woman, race neutralizes the effect of gender in my life while accenting it in hers. We take those same categories of analysis that have created cleavages in our lives, in this case, categories of race and gender, and use them as categories of connection in building empathy for each other's experiences.

Finding common causes and building empathy is difficult, no matter which side of privilege we inhabit. Building empathy from the dominant side of privilege is difficult, simply because individuals from privileged backgrounds are not encouraged to do so. For example, in order for those of you who are White to develop empathy for the experiences of people of color, you must grapple with how your white skin has privileged you. This is difficult to do, because it not only entails the intellectual process of seeing how whiteness is elevated in institutions and symbols, but it also involves the often painful process of seeing how your whiteness has shaped your personal biography. Intellectual stances against the institutional and symbolic dimensions of racism are generally easier to maintain than sustained self-reflection about how racism has shaped all of our individual biographies. Were and are your fathers, uncles, and grandfathers really more capable than mine, or can their accomplishments be explained in part by the racism members of my family experienced? Did your mothers stand silently by and watch all this happen? More importantly, how have they passed on the benefits of their whiteness to you?

These are difficult questions, and I have tremendous respect for my colleagues and students who are trying to answer them. Since there is no compelling reason to examine the source and meaning of one's own privilege, I know that those who do so have freely chosen this stance. They are making conscious efforts to root out the piece of the oppressor planted within them. To me, they are entitled to the support of people of color in their efforts. Men who declare themselves feminists, members of the middle class who ally themselves with anti-poverty struggles, heterosexuals who support gays and lesbians, are all trying to grow, and their efforts place them far ahead of the majority who never think of engaging in such important struggles.

Building empathy from the subordinate side of privilege is also difficult, but for different reasons. Members of subordinate groups are understandably reluctant to abandon a basic mistrust of members of powerful groups because this basic mistrust has traditionally been central to their survival. As a Black woman, it would be foolish for me to assume that White women, or Black men, or White men or any other group with a history of exploiting African-American women have my best interests at heart. These groups enjoy varying amounts of privilege over me and therefore I must carefully watch them and be prepared for a relation of domination and subordination.

Like the privileged, members of subordinate groups must also work toward replacing judgments by category with new ways of thinking and acting.

Refusing to do so stifles prospects for effective coalition and social change. Let me use another example from my own experiences. When I was an undergraduate, I had little time or patience for the theorizing of the privileged. My initial years at a private, elite institution were difficult, not because the coursework was challenging (it was, but that wasn't what distracted me) or because I had to work while my classmates lived on family allowances (I was used to work). The adjustment was difficult because I was surrounded by so many people who took their privilege for granted. Most of them felt entitled to their wealth. That astounded me.

I remember one incident of watching a White woman down the hall in my dormitory try to pick out which sweater to wear. The sweaters were piled up on her bed in all the colors of the rainbow, sweater after sweater. She asked my advice in a way that let me know that choosing a sweater was one of the most important decisions she had to make on a daily basis. Standing knee-deep in her sweaters, I realized how different our lives were. She did not have to worry about maintaining a solid academic average so that she could receive financial aid. Because she was in the majority, she was not treated as a representative of her race. She did not have to consider how her classroom comments or basic existence on campus contributed to the treatment her group would receive. Her allowance protected her from having to work, so she was free to spend her time studying, partying, or in her case, worrying about which sweater to wear. The degree of inequality in our lives and her unquestioned sense of entitlement concerning that inequality offended me. For a while, I categorized all affluent White women as being superficial, arrogant, overly concerned with material possessions, and part of my problem. But had I continued to classify people in this way, I would have missed out on making some very good friends whose discomfort with their inherited or acquired social class privileges pushed them to examine their position.

Since I opened with the words of Audre Lorde, it seems appropriate to close with another of her ideas. . . .

> Each of us is called upon to take a stand. So in these days ahead, as we examine ourselves and each other, our works, our fears, our differences, our sisterhood and survivals, I urge you to tackle what is most difficult for us all, self-scrutiny of our complacencies, the idea that since each of us believes she is on the side of right, she need not examine her position. (1985)

I urge you to examine your position.

references

Butler, Johnella. 1989. "Difficult Dialogues." *The Women's Review of Books* 6, no. 5.

Collins, Patricia Hill. 1989. "The Social Construction of Black Feminist Thought." *Signs.* Summer.

Gwaltney, John Langston. 1980. *Drylongso: A Self-Portrait of Black America.* New York: Vintage.

Harding, Sandra. 1986. *The Science Question in Feminism.* Ithaca, New York: Cornell University Press.

Jordan, June. 1985. *On Call: Political Essays.* Boston: South End Press.

Lorde, Audre. 1984. *Sister Outsider.* Trumansburg, New York: The Crossing Press.

_____. 1985. "Sisterhood and Survival." Keynote address, conference on the Black Woman Writer and the Diaspora, Michigan State University.

Spelman, Elizabeth. 1982. "Theories of Race and Gender: The Erasure of Black Women." *Quest* 5: 36–32.

Tate, Claudia, ed. 1983. *Black Women Writers at Work.* New York: Continuum.

20

winning hearts and minds

Mark R. Warren*

> John Brown worked not simply for black men—he worked with them;
> and he was a companion of their daily life, knew their faults and virtues,
> and felt, as few white Americans have felt, the bitter tragedy of their lot.
>
> —W. E. B. DU BOIS

With these words, W. E. B. Du Bois opened his biography of John Brown, the white abolitionist who led an armed assault against slavery. Brown had a religiously inspired moral vision of an America freed of the sin of slavery. As Du Bois indicated, Brown identified closely with African Americans, saw their cause as a common one, and deeply believed that he was working in the best interests of both blacks and whites. Brown certainly had fire in his heart. In the words of Reverend Joseph Lowery, referenced in the subtitle of this book, Brown came to deeply embrace the cause of racial justice. So do many white activists who work for racial justice today. How did they come to do so? . . .

How can white Americans come to care enough about racism that they move from passivity to action for racial justice? I decided to look for clues to answer that question by examining the lives and self-understanding of

*Mark R. Warren. "Winning Hearts and Minds." From *Fire in the Heart: How White Activists Embrace Racial Justice*. (2010) pp. 211–233. By permission of Oxford University Press, USA. Notes included in the original have been removed from this reprinted excerpt.

white people that have made that move and became committed activists for racial justice. . . .

Head, Heart, and Hand

Americans place great faith in education as a force for social change. If whites knew about racism, so this thinking goes, and understood that it continues to exist and oppress people of color, they would come to oppose it. I did find that awareness of racism proves important to the development of commitment on the part of the interviewees, but only partly so. Rather, I found that the activists in this study came to support racial justice through a combination of cognitive and emotional processes at the heart of which lay moral concerns.

Activists begin their journey to racial justice activism through a direct experience that leads to an awareness of racism, but the real action does not lie in the knowledge gained. What makes this experience a seminal one for them is that through it they recognize a contradiction between the values with which they have grown up and the reality of racial injustice. When they confront this value conflict, activists express anger at racial injustice. They care about racism at first because they believe deeply in the values that are being violated. They express what I call a moral impulse to act.

If we stop here, however, we are left with the do-gooder, the white person who helps people of color but remains at a distance. I find that relationships with people of color begin to undermine that separation. Whites learn more deeply about the reality of racism through these relationships. But more than the head is involved here, too. Personal relationships and stories tug at the heart; that is, they create emotional bonds of caring. Whites become concerned about racism because it affects real people they know. Rather than working *for* people of color, they begin to work *with* them, their commitment nurtured by an ethic of care and a growing sense of shared fate.

As whites take action for racial justice, they build more than individual relationships with people of color. Working collectively in activist groups, they prefigure the kind of human relationships they hope will characterize a future America. In other words, as they attempt to create respectful collaborative relationships, they construct a more concrete sense of the kind of society for which they are working, what I call a moral vision. They find purpose and meaning in a life that works for the kind of society they want for themselves, their children, and all people across racial lines. Some refer to this as a calling, but they all begin to express a direct interest for themselves in a life committed to racial justice activism. Activists come to see that racism harms whites, as well as people of color. It denies whites their full humanity and blocks progress toward a society that would benefit everyone, one that would be in the interest of whites, as well as people of color. Forging community in multiracial groups deepens a sense of shared fate and bonds of caring as it fosters hope for the possibilities of social change. If the moral impulse represents what activists are against, an emerging moral vision represents what they are for, a truly human or beloved community. It provides a foundation for shared identities as multiracial political activists.

Activists develop commitment and deepen their motivations over time, in part through their experiences taking action against racism. Activism provides whites an opportunity to build relationships with people of color, as well as other white activists, and to construct the kind of multiracial community in which they develop and implement a vision of a future society. This is not a linear process but rather a cycle or perhaps a spiral. Indeed, a model of motivation leading to action is too simplistic. Rather, I find that activists develop commitment over time and through activism. Indeed, there may be setbacks or a need for constant vigilance as the pressures of the dominant society constantly push whites back toward a white world and worldview.

For the sake of clarity, I have presented the processes in an ordered form, starting with a moral impulse and leading to a moral vision. To some extent, this order is represented in the activists' lives. However, some activists inherit a sense of a moral vision from their families or their religious traditions and so have elements of a vision at the beginning. For others, relationships come earlier rather than later. Meanwhile, activists continue to express moral outrage even after they deepen their commitment through relationships and construct a moral vision. Each of these processes has its own particular effects on developing commitment. Yet each represents a piece of the larger puzzle of commitment. I have illustrated below how they work together to forge a deep commitment to racial justice on the part of white activists (Figure 20.1).

It may be useful to summarize the relationship between these processes by visualizing them as a cycle. If we start with the heart, anger at the violation of deeply held values leads some white activists to take action for racial justice and thereby build relationships with people of color. These connec-

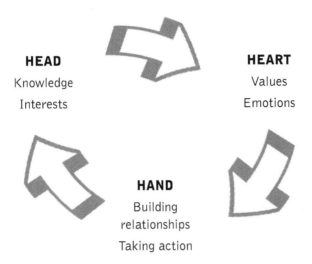

HEAD
Knowledge
Interests

HEART
Values
Emotions

HAND
Building
relationships
Taking action

Figure 20.1

tions create knowledge about the experiences of people of color and begin to shape a sense of common interests. By working in emergent multiracial communities, white activists develop caring and hope while generating a moral vision of a multiracial society with justice at its center. They continue to experiment with building respectful, collaborative associations in multiracial activist groups, all the while developing a sense of their personal interest in racial justice as they find that activism offers a meaningful life.

Within the context of the interactive approach just elaborated, I found moral concerns to play a key role in the development of commitment and action. This approach lies in stark contrast to most thinking on racial justice, which focuses on the cognitive domain. As noted earlier, we place great emphasis on educating white Americans about racism. Certainly, one must understand that racism is an important problem if one is to take action against it. In that sense I did find the processes of learning about the history and experiences of people of color and of developing a racial justice framework to be important to the activists in this study. Moreover, cognitive knowledge about racism, including research and analysis of how it works, is necessary to know what to do about it. However, by itself, knowledge does not motivate one to take action. It answers the "what" to do but not the "why" to do it.

Motivation comes primarily from a moral source even as its character develops from impulse to care and vision. White activists start with a moral impulse that racism is wrong because certain values they care about are being violated. Through relationships they deepen their commitment as they develop an ethic of caring. The many children of color who drop out of high school are no longer just numbers but rather real people to whom they are connected. Eventually activists make the cause their own through the construction of a moral vision of a just, multiracial, and human community.

The other way in which cognitive processes are typically emphasized is through a focus on the rational calculation of self-interest. If whites can come to see their common material interests with people of color (in better health care, for example), then they are likely to find common cause with people of color. Or if whites can see that it will cost them less to educate children than to incarcerate them after they drop out of high school and get into trouble, then they will likely support a more just educational system. These are important arguments. Yet I found almost no evidence that rational, interest-based understandings like these motivated the activists in my study.

I do not want to counterpose morality and interests. Rather, what I discovered is that activists find a way to get them to work together and to reinforce each other. In particular, as white activists construct a moral vision of a future society based upon their values, they develop a way to understand white interest in racial justice. As we have seen, these visions encompass material concerns. Activists are working today to address poverty, rebuild communities, and create better educational systems. The future society they envision would offer more equitable social provision for people of color and for most whites as well. Yet it would perhaps more fundamentally be a community based upon what activists see as deeply human values, where people treat each other with respect and caring across lines of race. Out of these values, better material provision can emerge. While interests and morality work together, in the end, activists embed an understanding of white people's interests into their vision of human community, and that is why I argue that moral sources are primary.

Pursuing a moral vision does not mean working altruistically *for* people of color. The activists in this study have developed a clear sense of their own direct stake in racial justice. In order to understand how morality and interests can work together at the individual level, we have to break from the notion that equates moral action with altruism—doing for someone else rather than for yourself. Nathan Teske, in his study of political activists, has criticized the duality of self-interested versus altruistic action. He shows instead that when activists uphold their most deeply held values by working for the common good, they are also benefiting themselves in ways that are quite rational. They construct an identity for themselves as moral persons, which allows them to gain a meaningful life and a place in history.

Teske reconciles morality and self-interest at the individual level, but I also found that activists resolve the dichotomy at the collective level, too, by embedding an understanding of the collective interests of white Americans in a moral vision. The two levels are in fact related. Activists derive meaning in their lives by pursuing that vision. As activist Roxane Auer captured it, "I'm contributing to the world I want to live in." In other words, activists develop a strong and direct interest in living their lives in the present in accordance with the principles on which that beloved community would be founded. Indeed, along with other activists they attempt to work out those principles by implementing them in the present.

It is also a mistake to counterpose cognitive understanding and emotions. Traditionally, we have understood emotionally based activity as nonrational and suspect in politics. Yet there is a large and growing literature in several fields that shows that emotions and cognition are closely connected. Political scientist George Marcus draws upon recent work in neuroscience to show the role of emotion in reasoning. He has argued that emotions are critical to democratic life, and so, in his view, "sentimental citizens" are the only ones capable of making reasoned political judgments and putting them into action. Political theorist Sharon Krause also shows that emotions can enhance, not detract from, democratic deliberation. She begins her critique of the distinction between passions and reason with words that echo the findings of this study: "Our minds are changed when our hearts are engaged."

Emotions play a particularly important role in cognitive processes regarding racial justice precisely because the minds of white Americans need to be changed. Whites need to break from the dominant color-blind ideology and adopt a racial justice framework. That seems to happen in crystallized moments when a direct experience of racism brings powerful emotions into play. These experiences shock whites out of a complacent belief in the fairness of American society and sear a new racial justice awareness into their consciousness.

In sum, many scholars of race relations and many policymakers have sought to make rational arguments that will convince whites that they have more to gain than lose by working together with people of color. Yet this study suggests that such an approach, however important, is ultimately too narrow. Rather, whites come to find common cause with people of color when their core values are engaged, when they build relationships that lead to caring and a sense of common identity, and when they can embed an understanding of their interests in a vision of a future, racially just society that would benefit all—that is, when the head, heart, and hand are all engaged. . . .

Moral, Visionary Leadership

I turn now to some of the broader lessons of this study for moving white Americans from passivity to action for racial justice. . . .

One of the key implications of this study is the need to bring values to the fore and assert moral leadership in the struggle for racial justice. There are two ways of thinking about morality in this regard, however, captured in my distinction between the moral impulse and a moral vision. Whites can be exhorted to do the right thing, or they can be offered a chance to join in an effort to pursue the moral project of a better society for all with justice at its core. To some extent, as we have seen, probably both appeals are necessary. Nevertheless, an appeal to conscience alone is insufficient. If whites feel only moral impulse, the result may be moralism rather than moral leadership. Perhaps that is the case for many well-meaning white people today. They believe racism is wrong, but they have not gone through the relationship-building and practice-based experiences that engage them in efforts to create and pursue values for a better society.

From this moralist point of view alone, the problem of racism is lodged in "bad" white people. Other whites are the problem, and moralists can easily denounce them. Even if they understand how racism functions in the institutional structure of American society, this still has nothing to do with them. Moralists have yet to discover two important and related lessons. First, as one activist in this study, Z. Holler, said, quoting Pogo, "The enemy is us." In other words, all white people have been affected by racial indoctrination. Rather than dichotomizing the world into good and bad and simply blaming others, all white Americans have to take a close look at their own beliefs and behaviors.

Second, the perpetuation of racism is a complex problem. Whites need a serious, sustained effort to create institutional change and to deal with difficult challenges as they arise. Denouncing racism can make some whites feel good. Laboring in the trenches of the educational and criminal justice systems for sustained racial justice change, for example, is not all feel-good work even if it results in a rewarding life. The IAF organizers in this study, Perry Perkins and Christine Stephens, balked at my labeling them as activists because, in IAF thinking, activism represents short-term, unfocused action. I do not think the label "activism" necessarily means inconsistency or lack of commitment, but I do think their concerns help us appreciate that making serious advances in racial justice requires long-term engagement in public work to build power and new kinds of relationships that lead to real and positive change.

Part of this serious work involves creating respectful, collaborative relationships with people of color. The moralists, the do-gooders working for people of color rather than with them, may continue to keep that separation. People of color are perhaps rightly suspicious of the white heroes who think they can solve problems for them. Rather, moral leadership involves building reciprocal relationships in common pursuit of justice goals. . . .

Moralism in relationship to other whites presents a constant challenge even for the most seasoned racial justice activists. They struggle with honest confrontation with the racial beliefs and behaviors of other whites in a way that does not create defensiveness. They foster a sense of responsibility on the part of whites for action against racism. Responsibility is one thing, however; shaming and guilt trips are another. We have not seen much evidence in this study that shaming individual whites motivates a great deal of action. Indeed, the moral impulse arises not from shaming an individual as a bad person but from engaging positive values that people believe in and care about. Moral leadership lies in offering a moral vision, something to work for, a chance to become part of the racial justice family, as activist Christine Clark put it.

This study lends little support to the idea that confronting whites with their racial privilege constitutes an effective strategy to move them to action. Racial privilege may be a complex reality that white people need to grasp. Indeed, much important work to move whites toward racial justice understanding and action occurs under this banner. However, stressing privilege as a strategy to engage whites seems to emphasize the wrong thing. It focuses on the narrow and short-term benefit whites receive from a racial hierarchy rather than their larger interest in a racially just future. Alone, it seems to engage shame and guilt rather than anger at injustice and hope for a better future. It is moralistic rather than visionary.

Moralism ignores interests in favor of altruism. By contrast, moral leadership takes interests seriously but reshapes white people's understanding of their interests and asks them to join a larger project that promises to create a better society for all. There is a material agenda here, one that offers better economic conditions and better social provision for people of color, as well as white families. However, this interest-based agenda is set and framed within a larger moral vision and political project.

There is evidence that suggests that this kind of moral leadership can be effective. Indeed, we are witnessing the rise of values-based activism in a variety of fields. For some, those values come from a religious faith that calls them to care for community and to act for social justice. Faith-based community organizing, for example, has emerged as a powerful force for engaging people in political action in their local communities. Indeed, several activists in this study are faith-based organizers and leaders. This kind of organizing engages value traditions while working for concrete, material improvements in the quality of people's lives in housing, jobs, and education.

These values can also have secular roots like those based in the American democratic traditions of fairness, freedom, and justice. They can also be newer creations. Many activists in the environmental movement, for example, work not just to prevent ecological devastation but also to establish a new kind of society based upon the principles of working in balance and harmony with the world and caring about all forms of life. Environmentalists today try to live those values out in their relationships to each other and to the environment. In practice, both old and new values can be blended, as can religious and secular ones. More and more we are realizing that people care deeply about their values and can be engaged around them in progressive politics and other activist endeavors.

In the end, moral leadership is about creating a vision that engages values to shape people's understanding of how their interests relate to racial justice. . . .

Building Multiracial Community

Another clear lesson of this study is the need to increase multiracial contact and collaboration in the United States. The activists in this study came to understand and care about racism through the people of color they knew personally. Certainly whites can teach other whites about racism. Indeed, the white activists in this study take that responsibility seriously. However, hearing stories directly from people of color engages the heart, as well as the head, and proves powerful. Through such relationships whites begin to care—and not just to know—about racism, and they begin to develop a sense of common identity and shared fate. Relationships, it appears, create the microfoundation for the broader visionary project of racial justice.

Studies of social capital, that is, social connections and ties between people, highlight the importance of these findings. Scholars of social capital like Robert Putnam have suggested that creating "bridging" ties across lines like race can create trust and cooperation and strengthen a sense of the common good. Yet we have far more "bonding" social capital, that is, ties among people who are like each other, than ties that bridge our differences. Nevertheless, despite persistent segregation, young people increasingly express a desire to be in a diverse setting. College may in fact be a particularly important place for whites to begin to create bridging ties.

Recent research by Robert Putnam highlights the importance of building these cross-racial ties. In studying racial diversity in localities across the United States, Putnam finds that areas with higher levels of racial diversity are lower in social trust. In other words, people appear to trust each other less when diversity is high. Whites trust blacks less and vice versa. Perhaps more surprisingly, however, people also trust other members of their own racial group less when diversity is high. In other words, diversity absent cross-racial relationships works against a sense of shared fate in the entire community. In this context, Putnam calls for investing in places where meaningful interactions across racial and ethnic lines occur, where people work, learn, and live together.

As Putnam and others realize, however, contact across race in and of itself may not move whites toward racial justice. Years ago, Gordon Allport put forward the "contact thesis," which argued that contact with black people lessens prejudice in whites but does so only under certain conditions. Contact reduces prejudice in situations where whites and blacks hold relatively equal status, share common goals, and cooperate with each other in some way and where social norms support the contact.

The findings of this study echo these themes. However, even more, they help us understand the processes that occur within these relationships to enhance support for racial justice. In other words, they open up the black box of bridging social capital to reveal what happens inside, which helps us understand how certain kinds of contact change minds.

Still, our interest goes beyond mere contact and the lessening of prejudice. We are concerned with the role of relationships in developing an understanding of racism and a commitment to racial justice. I find that many pressures work against racial equality within multiracial settings. Indeed, whites build relationships with people of color "under the weight of history," that is, in a context laden with unequal power relationships. Whites can unconsciously bring some of the prejudices they have learned from the larger society into multiracial settings, which leads people of color to mistrust their motives or commitments. In this context, positive action needs to be taken to construct institutional arrangements and policies that will promote truly collaborative relationships. . . . For example, explicit efforts to address racialized thinking or behavior prove important to lessening prejudice and moving whites toward racial justice. Moreover, I find that the more power that people of color hold in the situation, the more compelling the change in whites can be. More broadly, white activists emphasize the need for conversation based upon respect and honesty within these multiracial venues, as well as a genuine effort on their part to learn about the experience of people of color. To the extent that people can share stories across lines of race, mutuality and a sense of common cause develops.

We are also interested in more than creating one-on-one relationships across lines of race. Although those individual connections serve as a foundation for building collectivities, it is through creating community that whites can form shared identities with people of color and other justice-oriented whites. These groups, networks, and communities become the crucible where white activists develop a vision for a future multiracial society and work to implement it today. In other words, we are interested in fostering deeply democratic practices within multiracial institutions and communities.

discussion questions & activities

Discussion Questions

1 What do you see as the most significant overlapping issues faced in the study of race-privilege research and gender-privilege research? Can you identify other overlapping issues besides those raised in this section?
2. Ferber's chapter suggests there are also parallels with religious privilege. Do you see parallels with other systems of privilege? Identify at least three.
3. Why do you suspect some scholars or areas of study may resist embracing an intersectional approach? Do you think there are any specific cases where a unidimensional approach is called for?
4. Warren examines numerous reasons that compel white people to become anti-racist activists. Which of the reasons do you, personally, find most compelling?
5. Why is relationship-building so central to ally work?
6. Does Warren's research shift/add to your understanding about the work of social justice activism in any way?

Personal Connections

The following questions and activities are designed to be completed either on your own or in class and then discussed as a group with others. As you share your insights with others, think about the patterns and similarities that emerge, as well as the differences among your answers.

A. Be an Ally

What does it mean to be an ally? You will find many websites that discuss what it means for a person with privilege to be an ally. Peruse the plethora of sources, and create a definition of what it means to you to be an ally. Next, create a list of at least five ways in which you can and will strive to be an ally. Be realistic, and create a list that is doable for you. Consider the social-change act you chose to take in Section Two. Is this one thing you will continue? Why or why not?

B. Working for Social Justice

Surfing the Internet, identify at least five organizations working for social change and social justice, and describe what they do and why. Select one organization that you would be most interested in engaging with further (whether following, joining, learning from, etc., depending upon the type of organization).

C. Social Action Continuum

Online, search for the words "social action continuum." You will find popular continuums for self-assessment. Select one continuum, and discuss where you see yourself. Is this where you would like to be? Why or why not? What do you need to work on to advance to the next level?

D. Social Identity Development

Return to your examination of the stages of social identity development in section one. Do you think your stages have shifted at all? Why or why not?

index

Made in the USA
Middletown, DE
02 September 2015